A TAGMEMIC COMPARISON OF THE STRUCTURE OF ENGLISH AND VIETNAMESE SENTENCES

JANUA LINGUARUM

STUDIA MEMORIAE
NICOLAI VAN WIJK DEDICATA

edenda curat

C. H. VAN SCHOONEVELD
INDIANA UNIVERSITY

SERIES PRACTICA

110

1971
MOUTON
THE HAGUE · PARIS

A TAGMEMIC COMPARISON OF THE STRUCTURE OF ENGLISH AND VIETNAMESE SENTENCES

by

DƯƠNG THANH BÌNH

1971

MOUTON

THE HAGUE · PARIS

LIBRARY OF CONGRESS CATALOG CARD NUMBER: 74-123126

Printed in The Netherlands by Mouton & Co., Printers, The Hague.

ACKNOWLEDGMENTS

The completion of this project was made possible by the kindness and assistance of several persons. It is difficult for me to express my profound sense of obligation to these persons in only a few lines.

I wish to express my grateful appreciation to Professors Virginia F. Allen and Louis Forsdale for their initial encouragement and kind interest in the early stages of the project.

To all my friends at Teachers College I am indebted for their kind concern and encouragement throughout the study. I wish to thank especially Miss Vivian Horn for her untiring effort and unfailing patience in reading through the manuscript, Miss Jane Meyer for her helpful suggestions and comments, and Miss Gladys Burkhart for her help with the typing.

To my Vietnamese friends, Nguyễn Bích Lan, Nguyễn Ngọc Bích, Hàng Mỹ Hoa, and especially Đào Thị Hợi, I am grateful for their delightful and helpful discussions, concern, and encouragement.

My sincere thanks go to the members of the examining committee — Professors Robert L. Allen, Gerald Dykstra, Daniel P. Girard, Milton A. Kaplan, and Walter H. MacGinitie — for their valuable criticism and helpful suggestions for the improvement of this study. Particularly to Professor Allen, my major adviser, I wish to express my deep gratitude for his generosity in letting me use his studies as the basis for my project, for his kind and understanding guidance throughout the period of my work, and for his untiring efforts in helping to bring about the completion of this project.

For the scholarship grant which made it possible for me to come to the United States to study, I am indebted to the Vietnamese Department of National Education; to the United States Operations Mission in Saigon; to the Agency for International Development in Washington; and, through these agencies, to the American Government and the American people.

Finally, I wish to express my loving appreciation to my parents, sisters and brothers who have shared all my problems and who have given me constant moral support and encouragement throughout the critical period of this study.

D.T.B.

TABLE OF CONTENTS

VIETNAMESE ORTHOGRAPHY

Vietnamese is a tone language spoken by some thirty million people in Vietnam. The northern dialect of Vietnamese, which is the dialect of the present writer, is generally regarded to be the prestige dialect — that is, the 'standard language' of the country. It has six tones, while the southern and central dialects have five and four tones respectively. In writing Vietnamese, writers now regularly use the Latin alphabet, with certain modifications. (These are shown below.) Tones are indicated by means of diacritical marks.

The same combination of consonant(s) and vowel(s) will have different meanings when it is pronounced with different tones. The syllable /ta/, for example, will have any one of these six different meanings depending on its tone:

Tone	Pronunciation	Written Form	Meaning
level	/ta -/	ta	'I', 'we'
rising	/ta ↗/	tá	'a dozen'
falling	/ta ↘/	tà	'vicious'
falling-rising	/ta ∨↗/	tả	'to describe'
rising-falling	/ta ∧↘/	tã	'diapers'
level-falling	/ta /-↘ /	tạ	'one hundred kilograms'

It will be noted that one of the six tones is written with no diacritical mark.

Most Vietnamese letters are pronounced roughly like the corresponding letters in English. However, the /d/ sound that is similar to the sound of the English *d* is written with a bar across it: *đ*; the *d* without a bar is pronounced like the English *z*. Generally, in the northern dialect the letter *r* is pronounced like the /z/ sound in English, while in the central and southern dialects, it is pronounced roughly like the /r/ sound in English.

The consonant sounds in Vietnamese are written (and pronounced) as follows:

p /p/   t   /t/   ch /č/   c, k   /k/
               th   /th/

b /b/	đ /d/		g, gh /g/
m /m/	n /n/	nh /ñ/	ng, ngh /ŋ/
ph /f/	s, x /s/		kh /X/
	d, gi /z/	r /z/ or /r/	h /h'/
	l /l/		

The vowel sounds are written (and pronounced) as follows:

i, y /i/	u /u/		ư /U/
			ô /o/
e /ɛ/	ơ /ə:/	a /a:/	o /ə/
ê /e¹/	â /ə↗/	ă /a↗/	

The sounds /ə↗/ and /a↗/ as represented by the letters â and ă occur only in initial and medial positions.

INTRODUCTION

No two languages are exactly alike. The devices used to signal structural meaning differ from one language to another. The task of learning a foreign language is therefore different from that of learning one's own native language. One is called upon to learn new devices that signal structural meaning in the foreign language and to make contrasts which, in one's mother tongue, may not be contrasted at all. And, according to Robert Lado, one tends to transfer the form, meaning and distribution of the formal devices of one's native language to the foreign language.[1]

The problem of learning a foreign language, usually English, is a problem faced by many Vietnamese students nowadays. Due to the growing relationship between VietNam and the western countries, especially the United States, English has become one of the most important foreign languages used in VietNam. It has also become a school subject at the high school and university levels. Despite the students' efforts, they meet a great many difficulties in trying to achieve a good command of English. These difficulties stem from many factors including cultural differences and differences in the structural devices that are inherent in English and Vietnamese. Some of the greatest difficulties, in this writer's opinion, grow out of the differences to be found between the two languages in their use of word order or position.

Two studies by Robert L. Allen, *The Verb System of Present-Day American English*[2] and *A Modern Grammar of Written English*,[3] show that word order or position is the most important device used in present-day English. Allen's analysis is based on the different kinds of positions to be found in a sentence and on the different kinds of units that may occur in these positions.

Position also appears to be a highly important structural device used in Vietnamese. One characteristic feature of Vietnamese is that words are invariable in form. The

[1] Robert Lado, *Linguistics Across Cultures: Applied Linguistics for Language Teachers* (Ann Arbor, Mich., University of Michigan Press, 1957), pp. 52-58.

[2] Robert L. Allen, *The Verb System of Present-Day American English* (The Hague, Mouton & Co., 1966).

[3] Robert L. Allen, *A Modern Grammar of Written English* (New York, The Macmillan Company, in press).

structural meaning of a unit is often determined solely by the position of that unit in a sentence.

The purpose of this study is to identify the different kinds of positions that occur in a Vietnamese sentence and the different kinds of units that may occur in these positions, and to compare them with those in English with the aim of identifying the similarities and differences between the two languages. It is hoped that, on the basis of such a systematic comparison of the two languages, it will be possible to predict the points of difficulty that a Vietnamese student will meet when he studies English, and to make some suggestions for ways of improving the teaching of English to Vietnamese students and the preparation of materials for use in such teaching.

The kind of analysis to be made will be in part a tagmemic analysis, along the lines of sector analysis as proposed and used by Robert L. Allen in his works *The Verb System of Present-Day American English*[4] and *A Modern Grammar of Written English*.[5] For the purpose of clarity and simplicity in this contrastive analysis, the terms used in Allen's study of English will also be applied to Vietnamese grammar wherever possible. The analysis will also be reductive in that it will start on the sentence level and from there work down to the word level.

This study will be based on two types of materials:

(1) The analysis of the order of units in the English sentence will be based primarily on *A Modern Grammar of Written English* by Robert L. Allen.
(2) The materials used for the analysis of the order of units in the Vietnamese sentence will be based on a survey of studies of Vietnamese grammar. But the writer will use herself as her chief informant.

The kind of Vietnamese to be presented in this study will represent formal and informal written present-day Vietnamese. The dialect described is that of the northern part of VietNam; however, according to Lê Văn Lý, the structure of the Vietnamese language is the same in all parts of the country.[6] It is the same language, but is spoken with three different accents and with a very small number of different vocabulary items particular to each region. The Northern dialect is the dialect of the writer, who was born in the North and lived there to the age of twenty-one.

The following is a list of the letters used in the diagrams in this project for different positions or for different kinds of constructions or words (these symbols are based on Allen's *A Modern Grammar of Written English*[7]):

B: The B Sector (for particles)   *b*:   particle (e.g., *lên* 'up', *xuống* 'down', etc.)

C: The C Sector (for complements)   *c*:   construction modifier

[4] *Op. cit.*
[5] Robert L. Allen, *A Modern Grammar of Written English* (New York, The Macmillan Company, in press).
[6] Lê Văn Lý, *Le Parler Vietnamien* (Saigon, Department of National Education, 1960), p. 9.
[7] Allen, *op. cit.*

D:	The D (i.e., 'Droppable') Sector		
E:	The End Sector		
F:	The Front Sector		
H:	Non-Included Clausid		
I:	The Introductory Position	i:	includer, identifier
K:	Cluster		
L:	The L Sector (for sentence linkers)	l:	sentence linker
M_1:	The M_1 Position	m:	modifier
M_2:	The M_2 Position		
		n:	noun
O:	The Object Sector		
Q:	The Position for question words	q:	question word
R:	Prepositional Phrase	r:	preposition
S:	The Subject Sector		
T:	Trunk		
U:	The Sentence Level		
V:	The Verbal Sector	v:	verbid
Y:	The External Y Position	y:	words like *vâng*, *dạ* 'yes', etc.
Z:	The External Z Position	z:	words like *thế*, *vậy*, etc.
		aux:	auxiliary
Cld:	Clausid	*gn*:	noun denoting gender
Em.:	The Emphatic Sector	*mm*:	modi-modifier
Neg.:	The Position for Negative Particles	*nu*:	cardinal numeral
Pass.:	The Position for Passive Particles	*ord*:	ordinal numeral
Pd:	Predicatid	*pl.p.*:	plural particle
PdK:	Predicatid cluster	*pN*	personal pronoun
Pd*:	Predicatid nucleus	*pod*:	post-determiner
Qn:	Question	*prd*:	pre-determiner
St:	Statement	*tr*:	time-relationship particle
TR:	The Position for Time-Relationship Particles	$+$:	coordinator
Trans.:	Translation	*:	nucleus
Lit.:	Literal translation	$\pm$:	optional

1

REVIEW OF OTHER STUDIES OF VIETNAMESE GRAMMAR

This chapter, which is in three parts, presents a review of studies of Vietnamese grammar written in Vietnamese, French and English, respectively.

1.1. REVIEW OF VIETNAMESE GRAMMARS WRITTEN IN VIETNAMESE

Việt Nam Văn-Phạm (i.e., *Vietnamese Grammar*), written by Trần Trọng Kim with the collaboration of Bùi Kỷ and Phạm Duy Khiêm, was the first important modern Vietnamese book written in Vietnamese for the Vietnamese.[1] It has served not only as one of the widely-used textbooks in schools in Vietnam, but also as a model for most of the books on Vietnamese published more recently.

To the authors of *Việt Nam Văn-Phạm*, grammar, or the rules of speaking and writing correctly, must be based on logic as well as on people's use of words.[2] Their aim is to present and explain all the essential grammatical points in Vietnamese, and to illustrate them with examples taken from everyday speech or from poems and novels.[3]

According to Kim and his collaborators, there has never been a proper classification of word classes in Vietnamese, but only a traditional division of words into four groups, a division designed mainly as a help in the writing of poetry.[4] The groups in this traditional classification were: 'meaningful words', 'empty words', 'semi-meaning-ful words', and 'semi-empty words'.[5] The 'meaningful words' include what Kim calls nouns; the 'empty words' include adverbs, conjunctions, and prepositions; the 'semi-meaningful words' include adjectives and verbs; and the 'semi-empty words' include Kim's reduplicatives and suppletives.[6]

---

[1] Trần Trọng Kim, Bùi Kỷ, and Phạm Duy Khiêm, *Việt Nam Văn-Phạm* (8th printing; Saigon, Tân Việt, n.d.).
[2] *Ibid.*, p. 11.
[3] *Ibid.*, p. viii.
[4] *Ibid.*
[5] *Ibid.* (All translations from the Vietnamese have been made by the present writer.)
[6] *Ibid.*

Kim and his collaborators say that in order to learn a language, one must know the values and uses of each word class. They acknowledge that Western methods, especially French methods, should be used in classifying the different kinds of words in Vietnamese.[7]

They divide the words in Vietnamese into thirteen word classes or parts of speech, some of which are again sub-divided into smaller classes. The thirteen word classes are: nouns, articles, classifiers, demonstratives, pronouns, adjectives, verbs, adverbs, prepositions, conjunctions, interjections, suppletives, and reduplicatives.[8]

One unusual feature of *Việt Nam Văn-Phạm* is that the authors start with a discussion of sentence structure before they present their analysis of the thirteen word classes. In this book of more than two hundred pages, "Phép Đặt Câu" or the methods of sentence construction take up only one chapter of seventeen pages — but this chapter comes first. The rest of the book then deals with the thirteen classes and with different styles of writing.

In the opinion of the authors, the methods of sentence construction are "the methods of organizing words into propositions[9] and organizing these propositions into sentences".[10] The authors divide their chapter on sentence construction into two parts: the construction of propositions, and the construction of sentences. A proposition is composed of a subject, an adjective, and a verb. The subject is "to stand as head of the proposition", the adjective is "to designate the substance of the subject," and the verb is "to show the action of the subject".[11] Nouns, adjectives, and verbs can all have complements. The authors identify three kinds of verbal complements: object complements, indirect complements and *compléments circonstanciels*[12] of time, place, manner, etc.[13] Although the authors mention the positions of units in a proposition, they do not present a clear picture of their overall order. They say only that a certain unit stands before or after a certain other unit.

Concerning the sentence, the authors say that it is "formed by a proposition ex-

[7] *Ibid.*
[8] *Ibid.*, pp. 37-142.
[9] The French term *proposition* is used here instead of the English term *clause* because it reflects more faithfully the ideas of the authors. Since the authors use French methods of grammatical analysis, they also borrow French terminology for the ideas expressed. In *Việt Nam Văn-Phạm* and in other grammar books to be discussed later, the term *proposition* is used sometimes with the meaning of a clause and sometimes with the meaning of a sentence. Actually, a dependent or subordinate proposition is an included clause, and a principal or main proposition is the trunk or main part of a sentence.
[10] *Ibid.*, p. 19.
[11] *Ibid.*
[12] 'Compléments' as the term is used in *Việt Nam Văn-Phạm* and in other grammar books to be discussed later, are said to perform the same variety of functions in Vietnamese that constructions of the same name are supposed to perform in French. For example, one kind of verbal complement is called the *complément circonstanciel* of time, place, manner, etc. This type of complement actually performs the grammatical function that front and end adverbials of time, place, and manner perform in English. However, the French term *complément circonstanciel* is used here in order to adhere more closely to the ideas expressed by the authors under discussion.
[13] Ibid. p. 22.

pressing a complete thought, or by two or more propositions".[14] They then discuss different kinds of propositions: independent, main, and subordinate. They also discuss different kinds of subordinate propositions and their positions in sentences in relation to the main proposition.[15] The sentence is thus analyzed as consisting of a cluster of propositions with a main proposition preceded and/or followed by one or many subordinate propositions.

The word classes are discussed in greater detail than are the different kinds of propositions. But the information given about their positions in a sentence in relation to one another is quite fragmentary. The definitions and explanations of these word classes are based on meaning more than on their functions in propositions.

As stated in its preface, *Tiểu-Học Việt Nam Văn-Phạm* (i.e., *Vietnamese Grammar for Primary Schools*) came into existence because of the need for a textbook on Vietnamese grammar to be used in schools.[16] Trần Trọng Kim states that his earlier book *Việt Nam Văn-Phạm* (just discussed) included all the rules of Vietnamese grammar and instructions on how to use words and construct sentences. He felt, therefore, that it was too general and too difficult for use in primary schools.[17] With the collaboration of Bùi Kỷ and Nguyễn Quang Oánh, he wrote a new book, *Tiểu-Học Việt Nam Văn-Phạm*, which deals with only the essential grammatical points taken from *Việt Nam Văn-Phạm*, the points that he thought primary school students should know.

Sentence construction is again presented here on the basis of propositions. According to the authors, a proposition may be composed of "a subject and an adjective"; "a subject and a verb"; "a subject, a verb or an adjective and complement(s)"; or "an adjective or a verb with complement(s), but with no subject".[18]

The complements in the proposition include the direct complement, the indirect complement, and the noun complement.[19] The construction of sentences is described only in a presentation of the three kinds of propositions:

An independent proposition is a proposition which is complete in meaning and can stand alone to form a sentence. ...

A main proposition is a proposition which stands as the main part of a sentence. But it is by itself incomplete in meaning and needs to have one or more propositions subordinated to it to form a sentence.

A subordinate proposition is a proposition whose meaning is subordinate to the main proposition in the construction of a sentence.[20]

---

[14] *Ibid.*, p. 25.

[15] *Ibid.*, pp. 25-30.

[16] Trần Trọng Kim, Bùi Kỷ, and Nguyễn Quang Oánh, *Tiểu-Học Việt Nam Văn-Phạm* (3rd printing; Saigon, Tân Việt, n.d.).

[17] *Ibid.*, p. vii.

[18] *Ibid.*, pp. 25-26.

[19] *Ibid.*, pp. 31-32.

[20] *Ibid.*, p. 35. This passage appears in the Vietnamese original as follows:
Mệnh-đề độc-lập là mệnh-đề tự nó có cái nghĩa
lọn hẳn có thể đứng một mình mà thành một câu. ...
Mệnh-đề chính là mệnh-đề đứng làm chủ trong

Beyond the statements given above, nothing is said about the order of propositions in a sentence.

One of the shortcomings of this book that should be mentioned is that the rules given in the book are based for the most part on meaning rather than on such formal features as the syntactical devices used in Vietnamese.

Nguyễn Trúc Thanh divides his grammar book *Văn Phạm Mới* (i.e., *New Grammar*) into three unequal parts: the first part, which comprises half of the book, deals with the analysis of word classes; the second part, which is the shortest of the three, deals with sentence construction; the last part deals with different kinds of writing.[21]

The author presents two different classifications of word classes: one is based on word types, the other on function. On the basis of word type, Thanh analyzes Vietnamese as having six word classes: "meaningful words" (i.e., words that have lexical meaning), "empty words" (i.e., words that have grammatical but no lexical meaning), verbs, adjectives, numbers, and plural markers.[22] On the basis of grammatical function, he analyzes Vietnamese as having eleven word classes: nouns, classifiers, pronouns, verbs, adjectives, adverbs, front particles, end particles, conjunctions, interjections, and suppletives.[23]

Although Thanh tries to distinguish between classification on the basis of word type and classification on the basis of function, he does not really succeed in doing so. The analysis of word classes according to function is largely a re-statement of the analysis according to word type. Although the author uses different terms for his word classes, they are similar to those described in *Việt Nam Văn-Phạm*.[24] Thanh also makes some mention of the functions of the different word classes and of their positions in a sentence relative to one another, but the information given is always fragmentary and unconnected.

The section in Thanh's book that deals with syntax is very sketchy and incomplete. It takes up only sixteen pages, five of which deal with the problems of compounds and idioms. Like the other authors named above, Thanh talks about propositions first. He defines a proposition as consisting of enough words or idioms to express a 'judgment'.[25] According to him, a proposition may include a subject, a verb, an adjective, and/or complement(s). These units can be organized into three different kinds of patterns. The first pattern consists of a subject, a copulative verb, and an attribute; the second pattern consists of a subject, a verb, and complement(s); the

---

một câu, nhưng tự nó không đủ nghĩa, phải có một
hay nhiều mệnh-đề phụ vào mới thành câu.
    Mệnh-đề phụ là mệnh-đề có cái nghĩa phụ-thuộc
cho cái nghĩa của mệnh-đề chính để cho thành câu.

[21] Nguyễn Trúc Thanh, *Văn Phạm Mới* (Saigon, Liên-Hiệp, 1956).
[22] *Ibid.*, pp. 15-76.
[23] *Ibid.*, pp. 77-98.
[24] Trần Trọng Kim, Bùi Kỷ, and Phạm Duy Khiêm, *Việt Nam Văn-Phạm* (8th printing; Saigon, Tân Việt, n.d.).
[25] Nguyễn Trúc Thanh, *Văn Phạm Mới* (Saigon, Liên-Hiệp, 1956), p. 104.

third pattern consists of a subject, an adjective, and complement(s).[26] Thanh then discusses different kinds of propositions, such as independent propositions, main propositions, and subordinate propositions of various kinds.[27]

Thanh says very little about the sentence. He defines it as "including one or many propositions to express a complete thought".[28] A sentence can be composed of:

(1) One or many independent propositions. ...
(2) Two propositions linked together by a conjunction. ...
(3) One or many main propositions, and one or many completive subordinate propositions. ...
(4) One or many main propositions, and one or many determinative subordinate propositions. ...[29]

By completive subordinate propositions and determinative propositions, Thanh seems to mean adverbial included clausids and adjectival included clausids. Nothing is said about the order of propositions in a sentence.

Phạm Tất Đắc, in his book *Phân-Tích Tự-Loại & Phân-Tích Mệnh-Đề* (i.e., *The Analysis of Word Classes and the Analysis of Propositions*), devotes the first twelve chapters to a discussion and analysis of word classes.[30] Đắc's twelve word classes are similar to twelve of the thirteen classes described by Trần Trọng Kim, Bùi Kỷ and Phạm Duy Khiêm in their *Việt Nam Văn-Phạm*.

An unusual feature of the organization of Đắc's book is that the discussion of the subject and complements appears in the chapters dealing with nouns, the first word class to be described in the book.[31] Thus, the positions and functions of the various word classes are discussed even before the word classes themselves have been analyzed and classified. The complements discussed in Chapter II include noun complements, adjective complements and verb complements.[32] It seems that there is here a confusion of levels of analysis. While the discussion of noun and adjective complements is a discussion of the modifiers of nouns and modifiers of adjectives on the cluster level, the discussion of verb complements is actually a discussion of units on the predicate level.

---

[26] *Ibid.*, p. 105.
[27] *Ibid.*, pp. 108-111.
[28] *Ibid.*, p. 111.
[29] *Ibid.*, p. 111. This passage appears in the Vietnamese original as follows:
    (1) Một hay nhiều mệnh-đề độc-lập. ...
    (2) Hai mệnh-đề liên-lạc với nhau do liên-động-từ. ...
    (3) Một hay nhiều mệnh-đề chính, và một hay nhiều mệnh-đề-phụ bổ nghĩa. ...
    (4) Một hay nhiều mệnh-đề chính và một hay nhiều mệnh-đề phụ chỉ-định.
[30] Phạm Tất Đắc, *Phân-Tích Tự-Loại & Phân-Tích Mệnh-Đề* (4th printing; Saigon, Nhà Xuất-Bản ABC, 1950).
[31] *Ibid.*, pp. 9-27. The term *bổ từ* 'complement' is used by Đắc — just as the term *complément* is used in French grammars — to refer to modifiers of nouns and adjectives as well as to complements of verbs.
[32] *Ibid.*, pp. 13-27.

In the section dealing with the analysis of propositions, the author gives several possible patterns for propositions:

(1) A subject and a verb. ...
(2) A subject and a verb plus complement(s) (of the verb). ...
(3) A subject and an adjective. ...
(4) A subject and an adjective plus complement(s). ...
(5) A verb with complement(s) (elliptical subject). ...
(6) An adjective with complement(s) (elliptical subject). ...
(7) A verb (elliptical subject and complement). ...[33]

Đắc states that the two essential parts in a proposition are the subject and the verb.[34] He then cites and discusses three types of propositions: independent, main, and subordinate.[35] His 'independent propositions' are actually free sentences. His 'subordinate propositions' are again subdivided into three types: completive propositions, determinative propositions, and *propositions circonstanciels*.[36]

It seems to this writer that Đắc is more concerned with the analysis of propositions, especially subordinate propositions, than with the analysis of sentences. The only mention of sentence analysis in his book appears at the beginning of Chapter XIV (dealing with the analysis of propositions), where the author says:

The analysis of the propositions in a sentence (or to put it correctly, the analysis of a sentence) has the aim of:
(1) dividing the sentence into propositions;
(2) signaling the characteristics of each proposition (independent proposition, main proposition or subordinate proposition);
(3) signaling the functions of the subordinate propositions (whether they are determinative, completive, or *circonstanciel*).[37]

Like the other grammarians mentioned above, Đắc also says that the most important fact we must know in analyzing a sentence is the number of propositions, which are

---

[33]   *Ibid.*, pp. 87-87. This passage appears in the Vietnamese original as follows:
      (1) Chủ-từ và động-từ. ...
      (2) Chủ-từ và động-từ, thêm túc-từ (của động-từ). ...
      (3) Chủ-từ và tĩnh-từ. ...
      (4) Chủ-từ và tĩnh-từ, thêm túc-từ. ...
      (5) Động-từ với túc-từ (lẫn chủ-từ). ...
      (6) Tĩnh-từ với túc-từ (lẫn chủ-từ). ...
      (7) Mệnh- đề có thể chỉ có một động-từ (không chủ-từ, túc-từ). ...
[34]   *Ibid.*, p. 88.
[35]   *Ibid.*, pp. 101-112.
[36]   *Ibid.*, pp. 101-112.
[37]   *Ibid.*, p. 85. This passage appears in the Vietnamese original as follows:
    Phân-tích những mệnh-đề trong câu (hay nói cho đúng là phân-tích một câu) có muc-đích là:
      (1) Chia câu làm mấy mệnh-đề;
      (2) Nói tính-cách của từng mệnh-đề (mệnh-đề độc-lập, mệnh-đề chính hay mệnh-đề phụ);
      (3) Nói công-dụng của những mệnh-đề phụ (hoặc chỉ-định, hoặc bổ-túc, hoặc mệnh-đề phụ chỉ một trường-hợp nào).

determined by the number of verbs appearing in that sentence.[38] This preoccupation with propositions to the almost complete exclusion of any concern for sentences, coupled with the mixing of the levels of sentence and clause analysis, has, for a long time, handicapped Vietnamese grammarians in their efforts to analyze the true nature of sentences in Vietnamese.

Bùi Đức Tịnh has written three books on Vietnamese grammar, all of which were published between 1949 and 1956. His first book, *Những Nhận-Xét về Văn-Phạm Việt-Nam* (i.e., *Remarks on Vietnamese Grammar*), is a collection of revisions of articles previously published in magazines.[39] In this book he makes a detailed commentary on *Việt Nam Văn-Phạm* by Trần Trọng Kim, Bùi Kỷ and Phạm Duy Khiêm, while at the same time giving a preview of his second book on Vietnamese grammar.

Tịnh's ideas about language seem to be linguistically sound. For instance, he says that the grammar of a language consists of a set of rules or principles discovered through a careful study of the characteristics of that language, and based on what has been said or written in that language.[40] He believes that one cannot use the grammar of one language as a basis for the grammar of another.[41] Tịnh also says that one word class may have different functions, and that two different word classes may have the same function; so the discussion of functions of word classes is important if one is to understand them and use them effectively.[42]

Tịnh comments on the classification of certain words as so-called "special classifiers" in *Việt Nam Văn-Phạm*.[43] Although the authors of that book recognize the fact that these words are actually nouns which are used as classifiers before other nouns, Tịnh does not consider this sufficient justification for classifying them as a separate word class. According to him, if every noun that stands before another noun becomes a "special classifier", then there would be a limitless number of classifiers in the language. He points out that nearly all the concrete nouns in Vietnamese can perform the function of classifier. The solution Tịnh offers is to consider the "special classifier" and the noun that follows it as parts of a compound noun.[44]

Tịnh does not consider the reduplicative as a special word class, as do the authors of *Việt Nam Văn-Phạm*. He says that each reduplicative element is only a part of a word and functions together with the other elements in the word as a single unique unit in the language.[45]

With regard to the problem of sentence analysis, Tịnh agrees with the authors of *Việt Nam Văn-Phạm* that there are two essential parts in a proposition (a subject and

---

[38] *Ibid.*, p. 88.
[39] Bùi Đức Tịnh, *Những Nhận-Xét về Văn-Phạm Việt-Nam* (Saigon, Đại-Chúng, 1949).
[40] *Ibid.*, p. 21.
[41] *Ibid.*, p. 22.
[42] *Ibid.*, p. 34.
[43] Trần Trọng Kim, Bùi Kỷ, and Phạm Duy Khiêm, *Việt Nam Văn-Phạm* (8th printing; Saigon Tân Việt, n.d.), p. 47.
[44] Bùi Đức Tịnh, *Những Nhận-Xét về Văn-Phạm Việt-Nam* (Saigon, Đại-Chúng, 1949), pp. 44-47.
[45] *Ibid.*, pp. 59-60.

a predicate), and that the predicate can be either a verb or an adjective standing in the complement position.[46] Tịnh also distinguishes three kinds of propositions: a proposition expressing a single thought, a proposition expressing a main thought, and a proposition expressing a subordinate thought. The difference between a main and a subordinate proposition lies in the fact that the subordinate proposition often has a preposition (present or elliptical) standing in front of it.[47]

The second grammar book written by Bùi Đức Tịnh is called *Văn-Phạm Việt-Nam* (i.e., *Vietnamese Grammar*).[48] The statements about language in this book, like those in his first book, are very sound. Tịnh clearly recognizes the importance of a careful study of language. He sees the importance of syntax in the study of language, especially as regards the position of words in the flow of speech and of their functions. He criticizes the grammar books published before his for having put too much emphasis on the analysis and classification of word classes.[49] In paying too much attention to the parts, they have neglected to give an over-all, synthesized view of the language. According to Tịnh, it is necessary to analyze the units in a sentence and in a proposition in order to know the grammatical functions of the words and the meaning they express. It is also important to state rules in order to give the learner a notion of the grammar of the language. To be reliable, these grammatical rules should be related to one another, complementary to one another, and unified as the parts in an organized whole.[50]

Unlike the other grammarians mentioned above, Tịnh devotes almost as much space in his book to the discussion of syntax as he does to the discussion of the word classes. He says that to form a sentence one needs to know all the grammatical functions in a sentence and the word classes that perform these functions.[51] To identify these grammatical functions and to state the rules concerning their distribution is to describe the syntax of the language. Tịnh starts with the study of units in a simple sentence having only one proposition and goes on to sentences having more than one proposition.

According to Tịnh, a proposition has two parts:

(1) A subject: to designate persons or things spoken of.
(2) A predicate: to designate what is being said about the persons or things.[52]

The subject can be a noun, a pronoun, a verb, or an adjective.[53] The predicate can be a verb, a verb with its modifiers and complements, or an adjective with or without

---

[46] *Ibid.*, pp. 61-64.
[47] *Ibid.*, p. 71.
[48] Bùi Đức Tịnh, *Văn-Phạm Việt-Nam* (Saigon, P. Văn Tươi, 1952).
[49] *Ibid.*, p. 45.
[50] *Ibid.*, pp. 46-47.
[51] *Ibid.*, p. 243.
[52] *Ibid.*, p. 244. This passage appears in the Vietnamese original as follows:
    (1) Chủ-ngữ: chỉ người hay vật được nói đến.
    (2) Tuyên-ngữ: Những gì để nói về người hay vật ấy.
[53] *Ibid.*, p. 245.

complements, etc.[54] Three types of complements can occur in a single proposition: a noun complement, an adjective complement, and a verb complement. Verb complements are sub-divided into four types: direct objects, indirect objects, complements or passive verbs, and *compléments circonstanciels*. The last complement type is again divided into many sub-types.[55]

Tịnh's grammar seems to have been the first to mention the order of units in a proposition, although the description is inadequate. Tịnh says that in a Vietnamese proposition, the usual order of units is as follows:

$$\text{Subject} \begin{cases} \text{verb } \| \text{ direct object } \| \\ \text{indirect object} \\ \text{or} \\ \text{adjective } \| \text{ complement}^{56} \\ \text{(as predicate)} \end{cases}$$

Then he adds that the *compléments circonstanciels* can occur either at the beginning or at the end of the sentence, and that the two direct and indirect objects can interchange their positions, depending on their length. The shorter object will occur before the longer one.[57]

In a sentence having more than one proposition, the number of propositions depends on the number of predicates.[58] Like other grammarians before him, Tịnh classifies propositions into three kinds: independent, principal, and subordinate. Subordinate propositions are sub-divided into three kinds: determinative, completive, and *circonstanciels*.[59]

Near the end of the book, Tịnh advocates a method of analysis used by C. D. Tenney in his *English Lessons*. This method is called "Phương-Pháp Đồ-Biểu" or the diagram method.[60] Its purpose is to show what is essential in a sentence and what is not, and to show whether any essential part in a sentence is missing. On the first line of the diagram there are slots for the essential parts of a proposition, namely the subject and the predicate. Complement(s) of the subject and *compléments circonstanciels* of the predicate are put on lower lines. The following is an example taken rom Tịnh's book:

---

[54] *Ibid.*, pp. 247-249.
[55] *Ibid.*, p. 250.
[56] *Ibid.*, p. 263. This passage appears in the Vietnamese original as follows:

$$\text{CHỦ-NGỮ} \begin{cases} \text{Động từ } \| \text{ bổ-túc-ngữ thuộc-động } \| \\ \text{bổ-túc-ngữ can-động} \\ \text{hoặc} \\ \text{Tính-trạng-từ } \| \text{ bổ-túc-ngữ} \\ \text{(làm tuyên-ngữ).} \end{cases}$$

[57] *Ibid.*, p. 264.
[58] *Ibid.*, p. 265.
[59] *Ibid.*, pp. 266-270.
[60] *Ibid.*, p. 320.

Đêm nào[61] *ông cũng đọc sách đến khuya.*[62]
'Every night he reads until late'
(*Lit.*: Night whichever Mr. also read book until late.)

The diagram:

Apparently the author wants to show the two essential parts of the sentence, the subject and the predicate, separately from the other functional parts. The first row is divided into two parts by a double bar. If the predicate has a complement, a single bar appears between the verb and its complement(s). This method is useful in showing what is essential and what is not. But it is confusing when the order of the words in the sentence is taken into consideration. Moreover, some of the functional units, though not essential, belong to the same level of analysis as those in the first line. Thus, the levels of analysis on the lower lines are not clearly demarcated.

In the preface of Tịnh's third book, *Văn-Phạm Việt-Nam cho các Lớp Trung-Học* (i.e., *Vietnamese Grammar for Secondary Schools*), the author admits that he put too much emphasis on theory in his earlier book and thereby confused students and other readers with unfamiliar concepts and terminology.[64] In this book, therefore, he modifies his 'advanced' views on grammar and conforms to the type of analysis that has been popularized in the schools.[65]

In the preface of *Để Hiểu Văn-Phạm* (i.e., *To Understand Grammar*), Nguyễn Hiến Lê says that he does not claim to have written a complete grammar but only to have proposed a few grammatical principles for the preparation of a book dealing with the characteristics of the Vietnamese language, a book simple and easy enough to enable every Vietnamese to learn his own language.[66]

Lê criticizes other grammarians for not using the same terminology for the same parts of speech or word classes, and for imitating French grammar books too closely.[67] He proposes to leave out the analysis and classification of word classes since words in Vietnamese do not belong to any definite word classes.[68] He says that, instead, he will distinguish only the functions of the words in the language. He is right in realizing

---

[61]   In a question, *nào* means 'which'; in a statement sentence, *nào* means 'whichever' or 'any'. It is interesting to note that WH words in English also have two functions: they may function as question words in WH questions or as introducers in included clauses.

[62]   *Ibid.*, p. 320.

[63]   *Ibid.*

[64]   Bùi Đức Tịnh, *Văn-Phạm Việt-Nam cho các Lớp Trung-Học* (Saigon, Vĩnh-Bảo, 1956), "Preface".

[65]   *Ibid.*

[66]   Nguyễn Hiến Lê, *Để Hiểu Văn-Phạm* (Saigon, P. Văn Tươi, 1952), p. 6.

[67]   *Ibid.*, pp. 16-17.

[68]   *Ibid.*, p. 36.

that the function of a word is more important than its class, and that function changes with position. To discover the positions that each word can fill in the sentence is to discover the grammar of a language.[69]

The author divides the words in Vietnamese into five functional groups: *tiếng cốt yếu* 'essential words', *tiếng làm chủ* 'subjects', *tiếng bổ túc* 'complements', *tiếng để nối* 'linking words', and *tiếng phụ* 'subordinating words'.[70] But it is difficult to determine definitely the exact order in which these functional groups will occur in a given sentence. The following is Lê's summary of the positions for these five groups:

The essential word can occur anywhere, but in the question form, it often occurs at the beginning or at the end of a sentence or part of a sentence.
The subject word often occurs before the essential word.
The complement word usually occurs after the word being modified. But many words which are used to designate time and manner and which were originally Chinese words occur before the words they modify.
The linking word occurs between those parts that are being linked, but it occurs at the beginning of a sentence in an inversion.
The subordinating word does not have a definite position.[71]

From this summary, it is evident that Lê does not assign a particular position to any group. As there is no definite position for any functional group, and as there is no strict division into word classes, the analysis of a sentence in the manner proposed by Lê proves to be difficult. The author's attempt to identify the functional groups in a sentence is very commendable, but the method of analysis he proposes is too vague and inconsistent for someone else to understand or follow.

Several years later, Nguyễn Hiến Lê wrote another book on grammar. This time he collaborated with another grammarian, Trương Văn Chình. In 1963, the two of them together brought out *Khảo Luận về Ngữ Pháp Việt Nam* (i.e., *Studies in Vietnamese Grammar*).[72]

In the preface of this book, the authors state that they have followed the methods of structural linguistics in their research, primarily in connection with their examination of the "*structure de la pensée*". The authors do not adhere to any school of linguistics in particular but borrow what they think is good from various schools.[73]

---

[69] *Ibid.*, p. 68.
[70] *Ibid.*, p. 68.
[71] *Ibid.*, pp. 77-78. This passage appears in the Vietnamese original as follows:
Tiếng cốt-yếu có thể đứng ở đâu cũng được nhưng trong những câu
hỏi nó luôn-luôn đứng trước hay sau một câu hoặc một phần câu.
Tiếng làm chủ luôn-luôn đứng trước tiếng cốt-yếu.
Tiếng bổ-túc thường đứng sau tiếng được bổ-túc, nhưng nhiều
tiếng chỉ thời-gian và nhiều tiếng chỉ thể-cách mà gốc ở tiếng
Hán thì đứng trước.
Tiếng để nối đứng giữa những phần được nối, trừ trong phép
đảo-ngữ thì nó đứng đầu câu.
Tiếng phụ không có vị-trí nhất-định.
[72] Trương Văn Chình and Nguyễn Hiến Lê, *Khảo Luận về Ngữ Pháp Việt Nam* (Huế, Đại Học Huế, 1963).
[73] *Ibid.*, p. 8.

The authors' analysis of words and compounds is more than adequate. They recognize the existence of words which are composed of more than one syllable. They also recognize that syntactically compounds function as words and that therefore both compounds and words are to be treated alike on the syntactic level.[74]

The authors do not elaborate on the classification of word classes. Tentatively, they divide the words in Vietnamese into three groups: *thể từ* 'substantives', *trạng từ* 'adverbs', and *trợ từ* 'suppletive words'.[75] The *trạng từ* or 'adverbs' in this book correspond to three word classes in French, namely *verbe, adjectif qualificatif, ... adverbe de manière*.[76] While 'substantives' and 'adverbs' (as defined in this book) have real meaning and grammatical functions, the 'suppletive words' have no real meaning and perform no grammatical function.[77]

Chình and Lê classify grammatical functions into two different groups: the primary function, i.e., the function of the units in a sentence, and the secondary function, i.e., the function of units within sentence units.[78] Altogether, there are thirteen grammatical functions distributed in the following manner:

Primary Functions	(1) *Exposé du sujet*	
	(2) subject	
	(3) predicate	
	(4, 5, 6) modifier(s) of the sentence	subordinate word in the sentence
		complement of the sentence
		appositive of the sentence
	(7) sentence connector	
Secondary Functions		numeral
		classifier
	(8, 9, 10, 11, 12) modifiers of words	subordinate word in a word
		complement of a word
		appositive of a word
	(13) word connector[79]	

In the section on secondary functions, the authors include an analysis of both the adverb cluster and the substantive cluster. In an earlier part of the book, they describe

[74] *Ibid.*, pp. 61-148, 151.
[75] *Ibid.*, p. 152.
[76] *Ibid.*, p. 168.
[77] *Ibid.*, p. 180.
[78] *Ibid.*, p. 188.
[79] *Ibid.*, p. 189. This passage appears in the Vietnamese original as follows:

Từ vụ chính	(1) chủ đề	
	(2) chủ từ	
	(3) thuật từ	
	(4, 5, 6) gia từ của câu	phó từ của câu
		bổ từ của câu
		giải từ của câu
	(7) quan hệ từ của câu	

the functions as well as the positions of the modifiers of substantives and adverbs. Those which occur before the main word, they say, are the numeral, the classifier, and the subordinate. Those which occur after the main word include the complement and the appositive.[80] Then they give the following illustration:

Hai con chim non đang bay là là ngoài sân.[81]
'Two young birds were flying low in the courtyard'
(*Lit.*: Two animate thing bird young in the process of fly low courtyard.)

lượng từ	loại từ	phó từ	tiếng chính	bổ từ
numeral	*classifier*	*subordinate*	*main word*	*complement*
hai	con		chim	non
		đang	bay	là là, ngoài sân[82]

The order of units in clusters is presented in this fashion, but the authors do not distinguish between the order of units in a substantive cluster and the order in an adverb cluster.

The authors also describe classifiers and numerals in great detail.[83] Concerning the complement of the substantive which occurs after the main substantive, the authors do not say much. They say that they had intended to divide the complements of the substantive into demonstrative complements, adjective complements, possessive complements, and complements of place and time, but that, after concluding that this sort of division might not be useful or logical, they dropped the idea.[84]

In their description of the units in an adverb cluster, the authors distinguish *khách từ* 'the complement of the adverb', *bổ từ không gian, bổ từ thời gian* 'the complement of place and the complement of time of the adverb', *hình dung từ* 'the adjective', and *phó từ* 'the subordinate of the adverb'.[85] They mention all the possible positions of the modifiers of adverbs, but like other grammarians, they do not give a clear picture of the overall order of these modifiers. The reason that they place the analysis of these modifiers of adverbs in the section on the structure of clusters stems

---

			lượng từ
			loại từ
Từ vụ thứ {	(8, 9, 10, 11, 12) gia từ của tiếng		phó từ của tiếng
			bổ từ của tiếng
			giải từ của tiếng
	(13) quan hệ từ của tiếng		

It is to be noted that the authors use much the same terminology for both groups of functions. The chief distinction is in their labels for the functional levels: word or sentence. The term *bổ từ* 'complement' is used by Chình and Lê — just as the term *complément* is used in French grammars — to refer to modifiers of nouns and adjectives as well as to complements of verbs.

[80] *Ibid.*, p. 195.
[81] *Ibid.*
[82] *Ibid.*
[83] *Ibid.*, pp. 281-306.
[84] *Ibid.*, pp. 248-251.
[85] *Ibid.*, pp. 220-247.

from their belief that these modifiers modify the adverb alone.[86] In the section on sentences, the adverbs and their modifiers are described as forming one unit on the sentence level. This unit is called the predicate.

The authors give the following definition of a sentence:

A sentence is a construction of words used to express a situation or many situations which are related to one another; this construction of words can be by itself relatively complete in meaning, and is not grammatically included in any other construction.[87]

According to the authors, a simple sentence may have seven units:

(1) A subject,
(2) a predicate,
(3) an *exposé du sujet*,
(4) complement(s) (of the sentence),
(5) an appositive (of the sentence),
(6) a subordinate element (of the sentence),
(7) a sentence connector.[88]

The subject and the predicate are the two essential parts of a sentence; that is to say, a sentence must have at least these two units. The authors state that grammatically and semantically all the words in the sentence are directly or indirectly subordinate to the subject.[89] The complement, the appositive, and the subordinate elements have the function of modifying the essential parts of the sentence. These essential parts can be either the subject and the predicate, or the *exposé du sujet*, the subject, and the predicate.[90] The following patterns show their possible arrangement in a sentence:

(a) complement + exposé du sujet + subject + predicate,
(b) exposé du sujet + complement + subject + predicate,
(c) complement + subject + predicate,

---

[86] *Ibid.*, p. 219.
[87] *Ibid.*, pp. 476-744. This passage appears in the Vietnamese original as follows:
        Câu là một tổ hợp tiếng ... dùng để diễn tả một sự tình hay
        nhiều sự tình có quan hệ với nhau; tổ hợp ấy tự nó tương đối đầy đủ
        ý nghĩa, và không phụ thuộc về ngữ pháp vào một tổ hợp nào khác.
[88] *Ibid.*, p. 490. This passage appears in the Vietnamese original as follows:
        (1) chủ từ,
        (2) thuật từ,
        (3) chủ đề,
        (4) bổ từ (của câu),
        (5) giải từ (của câu),
        (6) phó từ (của câu),
        (7) quan hệ từ (của câu).
[89] *Ibid.*, pp. 495-496.
[90] *Ibid.*, p. 203.

(d) subject + complement + predicate,

(e) exposé du sujet + subject + predicate + complement.[91]

The adjective and the subordinate element may also precede the subject, but the authors do not mention their specific positions.[92]

In contrast to the other grammarians discussed above, the authors of *Khảo Luận về Ngữ Pháp Việt Nam* do make a distinction between *câu* 'sentences' and *cú* 'clauses' as two units on different functional levels.[93] But they also point out that a clause can be composed of the same functional units as a sentence.[94] Consequently, whenever they are discussing any functional unit on the sentence level, it is to be assumed that they are also discussing that unit on the clause level.[95] The authors also classify clauses into several types: independent clauses or sentences, main clauses, subordinate clauses, and sub-clauses.[96] While *cú phụ* or subordinate clauses can function as the complements and appositives of sentences, *bán cú* or sub-clauses function only as the complements and appositives of words.[97]

1.2. REVIEW OF VIETNAMESE GRAMMARS WRITTEN IN FRENCH

Cours d'annamite by R. Bulteau consists of fifty lessons dealing with the main "formes grammaticales" of Vietnamese.[98] It aims to help learners of Vietnamese, especially French-speaking learners, to speak, read and translate Vietnamese into French and French into Vietnamese.[99]

The book deals largely with an analysis of the functions and uses of the word classes in Vietnamese. Bulteau divides Vietnamese words into twelve word classes: articles, nouns, adjectives, possessives, demonstratives, indefinite determinatives, personal pronouns, verbs, adverbs, prepositions, conjunctions and interjections.[100]

Of the fifty lessons in this book, only five deal with the problems of Vietnamese syntax. Bulteau recognizes the importance of position in Vietnamese grammar. He

---

[91] *Ibid.*, p. 568. This passage appears in the Vietnamese original as follows:
  (a) bổ từ + chủ đề + chủ từ + thuật từ,
  (b) chủ đề + bổ từ + chủ từ + thuật từ,
  (c) bổ từ + chủ từ + thuật từ,
  (d) chủ từ + bổ từ + thuật từ,
  (e) chủ đề + chủ từ + thuật từ + bổ từ.

[92] *Ibid.*, pp. 583-586.

[93] *Ibid.*, p. 479.

[94] *Ibid.*, p. 492.

[95] *Ibid.*, p. 552.

[96] *Ibid.*, p. 628.

[97] *Ibid.*, pp. 634-635.

[98] R. Bulteau, *Cours d'annamite* (*Langue vietnamienne*) (4th printing; Paris, Editions Larose, 1953), p. vi.

[99] *Ibid* , pp. v-vi.

[100] *Ibid.*, pp. 17-194.

says that a word can change its word class by changing its position in the sentence.[101] He also recognizes the fact that Vietnamese uses certain particles to perform the functions of inflections in other languages.[102] According to Bulteau, the units in a Vietnamese sentence generally occur in the following order: subject, verb, attribute or complement.[103] He states that the negative particle occurs before the verb, that the "complément circonstanciel de temps" can occur either at the beginning or at the end of the sentence.[104] However, he does not go as deeply into the analysis of Vietnamese sentences as he does into the analysis of word classes.

L. Cadière spent nearly half a century in making a study of the Vietnamese language. On his death, he left his work without a title, but in 1958 it was published under the title *Syntaxe de la langue vietnamienne* by L'École Française d'Extrême-Orient.[105] Cadière's study includes a discussion of those grammatical points common to the three main dialects of Vietnam: the dialects of Huê (Center Vietnam), Saigon (South Vietnam), and North Vietnam.[106]

Cadière recognizes the important fact that Vietnamese, as a monosyllabic language, cannot have a syntax based on agreement. In his opinion, it can have only "LA SYNTAXE D'USAGE ou d'emploi et LA SYNTAXE DE POSITION".[107] Throughout his book, he concentrates on the uses of the grammatical units and on their positions.

His book is divided into two parts, the first of which deals with the analysis of word classes, and the second of which deals with the analysis of propositions.

In the section on substantives, Cadière classifies nouns which occur before other nouns as substantives of category. A substantive complement, as described by Cadière, is any noun, verb or adjective occurring after another noun.[108] It appears that there is no clear distinction between substantives of category and nouns acting as substantive complements. Below are two examples given by Cadière of substantives of category used with nouns, and two examples of nouns used with their substantive complements where the latter are also nouns:

Substantive of category + *Noun*		*Noun* + *Substantive complement*	
cây	chuối	nước	mắt
(tree)	(banana) = banana plant	(water)	(eye) = tear
trái	cam	cá	biển
(fruit)	(orange) = orange	(fish)	(sea) = sea fish[109]

[101]   *Ibid.*, p. 1.
[102]   *Ibid.*
[103]   *Ibid.*, p. 5.
[104]   *Ibid.*, pp. 13, 197, 199.
[105]   L. Cadière, *Syntaxe de la langue vietnamienne* (Paris, Publications de l'École Française d'Extrême-Orient, 1958), p. xi.
[106]   *Ibid.*, p. xxiii.
[107]   *Ibid.*, p. xxiv.
[108]   *Ibid.*, p. 20.
[109]   *Ibid.*, pp. 7, 21.

It is not clear on what grounds Cadière distinguishes between substantives of category followed by nouns and nouns followed by nouns functioning as substantive complements. He further sub-divides substantive complements into many groups, but he does so on the basis of the meanings they express rather than on the basis of their functions or of the positions in which they occur.[110] Although he notes that nouns, verbs, and adjectives can occur after the nouns they modify, he does not mention the order in which they may co-occur.

The second part of Cadière's book deals with the structure of propositions. According to Cadière, the units occurring in propositions include five major types: subjects, verbs, attributes, object complements, and various "compléments circonstanciels".[111] Cadière defines subjects as follows: "Le sujet, c'est l'être (personne ou chose) duquel on affirme une chose".[112] He says that the subject usually occurs before the verb, although he discusses cases where the subject is not expressed, as in coordinate propositions and in complex sentences.[113]

In his discussion of attributes, Cadière says that to show that a quality belongs to a subject, an adjective is placed immediately after it. In this case no copulative verb is needed to link the subject to the predicate. But in other cases, copulative verbs are needed.[114]

Cadière divides object complements into two kinds: direct object complements and indirect object complements. The former usually occur immediately after the verb, while the latter are introduced by prepositions such as cho, đến, cùng, etc.[115]

"Compléments circonstanciels" are used to complete the meaning of a verb by reference to time, place, manner, and the like.[116] A "complément circonstanciel" of time usually occurs at the beginning of an independent proposition, or after the verb in a subordinate proposition.[117] Cadière also classifies other "compléments circonstanciels" according to the meanings they express. These complements always occur after the verb.[118]

Cadière's description of the positions of the subject and verb is quite explicit, but his description of the positions of units following the verb in relation to one another is vague. He does not specify in what order they occur when they occur together in a proposition. In other words, although he analyzes each unit in great detail, he does not attempt to present an overall picture of the positions of all the possible units that might co-occur in a proposition.

[110] Ibid., pp. 20-22.
[111] Ibid., p. 81.
[112] Ibid.
[113] Ibid., pp. 83-85.
[114] Ibid., pp. 109-111.
[115] Ibid., pp. 112-115.
[116] Ibid., p. 115.
[117] Ibid., p. 118.
[118] Ibid., pp. 126-132.

With regard to the construction of propositions, Cadière states that Vietnamese syntax is governed by three "laws":

(1) LA LOI DE PRÉCISION,
(2) LA LOI DE SUCCESSION,
(3) LA LOI D'INDÉTERMINATION.[119]

He states "la loi de précision" as follows:

In a simple proposition, the words follow one another in such an order that each word clarifies the meaning of the preceding word or of one of the preceding words.[120]

According to Cadière, "la loi de précision" is the most important of the three.[121] "La loi de succession", in turn, "... requires that the facts mentioned succeed one another in their chronological order".[122] "La loi d'indétermination" is complementary to the other two laws. Cadière states this law as follows:

In fact, with the words in the sentence modifying one another according to the law of precision, and the facts following one another chronologically according to the law of succession, the Vietnamese language can dispense with the expression of certain secondary notions of time, person, cause, consequence, etc., already expressed in the normal sequence of words.[123]

Cadière then proceeds to describe the different kinds of propositions. He distinguishes two main types of subordinate propositions: completive propositions and different "propositions circonstancielles". He distinguishes two kinds of completive propositions: simple and indirect interrogative. A simple completive proposition can occur either immediately after the verb of the main proposition or separated from the verb by one of the conjunctions *rằng, là, cho*, etc.[124] Only a few verbs can occur with these conjunctions. An indirect interrogative completive proposition is an unchanged, normal question proposition occurring immediately after a main proposition.[125] Cadière distinguishes eight different kinds of "propositions circonstancielles" according to the meanings expressed by them.[126]

Le parler vietnamien by Lê Văn Lý consists of two parts, the first of which deals

---

[119] *Ibid.*, p. 137.
[120] *Ibid.*, p. 137. This passage appears in the French original as follows:
    Les mots, dans une proposition simple, se succèdent dans un ordre tel que chacun des termes précise le sens du terme précédent ou d'un des termes précédents.
[121] *Ibid.*, p. 138.
[122] *Ibid.* This passage appears in the French original as follows:
    "... veut que les faits énoncés se succèdent dans leur ordre chronologique."
[123] *Ibid.*, p. 140. This passage appears in the French original as follows:
    En effet, les mots dans la phrase, se déterminant réciproquement, selon la loi de précision, et les faits se succédant chronologiquement selon la loi de succession, la langue vietnamienne peut se dispenser d'exprimer certaines notions secondaires de temps, de personne, de cause, de conséquence, etc., déjà exprimés naturellement par l'enchaînement des termes.
[124] *Ibid.*, pp. 167-170.
[125] *Ibid.*, p. 170.
[126] *Ibid.*, pp. 170-189.

with the phonological structure of Vietnamese, and the second of which deals with the classification of words into word classes.[127]

To classify Vietnamese words, Lý examines the environments in which they occur and their capability of combining with words of other classes — that is, he examines certain elements that occur before or after the words belonging to one class in all their possible positions and thus tries to identify the characteristics that differentiate the words of one class from the words of other classes.[128] The elements that the author uses to differentiate one class of words from another are those particles which he calls "mots-témoins"[129] — that is, those words that can or cannot occur before or after members of the word class under consideration. In short, a given word is assigned to a word class on the basis of the presence or absence of certain "mots-témoins", i.e., by its potential co-occurrence with these "mots-témoins". By the use of this method, Lý comes up with three, or rather four, large "categories of words" (i.e., word classes), which he labels A, B and B', and C. Concerning the Word Class B', Lý only states that, among the words of category B, he distinguishes a special category of words called B' which is recognized by its potential occurrence after the lexemes $rất$ 'very', $khá$ 'rather', $khí$ or $hơi$ 'a little'.[130]

The members of his Word Class A correspond in general to traditional nouns.[131] The members of Word Class B correspond roughly to verbs; those of Word Class B' to adjectives.[132] Word Class C is sub-divided into C_1 ("mots-personnels"), C_2 ("mots de nombre"), and C_3 ("particules").[133] C_3 words account for all the words remaining in the language.[134] C_1 and C_2 words have their own "mots-témoins", but C_3 words do not. Instead, they are classified into four sub-groups according to their positions in utterances: initial particles, medial particles, final particles, and free particles. Free particles can occur either in initial or final positions.[135]

The "mots-témoins" of Word Classes A, B, B', and C are also analyzed and classified by Lý. The "mots-témoins" of Word Class A include plural markers, classifiers, and demonstratives.[136] The "mots-témoins" of Word Class B include words denoting aspect and words of negation.[137] The "mots-témoins" of Word Class B' include the lexemes $rất$, $khá$, $khí$ or $hơi$.[138] Word Class C has only one "mot-témoin", $chúng$, which is used as a plural marker for the "mots-personnels".[139]

[127] Lê Văn Lý, Le parler vietnamien (Sa structure phonologique et morphologique fonctionnelle) (Saigon, Bộ Quốc-Gia Giáo-Dục, Viện Khảo-Cổ, 1960).
[128] Ibid., pp. 150-151, 167.
[129] Ibid., p. 151.
[130] Ibid., p. 188.
[131] Ibid., pp. 189-192.
[132] Ibid., pp. 192-193.
[133] Ibid.
[134] Ibid., p. 193.
[135] Ibid., pp. 193-195.
[136] Ibid., pp. 200-231.
[137] Ibid., pp. 231-241.
[138] Ibid., p. 188.
[139] Ibid., pp. 241-242.

Lý also analyzes words which he calls "mots vides" or "mots usés". They are words which originally belonged to Word Classes A, B or B', but which have become prepositions or adverbs in present-day Vietnamese.[140]

It is clear that Lê Văn Lý does not use meaning but rather distribution and "mots-témoins" as the means for identifying word classes. Applied to Vietnamese, this has proved to be a very sound and effective method of classification.

1.3. REVIEW OF VIETNAMESE GRAMMARS WRITTEN IN ENGLISH

Introduction to Spoken Vietnamese by Robert B. Jones, Jr., and Huỳnh Sanh Thông consists of twenty Vietnamese lessons based on the Saigon dialect.[141] It aims to help learners of Vietnamese to speak fluently in normal, everyday conversation. Except for Lesson VII and the last six lessons, each of the lessons consists of a pronunciation drill, a dialogue, pattern drills, word study, exercises, conversations and narratives.[142] In the sections on pattern drills and word study the authors explain and clarify certain grammatical points and the uses of certain expressions. However, the present writer finds the grammatical sections too fragmentary: the authors' explanations are largely limited to the meanings and uses of individual words. Discussions of words of the same word class are not grouped together in one lesson or in two or three consecutive lessons but are scattered throughout the book. Furthermore, the uses of such words are 'taught' for the most part by means of long lists of model sentences printed after each explanation.

The only Vietnamese construction which the authors describe in detail is the nominal construction, which, they say, contains a maximum of five positions occurring in the following order:

quantifier classifier noun attribute demonstrative

(1)		con	chó	
(2)	hai	con	chó,	
(3)	hai	con	chó nhỏ,	
(4)	hai	con	chó	này,
(5)	hai	con	chó nhỏ	này,

(1) the dog
(2) two dogs
(3) two little dogs
(4) these two dogs
(5) these two little dogs[143]

---

[140] *Ibid.*, pp. 243-265.
[141] Robert B. Jones, Jr., and Huỳnh Sanh Thông, *Introduction to Spoken Vietnamese* (revised edition; Washington, D.C., American Council of Learned Societies, 1960).
[142] *Ibid.*, pp. vi-viii.
[143] *Ibid.*, p. 173.

Speak Vietnamese by Nguyễn Đình Hòa is a linguistically oriented book consisting of fifteen graded lessons for English learners of Vietnamese.[144] Conversations are used to introduce new sentence patterns and vocabulary items. Each lesson consists of a conversation presented in both Vietnamese and English, a list of Vietnamese vocabulary items with their English equivalents, sentence patterns, grammatical notes, a pronunciation drill, model sentences, and a test. According to Hòa, "The grammatical notes are intended to describe how Vietnamese is actually spoken. They are not offered as rules about how 'good' Vietnamese should be spoken."[145] Each lesson deals with one or two specific grammatical points. The sections on sentence patterns are the most relevant parts of the lessons for the purposes of this study. In each of those sections the author gives the order of the functional units within the sentence or construction to be learned. He is obviously aware of the importance of order in Vietnamese grammar. For example, in Lessons XI and XIV he shows the order of the auxiliary verbs by means of the following charts:

1	2		3[146]
cũng	đã sẽ	không chẳng	Main Verb
	sắp mới vừa vừa mới chưa		

1	2	3	4[147]
cũng	đã sẽ	không chẳng	Main Verb
	không chẳng chưa	có	
	sắp vừa mới vừa mới		

[144] Nguyễn Đình Hoà, *Speak Vietnamese* (Saigon, Publications of the School of Languages, 1957).
[145] *Ibid.*, p. x.
[146] *Ibid.*, p. 146.
[147] *Ibid.*, p. 205.

It can be seen that the order of the auxiliaries differs from one chart to the other. In the second chart, the addition of the auxiliary *có* moves *không* and *chẳng* to column 2. Hòa does not offer any explanation of this shift nor does he give any examples in which either *không*, *chẳng*, or *chưa* is used with the auxiliary verb *có*.

Hòa seems to regard adjectives as stative verbs denoting "a quality or condition or state of being".[148] He regularly presents sentence patterns in which he emphasizes the positions of the individual words to be learned. Some of these patterns follow:

Pattern: PR   (neg)   SV

Pattern: PR   (neg)   SV   A

Pattern: Subject *sắp/sẽ/vừa* Verb

Pattern: *Mấy giờ* Subject Predicate?

Pattern: Subject   *có* Verb (Object) *đâu!*[149]

(PR = pronouns, neg = negative, SV = stative verb, A = adverb)

Hòa seems to pay more attention to the individual words in a sentence than he does to the positions in which these words occur. This emphasis on the words themselves may cause difficulties for learners because words belonging to one word class can generally perform other functions as well, and hence can occur in more than one position. To illustrate his sentence patterns, Hòa follows each with a long list of model sentences (about twenty for each lesson) for learners to memorize.

Although Hòa's book consists of only fifteen 'introductory' lessons, he succeeds, within those narrow limits, in presenting some of the basic constructions and sentence patterns of Vietnamese.

M. B. Emeneau starts with the analysis of the 'word' in his *Studies in Vietnamese (Annamese) Grammar*.[150] According to him, words in Vietnamese are phonologically free but not all of them are syntactically free:

Many words cannot enter freely into the normal constructions of the language but occur only in restricted occurrences, i.e., in construction with certain other words, usually themselves similarly restricted in occurrence.[151]

Most of the restricted morphemes are substantives and verbs. They can be distinguished from free morphemes by the fact that they cannot freely combine with any word of "appropriate meaning and word class", but only with a limited number of words in a limited number of constructions.[152] Most of these restricted morphemes are Chinese loan words. Emeneau presents in great detail the ordinary and restricted

---

[148] *Ibid.*, p. 3.
[149] *Ibid.*, pp. 2, 3, 35, 47, 135.
[150] M. B. Emeneau, *Studies in Vietnamese (Annamese) Grammar* (= *University of California Publications in Linguistics*, Vol. 8), (Berkeley & Los Angeles, University of California Press, 1951). Annam is the former name of Vietnam and Annamese is the old term for Vietnamese.
[151] *Ibid.*, p. 2.
[152] *Ibid.*, pp. 144-145.

types of substantive phrases and verb phrases. The usual patterns of such two-word (or possibly three-word) constructions are the following: (1) restricted word + restricted word, (2) restricted word + free word, and (3) free word + restricted word.[153] Emeneau recognizes the fact that such constructions can often substitute for "single-word morphemes of the same class", i.e., they can perform the same syntactical function as free morphemes.[154]

Emeneau divides Vietnamese words into five major classes: substantives, verbs, conjunctions, final particles, and interjections.[155] He finds that substantives and verbs are more difficult to classify than the other word classes. He states that there are many subclasses of verbs but does not consider his analysis complete enough to make it possible to identify all the subclasses.[157] He does, however, give the following order for a "verb series":

1	2		3	4[158] ...
cũng	sẽ / đã	chớ / đừng không / chẳng	tự	.....
	chưa			

Emeneau assigns *sẽ* and *đã* to the subclass of "time verbs" and *chưa, chớ, đừng, không*, which are actually negators, to the subclass of "negative verbs".[159] He explains that *sẽ* can precede *chớ, đừng, không*, and *chẳng*, while *đã* can precede only *không* and *chẳng*; *chưa* can neither precede nor follow any element "within order 2".[160]

Emeneau subdivides substantives into classified nouns and nonclassified nouns, classifiers, numerators, demonstrative numerators, personal and place names, and pronouns, according to their occurrence in syntactic constructions.[161] He distinguishes three types of substantive phrases:

(1) Numeration, in which the noun is preceded by a numerator or followed by a demonstrative numerator, or both, with a classifier immediately preceding the noun if the latter belongs to the subclass called classified.

(2) Attribution, in which the noun, whether numerated or not, is immediately followed by an attribute or attributes, which may be noun, numerator (rarely), pronoun, personal name (rarely), verb or verb phrase, or complete predication (sometimes introduced by *mà*. ...)

153   *Ibid.*, pp. 145-154.
154   *Ibid.*, p. 44.
155   *Ibid.*, p. 45.
156   *Ibid.*, p. 79.
157   *Ibid.*, p. 45.
158   *Ibid.*, p. 74.
159   *Ibid.*
160   *Ibid.*
161   *Ibid.*, p. 45.

(3) In a third type of substantive phrase, the head is an additive series of nouns or pronouns, usually without any coordinating conjunction ... occasionally with a coordinating conjunction. ...[162]

He represents the order of elements in "numerated constructions" by the following schema:

Numerator	Classifier	Classified noun	± Attribute(s)	Demonstrative[163] numerator
	Nonclassified noun			

With regard to predications in Vietnamese, Emeneau notes that "the predication has as nucleus a predicate which may, but need not, be preceded by a subject."[164] He says that the presence of the subject is necessary only "... when it denotes something that is being identified for the first time in the context, or when it is anaphoric and its omission would lead to ambiguity."[165] Emeneau distinguishes two types of predicates: substantive and verb. Substantive predicates are not as numerous as verb predicates and consist of a substantive or of a substantive phrase.[166] Verb predicates consist of a verb or of a verb phrase. The verb phrase consists of a verb followed by one or more objects.[167]

With regard to complex predications, Emeneau says that there can be two predications in a sentence, one main and one subordinate. The subordinate predication usually precedes the main one and consists of "a substantive or substantive phrase, a verb or verb phrase, or a predication with subject and verb predicate. ..."[168] This last type can be preceded by a conjunction. Emeneau summarizes the different kinds of predications by the following formulas:

Formulas for the different types of predications so far described. P = predications; S = substantive or substantive phrase; V = verb; VPh = verb phrase; C = subordinating conjunction; ( ) indicates optional presence of that which is enclosed; ^{n} indicates one or more occurrences in series.

Simple predications (P)

(S)   S.

(S)   V $(S)^n$.

      V $(S)^n$S.

Complex predications

$\left. \begin{array}{l} S \\ V/VPh \\ (C)\ P \end{array} \right\}$, (thì) P.[169]

[162]   *Ibid.*
[163]   *Ibid.*, p. 84.
[164]   *Ibid.*, p. 46.
[165]   *Ibid.*
[166]   *Ibid.*, p. 47.
[167]   *Ibid.*, p. 48.
[168]   *Ibid.*, p. 65.
[169]   *Ibid.*, p. 61.

Emeneau's analysis of Vietnamese word classes is quite elaborate, but his analysis of predications is over-simplified. Too many sentence units remain unanalyzed; even the predicate itself requires more detailed analysis.

As the title suggests, *Verb Constructions in Vietnamese* by William W. Gage and H. Merrill Jackson describes the different kinds of verb constructions that occur in Vietnamese.[170] The method of analysis used by Gage and Jackson is the one used by Charles C. Hockett in his analysis of Chinese.[171] It seeks mainly to find out the positions of elements in the verb phrase. According to the authors, there are six positions in the Vietnamese verb phrase. These positions, if filled, would occur in the following order:

'a', an adverb
'v', the main verb
'r', a subsidiary
'i', an indirect object
'o', a direct object
'm', an adverbial modifier (in some cases, two).[172]

Gage and Jackson discover that $v + o$ is the most common pattern in predicates.[173] On a lower level, the units in a verb phrase are further divided until the last verb in the predicate is separated from its object or modifier. According to Gage and Jackson, the v position "is always filled" but any or all of the other five may be filled or may be vacant.[174]

The analysis of verb phrases in *Verb Constructions in Vietnamese* is largely accurate. But the assigning of words which are not verbs to the verb class has occasionally led the authors into analyzing verb phrases incorrectly. For instance, the authors first analyze the two words *đã* 'already' and *sẽ* 'will' as verbs.[175] They then state that "it is also possible to treat them as adverbs preceding the main verb ..."[176] and present examples in which they treat these words first as adverbs, then as verbs:

I   will carry things outside afterwards

(1) tôi sẽ   xách đồ   ra   sau

_____ 'I'll carry the things out later'
    S   P

— — — —   —

    a   v   o m^1 m^2

[170] William W. Gage and H. Merrill Jackson, *Verb Constructions in Vietnamese* (Southeast Asia Program, Data Paper Number 9, mimeographed), (Ithaca, New York, Department of Far Eastern Studies, Cornell University, July 1953).
[171] *Ibid.*, p. 14. ("Hockett, Charles F., Lectures on Chinese grammar given during a course in Linguistic Analysis in the spring of 1951").
[172] *Ibid.*, p. 2.
[173] *Ibid.*, p. 3.
[174] *Ibid.*, p. 2.
[175] *Ibid.*, p. 8.
[176] *Ibid.*, p. 10.

(2) tôi sẽ xách đổ   ra   sau

   S   P

    v   o

        v   o m^1 m^2

Mr. that already arrive not yet
(3) anh ấy đã   đến chưa 'Has he arrived yet?'

    (clause)   (final particle)

     S   P

     a   v

(4) anh ấy đã đến chưa

    (clause)   (final particle)

 S   P

    v o^{177}

Near the end of their analysis, Gage and Jackson re-state the positions of *đã* and *sẽ* as follows:

The pre-verbal position of the words *sẽ* and *đã* ... offers the best possibility yet discovered of establishing the verb as a formal category for the Vietnamese language. Thus, the verb class could be defined as the class of words which occur following, and in construction with, *sẽ* (or *đã* when it is not followed by what is known to be a substantive phrase). ...[178]

It appears that the authors do not consider *đã* and *sẽ* either as verbs or as auxiliaries, but rather as markers of verbs. The above examples could thus be re-analyzed as follows:

        S   TR V   O C
    U: Tôi sẽ   xách đổ ra sau.

        S   TR V D^{179}
    Qn: Anh ấy đã   đến chưa?

---

[177] *Ibid.*, pp. 10-11. The translation of the examples is given by Gage and Jackson.
[178] *Ibid.*, pp. 11-12.
[179] The method of analysis and the symbols used throughout this study are based on Robert L. Allen's "Sector analysis", described in *A Modern Grammar of Written English* (New York, The Macmillan Company, in press). For the explanation of the symbols, see the Introduction.

In other examples, the negator *không* 'not', the time relationship particle *chưa* 'not yet', and the preposition *cạnh* 'beside' are assigned by Gage and Jackson to the verbal position:[180]

(1)   I   not   know
     tôi không biết   'I don't know'

    — ————
    S   P
       ———   —
       v   o

(2)   sir   not yet go
     ông chưa   đi   'The gentleman hasn't gone yet'

    — ————
    S   P
       ———   —
       v   o

(3)   put beside charcoal cooking fire
     để   cạnh   bếp   'Put it beside the stove'

    — ————
    v   m
       ———   —
       v   o

These sentences may be re-analyzed as follows:

       S   Neg.   V
   U: Tôi   không biết.
       S   TR + Neg.   V
   Q: Ông   chưa   đi?[181]
       V   C[182]
  Pd: để   cạnh   bếp
   R: ⟨cạnh [bếp]⟩
         r   n

Since they assume that an adjective can function as a verb, Gage and Jackson do not take into account the possibility of its occurring in an adverbial position before or after the main verb. This diagram, for example, appears on page 1 of their book:

---

[180]   William W. Gage & H. Merrill Jackson, *op. cit.*, pp. 3-5.
[181]   In Vietnamese the time-relationship particles and the negators — with the exception of *chưa* — occur in separate positions. *Chưa* suggests both the idea of time and of negation and therefore occupies both positions.
[182]   For the explanation of the symbols, see the Introduction.

I   very feel honored can   know Miss
tôi rất   hân hạnh   được biêt   cô 'I'm very pleased to be able to know you'

S P
  ———   ————   ——————————
  a   v   m
         ——   ————————
         v   o
                 ——   ——————
                 v   o

But the sentence can be re-analyzed as follows:

S   M   Pass.[183] V   O
U: tôi   rất hân hạnh   được   biêt cô
K: |⟨rất hân hạnh⟩|
          ↶   *
         mm   m[184]

Aside from separating units in the predicate from the verb and identifying their positions, Gage and Jackson do not attempt to find the order of verbal units preceding the main verb in the verb phrase. They do not take into account the fact that a verb phrase may consist of a main verb as nucleus preceded by a group of auxiliary verbs. Instead, they treat both auxiliaries and verbs as similar items, and then analyze each verb phrase by separating these 'verbs' individually, in the order in which they occur, from the rest of the predicate. It has been shown by the re-analyses suggested above that Vietnamese verb phrases may be analyzed in a much simpler fashion.

In his "Word Classes in Vietnamese", P. J. Honey divides Vietnamese words into twelve classes which he numbers from "word class 1" to "word class 12".[185] He says, however, that instead of being designated by numbers, they can be called adjectives, verbs, qualified nouns, qualifiers, unqualified nouns, numerals, markers of plurality, personal pronouns, initial particles, medial particles, final particles, and polytopic particles.[186]

Honey does not claim that his classification of word classes is the only "true" one. But, according to him, his twelve word classes "do ... enable systematic syntactic statements to be made and are themselves wholly definable in terms of such statements".[187] He uses both distribution and a number of words called "indicators" as

---

[183]   The passive particle in Vietnamese is used to show that the subject of the sentence in which the particle occurs is neither the active performer of, nor a participant in, the action denoted by the predicate; the subject is rather a recipient — a passive recipient — of that action.
[184]   For the explanation of the symbols, see the Introduction.
[185]   Patrick J. Honey, "Word Classes in Vietnamese", *Bulletin of the School of Oriental and African Studies*, XVIII (1956), 534-544.
[186]   *Ibid.*
[187]   *Ibid.*, p. 535.

criteria for his classification.[188] Words are assigned to certain word classes on the basis of their co-occurrence or non-co-occurrence with certain indicators. For example, to identify word class 1, or adjectives, and word class 2, or verbs, Honey uses four words, *nhiều*, *lắm*, *rất*, and *hơi*.[189] First, the potentiality for co-occurrence with *nhiều* and *lắm* is used as a means of distinguishing word classes 1 and 2 from other classes; then the potentiality for co-occurrence with *hơi* and *rất* is used as a means of distinguishing word class 1 from word class 2.

By the use of distribution and indicators, and by the process of elimination, Honey has been able to base his classification of Vietnamese word classes on what seem to be linguistically sound criteria.

A Grammar of Spoken South Vietnamese by Laurence C. Thompson can be divided roughly into two parts.[190] The first part deals with the phonemes of spoken South Vietnamese and with the structures of morphs and compounds. The second part deals with problems of syntax. Thompson analyzes Vietnamese syntax in terms of constructions.

Thompson defines the terms PHRASE, CONSTRUCTION, ELEMENT, and POSITION as follows:

A PHRASE is a sequence of two or more lexemes as one of the constituents of a sentence (having a meaning greater than the sum of the meanings of the constituent lexemes) [sic]. A class of phrases having the same arrangement of forms and a core of common meaning is a CONSTRUCTION. An ELEMENT is one of the immediate constituents of a phrase; the class of all elements occurring in the same relative location in all phrases of a given construction is a POSITION.[191]

According to Thompson, there are two basic types of constructions in Vietnamese: exocentric and endocentric.[192]

There are three types of exocentric constructions:

(1) THE ACTOR-ACTION CONSTRUCTION. This type of construction consists of two positions which Thompson labels "SUBJECT", or actor, and "PREDICATE", or action.[193]

(2) THE ASSOCIATIVE CONSTRUCTION. This type of construction has two positions which Thompson labels "SUBJECT" and "ASSOCIATION".[194]

(3) THE RELATIONAL CONSTRUCTION. This type of construction consists of two positions which Thompson labels "RELATOR" and "GOAL".[195] Constructions of this type are prepositional phrases with prepositions in the relator position and nouns or pronouns in the goal position.

---

[188] *Ibid.*, p. 537.

[189] *Ibid.*, p. 536.

[190] Laurence C. Thompson, "A Grammar of Spoken South Vietnamese" (Unpublished Ph.D. dissertation, Yale University, New Haven, Connecticut, 1954).

[191] *Ibid.*, p. 103.

[192] *Ibid.*, p. 105.

[193] *Ibid.*, p. 107.

[194] *Ibid.*, p. 109.

[195] *Ibid.*, pp. 111-112.

There are also three sub-types of endocentric constructions:

(1) CORRELATIVE CONSTRUCTIONS, which have two positions, labeled "HEAD" and "CORRELATION" by Thompson.[196]

(2) COORDINATE CONSTRUCTIONS, which

... are classes of phrases having the same syntactic function as all their elements. ... They are ADDITIVE ... meaning 'all heads have equal application,' and SELECTIVE ... meaning 'one head is applicable to the exclusion of the others.'[197]

(3) ATTRIBUTIVE CONSTRUCTIONS, which

... have two positions: HEAD and ATTRIBUTE; they have the meaning 'head is modified or qualified by attribute.' They are RESTRICTIVE ... characterized by the order attribute-head and the meaning 'restrictive modification of scope'; and SPECIFYING ... characterized by the order head-attribute and the meaning 'particularization of head down to a specific unit.'[198]

Restrictive constructions are further divided into three sub-types:

(a) Aspectual constructions, which have two positions: aspect or attribute and head.[199] They fill the predicate position. Constructions of this type consist of verb clusters, with negators and time relationship particles in the attribute position, and with verbs in the head position.[200]

(b) Numerative constructions, which consist of two positions: numerator and head.[201] They fill the subject and goal positions. Constructions of this type consist of noun clusters made up of numbers and nouns.[202]

(c) Focal constructions, which consist of two positions: focus and head.[203] The focus is the position for a "front adverbial",[204] and the head is the position for the trunk or main part of a sentence.

Specifying constructions are also divided into three sub-types: substantival, verbal, and adverbial. Each of these consists of two positions: head and specifier.[205]

Thompson does not carry his analysis of positions to lower levels than those described above.

It is evident that Thompson is aware of the importance of positions in Vietnamese sentences. However, it should be noted that each construction which he describes (excluding the coordinate constructions, which may have several heads or consti-

---

[196]   *Ibid.*, p. 113.
[197]   *Ibid.*
[198]   *Ibid.*
[199]   *Ibid.*, pp. 119-121.
[200]   *Ibid.*, p. 121.
[201]   *Ibid.*, p. 119.
[202]   *Ibid.*
[203]   *Ibid.*, p. 122.
[204]   The terms "front adverbial" and "trunk" are borrowed from Robert L. Allen's *A Modern Grammar of Written English* (New York, The Macmillan Company, in press).
[205]   Thompson, *op. cit.*, p. 124.

tuents), consists of only two positions. It seems strange that all constructions, both exocentric and endocentric, should be made up of only two positions.[206]

Thompson says little about different kinds of sentences in Vietnamese. He discusses sentences only in the last few pages of his dissertation. He describes two types of sentences (compound and complex), each of which has as its head a construction that could occur as "a sentence by itself".[207] Compound and complex sentences are of two kinds: conjunctive and adjunctive.[208]

Thompson divides Vietnamese words into six major classes: aspects, verbals, relators, numerators, substantives, and particles.[209] On the basis of the positions in which they occur, aspects can be divided into three sub-classes: tenses, negatives, and qualifiers.[210] Adjectives, according to Thompson, are one kind of "verbals which do not occur as heads of action-goal phrases. ..."[211] The substantives have several sub-classes: demonstratives, pronouns, "categoricals", nouns and "focal substantives".[212] The particles are divided into five sub-types which Thompson labels interjections, "fixed particles", "predicative particles", "vocative particles", and "movable particles".[213]

[206]   Many linguists seem to assume that all constructions are binary. W. Nelson Francis, for instance, states that "*binary structure* is one of the most striking things about the grammatical organization of English. Because of it, virtually any English structure may be divided into two immediate constituents, each of which may in turn be divided into two, until the ultimate grammatical units, the words, are reached." W. Nelson Francis, *The Structure of American English* (New York, The Ronald Press Company, 1958), p. 312. However, there is no way of telling whether an expression like five young men should be taken as *five* → *young men*

or *five* ↘ *men.*
    young ↗

[207]   Thompson, *op. cit.*, p. 176.
[208]   *Ibid.*, pp. 176-178.
[209]   *Ibid.*, pp. 132-133.
[210]   *Ibid.*, pp. 137-139.
[211]   *Ibid.*, p. 141.
[212]   *Ibid.*, pp. 149-165.
[213]   *Ibid.*, pp. 166-173.

2

REVIEW AND SUMMARY OF
A MODERN GRAMMAR OF WRITTEN ENGLISH

One type of linguistic analysis which seems to hold great promise for the analysis of the grammar of Vietnamese is tagmemic analysis.

2.0. The present study, therefore, has as its primary goal a contrastive analysis of Vietnamese and English along tagmemic lines. Since the only detailed tagmemic analyses of English syntax known to the present writer are to be found in *The Verb System of Present-Day American English*[1] and in *A Modern Grammar of Written English*,[2] both by Robert L. Allen, this study will be based upon Allen's work.

In *A Modern Grammar of Written English*, Allen states that he had "worked out the broad outlines" of his own analysis of English — which he calls "sector analysis" — before he knew about the publications on tagmemics by Kenneth L. Pike and others at the Summer Institute of Linguistics in Norman, Oklahoma.[3] Although sector analysis does not "derive" from Pike's tagmemic theory, there is considerable similarity between the two.[4] Allen recognizes that Pike's tagmemic theory has provided "a strong theoretical foundation" for his own sector analysis.[5]

2.1. *A Modern Grammar of Written English* includes an evaluation of traditional grammars and a brief description of their origins and development in addition to the detailed presentation of the sector analysis of English, which is "basically 'tagmemic' in its approach".[6] The term WRITTEN in the title of the book is used to indicate that the kinds of English being analyzed are the kinds of English "one READS or WRITES,

---

[1] Robert L. Allen, *The Verb System of Present-Day American English* (The Hague, Mouton & Co., 1966).
[2] Robert L. Allen, *A Modern Grammar of Written English* (New York, The Macmillan Company, in press). References will be to pages in the typed manuscript. The present writer wishes to express her deepest gratitude to Professor Allen for allowing her to use his work as the basis for her research and for permitting her to quote extensively from his book.
[3] *Ibid.*, footnote 1, p. 1.
[4] *Ibid.*
[5] *Ibid.*
[6] *Ibid* , p. 1.

as opposed to the kinds of English one hears or speaks".[7] These include informal and conversational written English, as well as formal written English.[8] Sentences and constructions are defined in Allen's grammar "in terms of signals that a reader sees on the printed page, not in terms of sounds that one hears".[9]

2.2. Allen gives a summary of his grammar before presenting it in detail. His method of analysis is a reductive method, starting from the sentence level and working down to the word level.[10] Identification of the different positions in a sentence and of the different kinds of units that can occupy these positions is basic in Allen's grammar.[11] In his own words, Allen states that:

every sentence consists of a string of potential positions for different kinds of constructions, although in any given sentence one or more of these positions may be unoccupied; each of these constructions, in turn, consists of a string of positions for different kinds of units, on a lower level.
    In general, therefore, a sentence consists of a hierarchy of words or constructions nested within other constructions, on different levels.[12]

Allen emphasizes the importance of analyzing the constructions embedded in a sentence on succeeding levels instead of all on one level.[13] He says that the FUNCTION of any unit is determined by the position that it occupies in a larger construction; in identifying its FORM, however, we should take it out of the larger construction and bring it down to the next lower level all by itself.[14]

2.3. According to Allen, there are two kinds of sentences: "major sentences" and "minor sentences". He himself is mainly concerned with "major sentences", which, in addition to being grammatical, must meet the following criteria:

(1) The sentence must contain at least one "non-included" clause — that is, it must contain at least one clause that does not begin with one of the words traditionally called "subordinating conjunctions" or with one of the so-called "relative pronouns" (both of these word-classes will later be defined by listing);
(2) The non-included clause must have a subject (i.e., a word or combination of words in the "S" position as defined below);
(3) The non-included clause must contain a time-oriented "auxiliary" or a time-oriented verb form;
(4) The units in the sentence must occur in their "normal" order, as described below;
(5) The sentence must begin with a capital letter and end with a terminal punctuation mark.[15]

---

[7]   Ibid., footnote 1, pp. ii.
[8]   Ibid., p. 46.
[9]   Ibid.
[10] Ibid., p. 267a.
[11] Ibid., p. 1.
[12] Ibid.
[13] Ibid., pp. 2-4, 267a.
[14] Ibid., pp. 3-6.
[15] Ibid., p. 264.

A major sentence may be either "full" or "elliptical". A major elliptical sentence is distinguished from a "minor sentence" such as a request or a command by the fact that its missing units can be supplied from the immediately preceding linguistic context.[16] According to Allen,

> every major sentence is made up of a hierarchy of units on different levels. Every unit except the sentence itself occupies a fixed position on the next higher level; every unit except words and "idioms" is a sequence of *potential* positions for units on the next lower level.[17]

2.4. Allen starts his description of English with the finding of all "potential" positions on the sentence and predicate levels, which he calls "sectors". Then he identifies and describes the different kinds of constructions that can occur in each different sector. From the sector levels, he works down to the word level. He is careful to distinguish each level of analysis, and each of the different kinds of constructions that can function in one position or another.

2.5. Working from the sentence level down, Allen finds four "top" levels. The first or sentence level is a level for a cluster consisting of a "TRUNK" as its nucleus preceded and/or followed by modifiers called "FRONT" and "END" "SENTENCE ADVERBIALS".[18] This level can be schematically represented as follows:

$$U = F \quad) \qquad T \qquad (\quad E^{19}$$

(U = the sentence level; T = the trunk; F = the front sector; E = the end sector.)

2.5.1. According to Allen, the chief characteristics of sentence adverbials or of the F and E sectors are that they modify the trunk as a whole, that they can be dropped from a sentence without affecting the grammaticality of that sentence, and that they can shift from the F to the E position, or from the E to the F position.[20] For example:

> Last winter) my parents moved to Florida.
> My parents moved to Florida (last winter.[21]

2.6. On the second or trunk level, the trunk, consisting of a "SUBJECT" and a "PRE-DICATE", can be schematically represented as follows:

$$T = \boxed{\;S\;} \quad P^{22}$$

(T = the trunk level; S = the subject sector; P = the predicate.)

---

[16] *Ibid.*, pp. 266-267.
[17] *Ibid.*, pp. 267-267a.
[18] *Ibid.*, p. 7.
[19] *Ibid.*, p. 8.
[20] *Ibid.*, pp. 7-8, 267a.
[21] *Ibid.*, p. 4.
[22] *Ibid.*, p. 9.

2.6.1. Allen recognizes that in a major sentence the subject position must always be filled. This makes it possible for a statement to become a question by shifting one of the carrier words from the nonshifted X position to the shifted X position preceding the subject.[23] He defines the subject as follows:

THE SUBJECT of a sentence is here defined as that unit around which one of the following words (called "X WORDS" or "CARRIERS") shifts when a statement is changed to a Yes-No question, or when a question is changed to an (emphatic) statement. ...[24]

For example:

	$\tilde{X}$		X
U & T:	The man who lives in the house across the street		likes cats.
T:	*Does* the man who lives in the house across the street		like cats?
	The man who lives in the house across the street		*does* like cats.

	S	P
T:	The man who lives in the house across the street	likes cats.[25]

2.7. The third or predicate level is the level for a "PREDICATE CLUSTER" consisting of a "PREDICATE NUCLEUS" preceded and/or followed by predicate adverbials as modifiers.[26] Allen calls these two modifier positions the "M" or "MIDDLE POSITION" and the "D" or "DROPPABLE POSITION".[27] This level can be schematically represented as follows:

$$PK = M \quad) \qquad P* \qquad (\quad D^{28}$$

(PK = the predicate cluster; M = the middle sector; P* = the predicate nucleus; D = the D or droppable sector.)

According to Allen, predicate adverbials are different from sentence adverbials in that they cannot shift from the M to the D position or from the D to the M position.[29]

2.7.1. Allen states that the M sector is also called the middle sector because it occurs approximately in the "middle of the trunk", between the X and the V positions.[30] The middle sector is the position for members of a listable-lexeme class called "MIDDLE ADVERBS".[31] For example:

[23] *Ibid.*, p. 320.
[24] *Ibid.*, pp. 8-9.
[25] *Ibid.*, p. 9.
[26] *Ibid.*, p. 10.
[27] *Ibid.*, p. 11.
[28] *Ibid.*, p. 13.
[29] *Ibid.*, p. 10.
[30] *Ibid.*
[31] *Ibid.*, p. 465.

$$\text{X} \quad \text{M} \quad \text{V}$$
Mrs. Zobel has always {kept her eggs in the refrigerator}[32]

2.7.2. Allen states that the "D" or droppable sector is the position for units which can be dropped without making the sentence in which they occur ungrammatical, but which cannot be shifted to the beginning of the sentence.[33] According to him, it is the verb that determines whether the following units can or cannot be dropped from the sentence.[34] In the following sentences, for instance, the unit *on the floor* cannot be dropped from the first sentence, but it can be dropped from the second:

$$\text{C} \qquad \text{D}$$
Mrs. Clark   *put*   an egg *on the floor.*
Mrs. Clark *dropped* an egg   *on the floor.*[35]

2.8. On the fourth or predicate nucleus level, there are four positions which Allen calls "THE VERBAL POSITION", "THE OBJECT POSITION", "THE PARTICLE POSITION", and "THE COMPLEMENT POSITION".[36] This level can be schematically represented as follows:

$$\text{P*} = \text{V} + \text{O} + \text{B} + \text{C}^{37}$$

(P* = the predicate nucleus level; V = the verbal sector; O = the object sector; B = the particle sector; C = the complement sector.)

2.8.1. According to Allen, the verbal sector is the position not for the verb alone but for all elements in a verb cluster minus the X word.[38] The X word is a word occurring in the X sector. A verb cluster consists of a verb which is the nucleus, plus one or more members of a listable-lexeme class called auxiliaries.[39] According to Allen, every verb has six forms, except the verb *BE* which has only three forms: *be, been,* and *being.*[40] Three of the verb forms which show time-orientation are called "VER-BEXES", while the other three which do not show time-orientation are called "VER-BIDS".[41] The three verbex forms are "THE PAST FORM" and "THE PRESENT FORMS" or "NON-PAST FORMS".[42] One of the present forms always ends in "-*s*" or "-*es*" and is called "THE S FORM"; the other form is similar to the base form and is called "THE NO-S FORM".[43] The three verbid forms of every verb are the base form, the D-T-N

---

[32]   *Ibid.,* p. 467.
[33]   *Ibid.,* pp. 468-469.
[34]   *Ibid.,* pp. 12, 471.
[35]   *Ibid.,* p. 12.
[36]   *Ibid.,* p. 13.
[37]   *Ibid.*
[38]   *Ibid.,* p. 474b.
[39]   *Ibid.,* pp. 476-478.
[40]   *Ibid.,* p. 479.
[41]   *Ibid.,* pp. 35, 480.
[42]   *Ibid.,* pp. 35, 490.
[43]   *Ibid.*

form, and the ING form.[44] Allen notes that it is the preceding auxiliary or the preceding X word which determines the form of the following verbid.[45] For example:

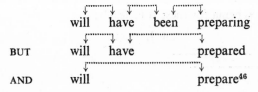

will   have   been   preparing

BUT   will   have   prepared

AND   will   prepare[46]

2.8.2. According to Allen, the O sector is the position for the object of the verb. The object of the verb does not have the same referent as the subject except when some members of the listable-lexeme class called "reflexives" occur.[47] In the following sentences, *a good life* in the second sentence is the object of the verb while *a poor man* in the first sentence is not.

Stephen lived *a poor man.*
Stephen lived *a good life.*[48]

The object of the verb in an active sentence may become the subject in a passive sentence.[49]

2.8.3. According to Allen, the B sector follows the O sector and is the position for listable particles, either single or compound particles.[50] Some of those particles are similar in form to some of the prepositions, but they are different from the prepositions because they are used without an object.[51] The particle in the B sector can also shift to the shifted B sector preceding the O sector. For example:

(V)   B̃ O   B C
Pd*: (take) *up* a cup of coffee   to his mother.[52]
     (take)   a cup of coffee *up* to his mother.

2.8.4. The fourth position on the predicate nucleus level — that is, the complement sector — is defined by Allen as follows:

Any unit that follows the verb in a predicate or predicatid which is not the object and not a particle and which cannot be dropped occoupies the C sector. Such a unit may be called a COMPLEMENT.[53]

[44] *Ibid.*, pp. 36, 481.
[45] *Ibid.*, p. 481.
[46] *Ibid.*, p. 482.
[47] *Ibid.*, pp. 538-540.
[48] *Ibid.*, p. 541.
[49] *Ibid.*, p. 543.
[50] *Ibid.*, p. 545.
[51] *Ibid.*, pp. 545-546.
[52] *Ibid.*, p. 546.
[53] *Ibid.*, p. 551.

(A predicatid is defined by Allen as "a predicate without time-orientation".[54] Allen notes that many kinds of constructions can occur in the C sector.)

Allen then presents the following schema for these four levels:

$$
\begin{array}{ccc}
\text{U} = \text{F} \,) & \text{T} & (\ \text{E} \\
\end{array}
$$

T =	S	PK	
PK =	M)	P*	(D
P* =		V + O + B + C[55]	

2.9. Allen notes that every clause that is not introduced by a WH word has two X positions: the "NON-SHIFTED X POSITION" which follows the subject position, and the "SHIFTED X POSITION" which precedes the subject position.[56] The shifted $\tilde{X}$ position (with a tilde over the X) is vacant in a statement sentence, but is always filled by a carrier in a "Yes-No question".[57] For example:

    $\tilde{X}$ X
St: Percy *can* speak a few words of Arabic.
Q: *Can* Percy   speak a few words of Arabic?[58]

The "CARRIERS" or "X WORDS" which occur in the X or shifted X sectors belong to a listable-lexeme class of lexemes such as *am, are, is, do, can, will*, etc.[59]

The X sector is also the position for emphatic stress and for the negator *not* or its contracted form *n't*.[60] For example:

        X
Percy   took a cup of coffee up to his mother before breakfast.
Percy *didn't* take a cup of coffee up to his mother before breakfast.
Percy *did*   take a cup of coffee up to his mother before breakfast.[61]

2.10. Allen identifies four "shifted sectors", which he designates by letters with tildes over them. These are the shifted $\tilde{X}$, $\tilde{M}$, $\tilde{B}$, and $\tilde{C}$ sectors.[62] Since end adverbials in the E sector are identified by their potentiality for shifting to the F sector, the F sector may also be thought of as a "shifted position" for sentence adverbials. The following are examples of these shifted sectors:

[54] *Ibid.*, p. 570.
[55] *Ibid.*, p. 13.
[56] *Ibid.*, pp. 9, 301.
[57] *Ibid.*, pp. 301-302.
[58] *Ibid.*, p. 302.
[59] *Ibid.*, p. 300a.
[60] *Ibid.*, pp. 304-304a.
[61] *Ibid.*, p. 304.
[62] *Ibid.*, pp. 16-18.

X̃   X

St: Percy *can* speak a few words of Arabic.

Q: *Can* Percy   speak a few words of Arabic?[63]

          X   M   V

Mrs. Zobel has always kept her eggs in the refrigerator.

         M̃   X V

Mrs. Zobel always has kept her eggs in the refrigerator.[64]

        B̃   B

I can turn   the television set *on* (Sunday.

I can turn *on* the television set   (Sunday.[65]

        C̃   C

Percy bought   an apple *for his teacher*.[66]

Percy bought *his teacher* an apple.

F   E

Last winter   my parents moved to Florida.

          Did my parents move to Florida *last winter*?[67]

The following is a schema of the order of both shifted and non-shifted sectors:

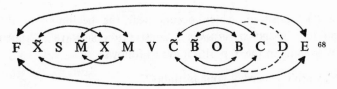

F X̃ S M̃ X M V C̃ B̃ O B C D E [68]

Allen states that more than one unit may occur in the F, E, C and D sectors.[69]

2.11. There are two more sectors on the sentence and trunk levels.

2.11.1. The first is the "L" sector for sentence linkers, which precedes the F sector.[70] Sentence linkers such as *Now, Indeed, But*, etc., are words used to "link their own sentences with the sentences preceding them".[71] For example:

"*Now* there's no reason to get annoyed. I must have been mistaken."
"*Indeed* you were."[72]

[63] *Ibid.*, p. 302.
[64] *Ibid.*, p. 467.
[65] *Ibid.*, p. 548.
[66] *Ibid.*, p. 559.
[67] *Ibid.*, p. 16.
[68] *Ibid.*, p. 18.
[69] *Ibid.*, p. 19.
[70] *Ibid.*
[71] *Ibid.*, p. 270.
[72] *Ibid.*, p. 271a.

2.11.1. The second is the "I" sector for WH words and WH units such as *why*, *where*, *how often*, etc., which are used to introduce the trunk in "questions other than Yes-No questions" (i.e., questions that can be answered by "Yes" or "No"), for includers in included clauses, and for inverters.[73] Inverters such as *not only*, *no sooner*, *little*, etc., belong to a listable-lexeme class which causes the inversion of the subject and the X word.[74] Following are examples of these three types of units in the I sector:

>   I
>
> (1) *Why* | did you order such a large meal?
>
>   I   Pd
>
> *How often* | does | Percy | {take coffee up to his mother before breakfast}
>   I
>
> (2) I asked you [*why* you ordered such a large meal.]
>   I   X̃ S
>
> (3) *Little did we* realize what was in store for us when we entered the boys' room.[75]

2.12. In Allen's analysis, there are also four other positions which occur on the sentence level but which do not form part of the "sentence proper". These are the "Y", the "PP" and the "Z" positions.

2.12.1. The "Y" position, which occurs near the beginning of the sentence, is the position for "RESPONSE SIGNALS", "HESITATION SIGNALS", "GREETINGS", etc.[76] Sentences with units in the Y position are as follows:

> "*Percy*, wasn't yesterday your birthday?"
> "*No*, it wasn't."[77]

2.12.2. The two "PP" positions are positions for a postponed subject or a postponed object.[78] The subject or the object sector is then filled by the filler *it*, as in the following sentences:

>   PP
> "*It*'s not true *that yesterday was my father's birthday*."
> "I find *it* hard *to believe that Percy really knows Arabic*."[79]

2.12.3. The "Z" position, occuring at the end of the sentence, in the position for "TAG QUESTIONS", for nouns of address, and for words like *too*, *either*, etc.[80] For example:

[73] *Ibid.*, pp. 19, 325-326, 568.
[74] *Ibid.*, p. 568.
[75] *Ibid.*, footnote 1, pp. 325, 569.
[76] *Ibid.*, p. 269.
[77] *Ibid.*
[78] *Ibid.*, p. 270.
[79] *Ibid.*, pp. 270, 544.
[80] *Ibid.*, pp. 20, 270.

"Just a minute! I haven't finished *yet*."
"Yesterday was your father's birthday, *wasn't it?*"
"Wasn't it, *Percy?*"[81]

2.13. The "total sector spectrum" of the sectors on the sentence, TRUNK, PREDICATE CLUSTER, and PREDICATE-NUCLEUS levels is presented in Allen's grammar as follows:

$$L \ Y \ F \ I \ \tilde{X} \ S \ \tilde{M} \ X \ M \ V \ \tilde{C} \ \tilde{B} \ O \ B \ C_1 \ C_2 \ C_3 \ D_1 \ D_2 \ PP \ E_1 \ E_2 \ E_3 \ PP \ Z^{82}$$

2.14. After finding all the potential sectors on these four top levels, Allen proceeds to examine the constructions which can occur in each sector.

2.14.1. Allen distinguishes eight basic construction-types in English: TRUNKS, PREDICATES, PREDICATIDS (i.e., non-finite predicates), INCLUDED (i.e., 'subordinate') CLAUSES, CLAUSIDS (i.e., non-finite clauses), (prepositional) PHRASES, POSSESSIVES (i.e., constructions ending in *'s, s'*, or *'*), and CLUSTERS.[83] Clusters, in turn, may be subdivided into such categories as noun clusters, verb clusters, adjective clusters, and the like.[84]

2.14.2. After all constructions in a sentence have been analyzed on successively lower levels, one eventually reaches "the word level" (which will differ for each construction). In the last step of syntactic analysis, the words in a sentence are assigned to different "parts of speech" or word classes. But as Allen remarks, some combinations of words cannot be analyzed further without affecting the meaning expressed by them.[85] He calls such combinations of words "lexemes". A lexeme is defined as "either a single word or a combination of words which has a single lexical meaning that cannot be predicted on the basis of the meanings of the words so combined".[86] In the following example, the two words *a* and *little* are two lexemes when they appear before the word *boy*, but constitute only one lexeme when they occur before *annoying*:

Incessant questioning by *a little* boy can be more than *a little* annoying.

2.15. According to Allen, lexemes are of two kinds: those belonging to "LISTABLE LEXEME CLASSES" and those belonging to "NON-LISTABLE LEXEME CLASSES".[87] A listable lexeme class can be defined by listing its members, while a non-listable lexeme class is defined by describing the formal characteristics of its members (including the positions

---

[81] *Ibid.*, p. 270.
[82] Lecture notes on *Sector Analysis* given by Dr. Robert L. Allen (Course No. TL 4102), New York Teachers College, Columbia University, Spring Session, February 3, 1965.
[83] Allen, *op. cit.*, pp. 34-35, 43, 344-347.
[84] *Ibid.*, pp. 344-345.
[85] *Ibid.*, pp. 271-272.
[86] *Ibid.*, p. 272.
[87] *Ibid.*, p. 273.

in which they may occur).[88] Allen notes that some lexemes belong to more than one lexeme class.[89] The non-listable lexeme classes are nouns, verbs, adjectives, and LY adverbs.[90] The listable lexeme classes are determiners such as *the, a, an,* etc.; prepositions such as *of, for, beneath, according to,* etc.; and construction modifiers such as *especially, just, only,* etc.[91]

2.16. Following are the lists of constructions which may occur in the F, E, S, O, C, D, and PP sectors.

2.16.1. *The F and E sectors.* — Allen distinguishes six kinds of sentence adverbials occurring in the F and E sectors: single-word adverbials, adverbial phrases, adverbial clauses, clusters, predicatids, and clausids.[92] Following are examples of these six adverbials:

2.16.1.1. *Single-word adverbial:*

F   E
Carefully) Percy took a cup of coffee up to his mother.
            Percy took a cup of coffee up to his mother (*carefully.*[93]

2.16.1.2. *Adverbial phrase:*

         F   T   E
U: Yesterday Percy took a cup of coffee up to his mother *before breakfast.*
R: ⟨before │ breakfast │⟩[94]

(F = the front sector; E = the end sector; T = the trunk; U = the sentence level; R = the phrase level.)

In Allen's analysis, phrases are enclosed between ⟨ ⟩ and nominals within rectangles.[95] Phrases are defined by Allen as constructions made up of nominals introduced by members of a listable lexeme class called "prepositions".[96]

2.16.1.3. *Adverbial clause:*

         F   T
U: *Before he ate breakfast,*) Percy took a cup of coffee up to his mother.

         I
Cl: [before │ he ate breakfast[97]]

[88] *Ibid.,* p. 274.
[89] *Ibid.*
[90] *Ibid.,* p. 33.
[91] *Ibid.,* pp. 436, 278-279, 425.
[92] *Ibid.,* pp. 297-298.
[93] *Ibid.,* p. 275.
[94] *Ibid.,* p. 281a.
[95] *Ibid.,* p. 281.
[96] *Ibid.,* pp. 281, 285.
[97] *Ibid.,* p. 289a.

(Cl = the included clause level; I = the introductory sector.)

In Allen's analysis, included clauses are enclosed between square brackets, and the "I" position is cut off from the rest of the clause by a vertical line.[98] Allen finds that a clause is similar to a major sentence, but it does not begin with a capital letter and does not end with a punctuation mark.[99] An included clause is a clause introduced by a clause includer.[100]

2.16.1.4. *Adverbial cluster:*

     T   E

H: Percy took a cup of coffee up to his mother (*very carefully.*

K: |⟨*very carefully*⟩|

a: *carefully*[101]

(H = the non-included clause level; K = the cluster level; a = the LY adverb.)

In Allen's analysis, the symbols "|⟨ ⟩|" are used to enclose clusters.[102] A cluster is defined by Allen as a construction with a "nucleus" and one or more modifiers where the nucleus is the essential component. (The modifiers are often droppable.) The nucleus of a cluster can often function in place of the whole cluster.[103] In the example above, *carefully* is the nucleus of the cluster *very carefully*.[104]

2.16.1.5. *Adverbial predicatid:*

F

Crossing the street against the light one day last week, Leroy was almost hit by a taxi.

E

The boys did not notice me, *carried away as they were by what they were doing.*[105]

A predicatid is defined by Allen as a predicate that does not have "time-orientation".[106]

2.16.1.6. *Adverbial clausid:*

The moon coming out from behind the clouds, we could see the Spanish galleon only a short distance away.

Our captain decided that the best course of action would be to surrender, *things being what they were.*[107]

---

98 *Ibid.*, p. 289a.
99 *Ibid.*, p. 286.
100 *Ibid.*, p. 332.
101 *Ibid.*
102 *Ibid.*
103 *Ibid.*
104 *Ibid.*
105 *Ibid.*, pp. 583, 574.
106 *Ibid.*, p. 570.
107 *Ibid.*, p. 588.

According to Allen, a clausid is a non-included clause that does not have "time-orientation" and that consists of a nominal or a pro-nominal and a predicatid.[108]

2.16.1.7. Allen finds that three different kinds of adverbials, requiring different kinds of substitutes, can co-occur in the E sector. They are often referred to as "adverbials of manner", "adverbials of place", and "adverbials of time". These adverbials "commonly" occur in the order "manner-place-time" in the E territory.[109] For example:

> Zilk stabbed his wife to death *with a pair of scissors in the basement of their house in 1962.*[110]

2.16.2. *The S sector.* — Besides the fillers *it*, *there*, and any substitutes, five kinds of constructions may occur in the subject position. These are the nominal noun cluster, the nominal included clause, the nominal ING predicatid and TO predicatid, the nominal clausid, and the nominal phrase. Following are examples of these constructions:

2.16.2.1. *Fillers "it" and "there":*

S   X
It   is five o'clock.
There is no bread in that bread box.[111]

2.16.2.2. *Pro-nominal:*

> Joel took special care of *the rose bushes in the back yard* because *they* belonged to him.[112]

2.16.2.3. *Nominal noun cluster:*

S   X Pd
Last Saturday was Percy's birthday.
|⟨last Saturday⟩|[113]
  →   *

According to Allen, "A NOMINAL is any construction (or lexeme) that may be replaced in its own sentence (or in a succeeding sentence echoing its own sentence) by one or another of the pro-nominals."[114]

And a noun cluster is defined by Allen as a construction which has a noun as its nucleus "preceded and/or followed by one or more adjectivals."[115]

---

108   *Ibid.*, p. 585.
109   *Ibid.*, pp. 298-300.
110   *Ibid.*, p. 298.
111   *Ibid.*, pp. 320-321.
112   *Ibid.*, p. 365b.
113   *Ibid.*, p. 395.
114   *Ibid.*, p. 396.
115   *Ibid.*, p. 397.

2.16.2.4. *Nominal included clause:*

That you do not want to go is all too evident.[116]

2.16.2.5. *Nominal ING predicatid and TO predicatid:*

S

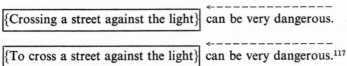

{Crossing a street against the light} can be very dangerous.

{To cross a street against the light} can be very dangerous.[117]

2.16.2.6. *Nominal clausid:*

‖Leroy {crossing the street like that}‖ frightens his sister.[118]

In Allen's analysis, the subject is enclosed in a rectangle, and the predicate is marked by a wavy arrow pointing toward the subject.[119]

2.16.2.7. *Nominal prepositional phrase:*

S

⟨In the closet⟩ is no fair.

⟨For ‖Leroy {to cross the street against the light}‖⟩

is very foolish.[120]

According to Allen, a phrase such as that in the first example above is not frequently used in the subject position, but a phrase consisting of the preposition *for* and a TO clausid, as in the second example, is often used in place of the TO clausid alone.[121]

2.16.3. *The O sector.* — According to Allen, the filler *it*, a noun cluster (or noun), a pro-nominal or a nominal substitute, a nominal clause, and an ING predicatid or TO predicatid may occur in the position for the object of the verb. Following are examples of these constructions:

2.16.3.1. *The filler it:*

O   PP

I consider *it* very foolish {to cross a street against the light}.[122]

---

[116]   *Ibid.,* p. 411.
[117]   *Ibid.,* p. 415.
[118]   *Ibid.,* p. 417.
[119]   *Ibid.,* p. 315a.
[120]   *Ibid.,* pp. 419-420.
[121]   *Ibid.*
[122]   *Ibid.,* p. 416.

2.16.3.2. *Noun cluster:*

      O   C

I told *a story to the children.*[123]

2.16.3.3. *Pro-nominal:*

      O C

I told *him that he was a fool.*[124]

2.16.3.4. *Nominal clause:*

I wish (*that*) *you had never suggested our going.*
I always say *what I think.*[125]

2.16.3.5. *Clausid:*

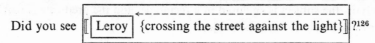

Did you see ⟦ Leroy ⟧ {crossing the street against the light}⟧ ?[126]

2.16.3.6. *ING predicatid or TO predicatid:*

            O

Percy dislikes {crossing a street against the light} .

He doesn't like {to cross a street against the light} .[127]

2.16.4. *The C sector.* — The complement sector is the position for many kinds of constructions. Following are examples of these constructions:

2.16.4.1. *Noun cluster or complement nominal:*

         C

Olga and Melanie are *quiet girls.*[128]

2.16.4.2. *'Complement adjective' or 'complement adjective cluster':*

         C

Olga and Melanie are   *quiet.*
Olga and Melanie are *very quiet.*[129]

2.16.4.3. *'Complement adverb':*

         C

That car moves *fast.*[130]

[123] *Ibid.*, footnote 1, p. 413.
[124] *Ibid.*
[125] *Ibid.*, p. 412.
[126] *Ibid.*, p. 417.
[127] *Ibid.*, p. 415.
[128] *Ibid.*, p. 552.
[129] *Ibid.*
[130] *Ibid.*, p. 553.

2.16.4.4. *Phrase or pro-phrase:*

C
We're (*almost*) at the Baxters' house.
We're (*almost*) there.[131]

2.16.4.5. *Nominal 'complement clause':*

O   C
Mr. Crump told me *that he was going to Burma.*[132]

Allen distinguishes two special includers, *as if* and *as though*, which are used to introduce complement clauses that are not nominal clauses, as in the following examples:

Mr. Crump acts *as if he were eager to get back to Nagaland.*
Mr. Crump acts *as though he were eager to get back to Nagaland.*[133]

2.16.4.6. *'Complement verbid':*

C
I went *fishing.*[134]

2.16.4.7. *'Complement predicatid':*

C
I went *fishing for trout.*[135]

2.16.5. *The C̃ sector.* — Some of the phrases introduced by *to* or *for* may be shifted from the C sector to the shifted C sector preceding the O sector. By so shifting, these phrases lose their introducers and become clusters.[136] For example:

V   O   C
Percy bought an   apple *for his teacher.*
Percy brought the apple *to his teacher.*

These become:

C̃   O
Percy bought *his teacher* an apple.
Percy brought *his teacher* the apple.[137]

2.16.6. *The D sector.* — A phrase or a predicatid may occur in the droppable sector. Following are examples of these constructions:

131 *Ibid.*, p. 554.
132 *Ibid.*, p. 555.
133 *Ibid.*
134 *Ibid.*, p. 556.
135 *Ibid.*
136 *Ibid.*, footnote 1, p. 558.
137 *Ibid.*, p. 558.

2.16.6.1. *Phrase:*

D

Mrs. Zobel dropped an egg *on the floor.*[138]

2.16.6.2. *Predicatid:*

I had sent them to their room *dejected and disheartened* — or so I had thought.[139]

2.16.7. *The PP sectors.* — A predicatid or a clause may occur as a postponed object or a postponed subject in any one of the two PP sectors. Following are examples of these constructions:

2.16.7.1. *Predicatid:*

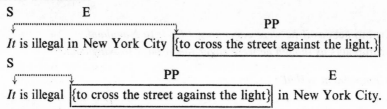

2.16.7.2. *Clause:*

PP

"*It*'s not true *that yesterday was my father's birthday.*"

"I find *it* hard to believe *that Percy really knows Arabic.*"[140]

2.16.8. The sectors that are not mentioned in this section have already been dealt with in the earlier sections.

2.17. *Minor sentences.* — According to Allen, minor sentences are used more often in informal spoken English than in formal written English.[141] The most common types of minor sentences are commands, requests, half sentences used as questions, inverted sentences like *Here comes the teacher,* sentences introduced by *what a,* or by *how* and an adjective like *What a lovely dress* and *How kind of you,* and clausids like *Heaven forbid,* etc.[142]

2.18. *Conclusion.* — By his strict separation of levels of analysis, Allen is able to show that constructions can occur in many different positions, that constructions which function on higher levels can also function as parts of units on lower levels, and that a construction can function as part of a unit within the same kind of construction. For example, while a clause and a predicatid can function as units on the

---

[138]   *Ibid.,* p. 470.
[139]   *Ibid.,* p. 574.
[140]   *Ibid.,* pp. 270, 544.
[141]   *Ibid.,* p. 616.
[142]   *Ibid.,* pp. 616-619.

sentence level, they can also function as modifiers of nouns on the cluster level; and a phrase can function within another phrase.

The strict observance of the distinction between function and form enables Allen to show that constructions function differently according to the positions or slots they fill. For instance, an adverbial clause in the F sector functions differently from an adjectival clause in a noun cluster. Allen is also able to show that many kinds of constructions can occur in one position while one kind of construction can occur in many different positions. For instance, the E, S, O sectors are positions for many kinds of constructions, while a construction like the noun cluster can occur in the S, O, C sectors, or in the slot for the object of a preposition.

The symbols and new terminology used by Allen also help to make the levels of analysis, and the various functions and forms, stand out more clearly.

Although Allen puts primary emphasis on positions of units in his sector analysis, he also takes into consideration other devices used in English, such as ties and valences between various forms which can influence a change in construction, and especially the importance of the various verb endings and various types of verbs in the classification of different kinds of constructions. Allen recognizes that the verb plays a very important role in English syntax.[143] It is the verb which determines the type of sentence pattern "to which its sentence belongs" and the kinds of construction that can occur after it.[144] Allen also shows that predicatids and clausids are among the most important constructions used in formal written English since these constructions can occur in many positions and can therefore help to vary the style of writing.

Allen has clearly demonstrated that position is the most important device used in present-day English.

[143] *Ibid.*, p. 613.
[144] *Ibid.*

A GRAMMAR OF PRESENT-DAY WRITTEN VIETNAMESE: THE SECTORS ON THE SENTENCE LEVEL

Like the English grammar presented in Chapter 2, the Vietnamese grammar about to be presented in this chapter is also a tagmemic analysis of written Vietnamese, that is, an analysis of Vietnamese along the lines of sector analysis, which primarily emphasizes the positions of units on the sentence, trunk, and predicate or predicatid levels.

3.1. THE SENTENCE

The present writer is mainly concerned with major sentences that would be accepted as grammatical by native speakers of Vietnamese. A major sentence in Vietnamese is defined as one which meets the following criteria:

(1) The sentence must have at least one non-included clausid[1] — that is, a clausid which does not begin with one of the listable includers. (These includers are traditionally called 'subordinating conjunctions'.)
(2) The non-included clausid must have a subject (except in some special cases where the subject is omitted), and at least one unit in the predicatid.
(3) The units in the sentence must occur in the sequence described below.
(4) The sentence must begin with a capital letter and end with a terminal punctuation mark.

A major sentence may be either full or elliptical. A major elliptical sentence cannot occur at the beginning of a body of writing or conversation; it must be possible to supply all the missing elements from the immediately preceding linguistic context.

---

[1] Vietnamese is a language with a 'one-time' verb system. Since every Vietnamese verb has only one invariable form, and since the particles that are used to express time in the sentence actually express time-relationship rather than definite time, it seems more appropriate to refer to the sentence in Vietnamese as a non-included clausid. For a more detailed discussion of time in Vietnamese, see Đaò Thị Hợi's "Representation of Time and Time Relationship in English and in Vietnamese" (unpublished doctoral project report, Teachers College, Columbia University, New York, 1965).

3.2. THE SECTORS IN THE VIETNAMESE SENTENCE

When analyzing a sentence from the sentence level down to the word level, it is possible to distinguish four levels at the top. The positions on these four levels will be called SECTORS.

3.2.1. *The Sentence Level*

The first or sentence level is a level for a cluster consisting of a TRUNK as its nucleus preceded and/or followed by modifiers called FRONT and END SENTENCE ADVERBIALS. This level may be schematically represented as follows:

$$U = F) \qquad T \qquad (E^2$$

For example:

F   E

U: (1) a. *Sáng hôm qua* tôi về Saigon.
      b.   Tôi về Saigon *sáng hôm qua*.

Trans.: (1) a. *Yesterday morning* I came back to Saigon.
          (Lit.: Morning day past I return Saigon.)
      b. I came back to Saigon *yesterday morning*.
         (Lit.: I return Saigon morning day past.)

Front and end sentence adverbials modify the trunk as a whole and are identified by their potentiality for shifting from one position to the other.

3.2.2. *The Trunk Level*

The second or trunk level, which consists of positions for a SUBJECT and a PREDICATID CLUSTER, may be schematically represented as follows:

$$T = \qquad \boxed{\pm S} \qquad PdK^3$$

A predicatid is a predicate without time-orientation. Since Vietnamese sentences lack time-orientation, the trunk is considered to consist of a subject and a predicatid. For example:

          S   Pd[4]
U: (2)   Tôi   về Saigon.

Trans.: (2)   'I came back to Saigon'.
            (*Lit.*: I return Saigon.)

---

[2]   For the explanation of the symbols, see the Introduction.
[3]   For the explanation of the symbols, see the Introduction.
[4]   *Ibid.*

3.2.3. *The Predicatid Cluster Level*

The third or predicatid cluster level is the level for a PREDICATID CLUSTER consisting of a PREDICATID NUCLEUS preceded and/or followed by PREDICATID ADVERBIALS as modifiers. The three modifier positions are called the M_1 or THE FIRST MIDDLE POSITION, the M_2 or THE SECOND MIDDLE POSITION, and the D or THE DROPPABLE POSITION. This level may be schematically represented as follows:

$$PdK = M_1 \ M_2 \ ) \qquad Pd* \qquad (\ D^5$$

The M_1 position occurs after the subject position, the M_2 position occurs between the time-relationship position and the verbal position, and the droppable position occurs between the complement position and the end adverbial position. Unlike the sentence adverbials, units in the M_1, M_2, and D positions can be dropped but cannot be shifted from one position to another. For example:

		S	M_1	V	C
(3)		Tôi cũng về Saigon.			

		S	TR M_2		V	O
(4)		Tôi sẽ luôn luôn học tiếng Anh.				

		S	V	O	D^6
(5)		Cô Lan nói tiếng Anh rất giỏi.			

Trans.: (3)   I also came back to Saigon.
(*Lit.*: I also return Saigon.)

(4)   I will often study English.
(*Lit.*: I later time often study sound Britain.)

(5)   Miss Lan speaks English very well.
(*Lit.*: Miss Lan speak sound Britain very brilliant.)

3.2.4. *The Predicatid Nucleus Level*

On the fourth or predicatid-nucleus level, there are four positions which will be called THE VERBAL POSITION, THE OBJECT POSITION, THE PARTICLE POSITION, and THE COMPLEMENT POSITION. This level may be schematically represented as follows:

$$Pd* = V + O + B + C^7$$

For example:

		S	V	O	B	C^8
(6)		Tôi cầm cái lược lên cho Lan.				

Trans.: (6)   I took a comb up to Lan.
(*Lit.*: I hold inanimate determiner comb up for Lan.)

---

[5] *Ibid.*
[6] For the explanation of the symbols, see the Introduction.
[7] *Ibid.*
[8] *Ibid.*

All the four levels may be represented as follows:

$$U \quad = F \,) \qquad\qquad T \qquad\qquad (\ E$$

$$T \quad = \quad \boxed{\pm\ S} \qquad PdK$$

$$PdK = \qquad M_1\ M_2 \quad Pd^* \quad (\ D$$

$$Pd^* = \qquad\qquad V + O + B + C$$

They may also be represented in a single linear sequence as follows:

$$U = F\ )\pm S + M_1 + M_2\ ) + V + O + B + C\ (+ D\ (+ E^9$$

There are also three other sectors: THE TIME-RELATIONSHIP POSITION, which occurs between the M_1 and M_2 sectors; and THE NEGATOR POSITION and THE PASSIVE POSITION, which precede the verbal sector. For example:

		S	M_1	TR	M_2	V	O
U:	(7)	Tôi	cũng	sẽ	luôn luôn	ăn	cam.

		S	TR	Neg.	V	C
	(8)	Tôi	sẽ	không	về	Việt Nam.

		S	Pass.	V[10]
	(9)	Tôi	bị	đánh.

Trans.: (7)   I will often eat oranges too.
        (*Lit.*: I also later time often eat orange.)

       (8)   I will not go back to Vietnam.
             (*Lit.*: I later time no return Vietnam.)

       (9)   I was beaten.
             (*Lit.*: I passive beat.)

There are in addition two shifted sectors, which will be represented by tildes over their symbols. These are the $\tilde{B}$ and $\tilde{C}$ sectors. Since front adverbials in the F sector are identified by their potentiality for shifting to the E sector, the E sector may also be considered to be a shifted position for sentence adverbials. The following examples show the shifted sectors:

		S	V	$\tilde{B}$	$\tilde{C}$	O	B	C
U: (10)	a.	Lan	cầm			cái lược này	*lên*	*cho mợ*.
	b.	Lan	cầm	*lên*		cái lược này		*cho mợ*.
	c.	Lan	cầm	*lên*	*cho mợ*	cái lược này.		

---

[9]   For the explanation of the symbols, see the Introduction.
[10]   *Ibid.*

Trans.: (10) a. Lan took this comb *up to mother.*

                (*Lit.*: Lan hold pre-determiner comb post-determiner up for mother.)

          b. Lan took *up* this comb *to mother.*

                (*Lit.*: Lan hold up pre-determiner comb post-determiner for mother.)

          c. Lan took *mother up* this comb.

                (*Lit.*: Lan hold up for mother pre-determiner comb post-determiner.)

             F   S   TR V C   E

U: (11) a. *Ngày mai* Lan sẽ   về Saigon.

        b.   Lan sẽ   về Saigon *ngày mai.*

Trans.: (11) a. *Tomorrow* Lan will go back to Saigon.

                (*Lit.*: Day tomorrow Lan later time return Saigon.)

          b. Lan will go back to Saigon *tomorrow.*

                (*Lit.*: Lan later time return Saigon day tomorrow.)

The following schema shows both shifted and non-shifted sectors in a single linear sequence:

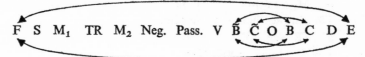

There are four more sectors on the sentence and trunk levels. The first is the L sector for sentence linkers, the second is the I or introductory sector, the third is the Q sector for question words, and the fourth is the 'Em.' or emphatic sector.

Two more sectors which might be considered to be on the sentence level but which are not really part of the sentence proper are the Y sector occurring at the very beginning of the sentence, and the Z sector occurring at the very end of the sentence.

The complete spectrum of the sectors on the sentence, trunk, predicatid-cluster, and predicatid-nucleus levels is as follows:

      Y Em. L F I S M_1 TR M_2 Neg. Pass. V B̃ C̃ O B C D E Q Z

There are five basic types of constructions in Vietnamese: trunks, predicatids, clausids, phrases, and clusters. Clusters may be sub-divided into noun clusters, verb clusters, and modifier clusters.

3.3. LEXEMES

Because of the possibility that a name like *Qui Nhơn* could be read either as *Quin Hơn* or *Qui Nhơn*, it is conventional in Vietnamese orthography to write every syllable as a separate word (that is, with spaces before and after it), whether it is meaningful by itself or not. The majority of lexemes in Vietnamese are, indeed, one-word lexemes. But many lexemes consist of two, three, or even four words. Lexemes are of three types: simple, complex, and compound.

3.3.1. Simple lexemes are one-word lexemes, such as:

nhà   cửa   sách
house door   book

3.3.2. Complex lexemes are of four types:

(1) Two-word lexemes consisting of two words which are phonetically identical. Either of the two words may be regarded as the 'perfect reduplicative' of the other.[11] For example:

tròn tròn   luôn luôn   to to   vàng vàng
round round   often often   big big   yellow yellow
rather round   often   rather big   rather yellow

(2) Two-word lexemes consisting of a word followed by a 'partial reduplicative'.[11] For example:

rộng rải   vội vàng   chim chóc
large   hurry   bird

(3) Two-word lexemes consisting of a word preceded by a partial reduplicative. For example:

mong mỏng   nho nhỏ   khang khác
thin   small   different

The meaningful part or base of a complex lexeme may occur as a simple lexeme, without its reduplicative. Reduplicatives, on the other hand, are neither morphologically nor syntactically free, although they are free phonologically. They are always bound to base words, with which they form meaningful units on the 'word' level. Reduplicatives are added to bases either to modify the meaning of the bases or else for stylistic reasons — in order, for example, to make the resulting lexemes more melodious. Almost any word in Vietnamese may have its own reduplicative. Some base words even take two or three different reduplicatives. For example:

lành lạnh   lạnh lùng   lạnh lẽo
   cold   cold   cold
a bit cold cold or indifferent cold or desolate

già giêc   già giặn
old   old
old of age or mature in character   mature in character

---

[11] The terms PERFECT REDUPLICATIVE and PARTIAL REDUPLICATIVE have been taken from Laurence C. Thompson's "A Grammar of Spoken South Vietnamese" (unpublished Ph.D. dissertation, Yale University, New Haven, Connecticut, 1954), p. 59. Thompson uses the term REDUPLICATIVE to designate "dissyllabic morphs" which are either "PERFECT", i.e., totally similar phonetically, or else "PARTIAL", i.e., only partially similar phonetically.

A number of Vietnamese lexemes are made up of base words in combination with other words which are not reduplicated from the base words but which have some of the same characteristics as reduplicatives: they are free phonologically but not morphologically nor syntactically, and they are always bound to base words with which they form meaningful units on the 'word' level. These words may be regarded as additive words which, like the reduplicatives, are added to bases either to modify the meaning of the bases or else for stylistic reasons. The following are examples of the lexeme *già* 'old' combined both with its reduplicative and with an additive word:

già giặn	già nua
old	old
mature in character	old of age

(4) Two- or three-word lexemes borrowed from French or English. For example:

va li	cà phê	sà phòng	búp bê	ô tô	ci nê
suitcase	coffee	soap	doll	car	movies
mít tinh	bin đinh	bít têt	cao bồi (cowboy)		
meeting	building	beefsteak	delinquent		

3.3.3. Compound lexemes consist of two or three one-word lexemes joined in a fairly fixed order to form a new lexeme whose meaning is different from the meaning suggested by the combination of the constituent lexemes.

(1) The following are examples of two-word compound lexemes:

bàn ghê	quần áo	trâu bò	nhà cửa
table chair	trousers shirt	buffalo cow	house door
furniture	clothes	cattle	house

đánh rơi	hỏi thăm	buôn bán	khâu vá
beat fall	ask visit	buy sell	saw mend
lose	inquire	trade	saw

In some cases, the meaning of a compound does not change even when there is a change in the order of its constituent lexemes. For example:

ao ước = ước ao	than thở = thở than
long(ing)	complain

But in other cases, a change in the order of the constituent lexemes does change the meaning of the compound. For example:

thanh bình	bình thanh
peace	level tone

(2) The following are examples of four-word compound lexemes:

nói   đi   nói   lại   đi đi lại   lại
speak forth speak back   go go return return
speak again and again   go back and forth

All the compound lexemes cited above are made up of only Vietnamese words. There are also compound lexemes made up of Sino-Vietnamese words[12] or of both Sino-Vietnamese and Vietnamese words.

(3) The following are compound lexemes made up of two Sino-Vietnamese words:

quốc gia   sơn   hà   ái quốc   tiến   bộ
nation family   mountain river love nation advance step
state   nation   patriotism progress

Sino-Vietnamese words rarely occur alone, but generally combine with other Sino-Vietnamese or Vietnamese words into compound lexemes which function as single units on the 'word' level.

(4) The following are examples of compound lexemes made up of Vietnamese words followed by Sino-Vietnamese words:

sách giáo khoa   bạn   hữu   tàu hỏa
book teach subject friend friend ship fire
textbook   friendship   train

(5) The following are examples of compound lexemes made up of three or four Sino-Vietnamese words:

hàn thử biểu   chiến đầu   hạm   hàng   không mẫu   hạm
cold heat show   war combat ship   transport air   mother ship
thermometer   warship   aircraft carrier

(6) The following are examples of compound lexemes made up of Sino-Vietnamese words followed by Vietnamese words:

danh tiếng   ngu   dốt   hiền lành
name sound   stupid ignorant gentle gentle
famous   ignorant   gentle

(7) There are a few Sino-Vietnamese lexemes which usually combine with Sino-Vietnamese words or compounds. They may either precede or follow the word or compound with which they combine.

Those which regularly follow are: *nhân* 'man', *gia* 'man', *giả* 'man', *sĩ* 'educated man', *hóa* 'become'. For example:

---

[12]   Sino-Vietnamese words are words borrowed from Chinese. They behave differently from pure Vietnamese words.

ân nhân	thính giả	nhạc gia	họa sĩ	giản dị hóa
grateful man	hear man	music man	paint man	simple easy become
benefactor	listener	composer	painter	simplify

Those which regularly precede are: *vô* 'no', *phi* 'contrary', *bất* 'no', *khả* 'worthy of', *đại* 'big', *tiểu* 'small'.

vô nhân đạo	phi nghĩa	bất động sản
no man way	contrary right	no move property
inhumane	dishonest	real estate

khả ái	đắc lực	đại thương gia	tiểu quốc
worthy of love	gain power	big commerce man	small nation
lovely	efficient	big merchant	small nation

All the lexemes described above, whether simple or compound, will be treated in this analysis as single units functioning syntactically on the 'word' level.

3.4. LEXEME CLASSES

There are two kinds of lexemes in Vietnamese: those belonging to LISTABLE LEXEME CLASSES, and those belonging to NON-LISTABLE LEXEME CLASSES. A listable lexeme class can be defined by listing its members, while a non-listable lexeme class is defined by listing the positions in which its members may occur. The non-listable lexeme classes are nouns, verbs and modifiers. The most important listable lexeme classes include the following:

— the introducers of constructions and words, such as: *khi* 'when', *nếu* 'if', *trong* 'in', etc.;
— the coordinators, such as *và* 'and', *rồi* 'then', etc.;
— the listable adverbs, such as *luôn* 'often', *thỉnh thỏang* 'sometimes', etc.;
— the particles, such as *lên* 'up', *xuống* 'down', etc.;
— the sentence linkers, such as *vậy thì* 'then', *nhưng* 'but', etc.;
— the time-relationship particles, such as *sẽ* 'later time', *đã* 'earlier time', etc.;
— the Y-sector words, such as *dạ* 'yes', *không* 'no', etc.;
— the negators, such as *không*, *chẳng* 'no', etc.;
— the substitutes, such as *chị* 'elder sister', etc.;
— the question words, such as *sao* 'why', *ai* 'who', etc.;
— the modi-modifiers, such as *rất*, *lắm* 'very'.

Each sector will now be examined in turn to find the kinds of constructions that may occur in each.

3.5. THE Y SECTOR

The Y sector is the position for:

— RESPONSE SIGNALS or YES-NO WORDS, such as *chưa, có, dạ, được, ờ, ừ, không, rồi, vâng*;

— EXCLAMATION SIGNALS, such as *à, ái, áichà, chà, chao ôi, chết, hỡi ơi, ôi, ô hô, than ôi, trời ơi, ủa*;

— SURPRISE SIGNALS, such as *thật à, thật không, thể à, vậy à*;

— ATTENTION SIGNALS, such as *ấy, bẩm, đấy, kìa, nào, này, thôi, thưa. Thưa* and *bẩm* are usually used with an honorific noun appropriate to the age of the person whom one is addressing;

— and GREETINGS, such as *chào* or *lạy*, which are used with an honorific noun appropriate to the age of the person whom one is greeting.

The italic expressions in the following examples fill the Y sector in their respective sentences:

      (12) a. *Dạ*, con ăn cơm rồi ạ.

          b. *Trời ơi*, chị đẹp quá!

          c. *Vậy à*, chị có khóc không?

          d. *Này anh*, bao giờ anh đi?

          e. *Chào bà ạ*.

Trans.: (12) a. *Yes*, I have already eaten.

            (*Lit.*: Yes child eat rice already final particle.)

          b. *Heavens*, you are so beautiful!

            (*Lit.*: God oh elder sister beautiful very!)

          c. *Indeed*, did you cry?

            (*Lit.*: Indeed elder sister emphatic particle cry no?)

          d. *Hey*, when will you go?

            (*Lit.*: Hey older brother when older brother go?)

          e. *Good day, Madam*.

            (*Lit.*: Salutation Mrs. final particle.)

3.6. THE Z SECTOR

The Z sector is the position for NOUNS OF ADDRESS and for final particles such as:

— EXCLAMATION SIGNALS like *làm sao, thay, ru, vay, ư, tá, vậy*;

— ATTENTION GETTERS like *chứ, đấy, đấy chứ, đi, đi mà, kia, nao, nghe*;

— THE POLITE SIGNAL *ạ*;

— FINAL PARTICLES added to questions like *đấy, thể, vậy*.

The following are examples of the use of each type of final particle:

  (13) a. Núi này đẹp lắm *thay*!
    b. Chúng ta đi chơi *nào*.
    c. Con ăn rồi *ạ*.
    d. Anh đi đâu *thế*?
    e. Ai cũng biết học là cần *vậy*!
    f. Chị đi đâu *thể*, *chị Lan*?

Trans.: (13) a. This mountain is very beautiful!
     (*Lit.*: Mountain post-determiner beautiful final particle!)
    b. Let's go out.
     (*Lit.*: We go play final particle.)
    c. I have already eaten.
     (*Lit.*: Child eat already final particle.)
    d. Where are you going?
     (*Lit.*: Older brother go where final particle?)
    e. Everyone knows that education is indispensable!
     (*Lit.*: Who also know study is necessary final particle!)
    f. Where are you going, *Lan*?
     (*Lit.*: Older sister go where final particle older sister Lan?)

3.7. THE L SECTOR

The L sector is the position for items which are used to link the sentence in which they occur to the preceding sentence. Sentence linkers include such words as:

bất luận	gỉa dĩ	sau đó	tuy vậy mà
bất quá	hay là	song le	trước hết
bất đắc dĩ	hóa ra	sau hết	tuy nhiên
bởi thế	huống chi	té ra	tóm lại
bởi vậy	hèn nào	thật quả	vậy
bởi thế nên	hơn nữa	thế rồi	vậy thì
bởi vậy nên	liền đó	thế thì	vậy là
bởi vậy cho nên	lẽ dĩ nhiên	thành thử	vì vậy
bởi thế cho nên	như vậy thì	thật vậy	vậy mà
bởi đó cho nên	nhưng	thật ra	vả
chẳng qua	như vậy	tuy nhiên	vả lại
chung qui	nhưng mà	thế mà	vả chăng
cùng lắm	nếu thế	thảo nào	với lại
cố nhiên	nếu vậy	tuy vậy	vì thế
dẫu thế	nhưng vì thế	tuy thế	vậy nên
đại khái	nói tóm lại	tuy thế nhưng	

để kết luận   rồi   tuy vậy nhưng
dù thế nào chăng nữa   tuy thế mà

The following are examples of the use of sentence linkers in the L sector:

> (14) a. Chị đang làm cơm, phải không?
>   L
>   b. *Thật vậy*, tôi đang thổi cơm.
>   c. *Thế rồi*, chị phải làm gì nữa?
>   d. *Sau đây*, tôi phải luộc rau.

Trans.: (14) a. You are preparing the meal, aren't you?
>   (*Lit.*: Elder sister in the process of do rice, tag question words?)
>   b. *Indeed*, I am cooking rice.
>   (*Lit.*: Indeed I in the process of cook rice.)
>   c. *Then* what else do you have to do?
>   (*Lit.*: Then older sister must boil what else?)
>   d. *After this* I have to boil some vegetables.
>   (*Lit.*: After this I must boil vegetable.)

Some of the sentence linkers, such as *nhưng*, *rồi*, etc., are also used as coordinators.
The Y, Z, and L positions are positions for lexemes, not for constructions.

3.8. THE F AND E SECTORS

It was shown in section 3.2.1. that, on the sentence level, a sentence may consist of
three units: a trunk, and two sentence adverbials. Sentence adverbials are identifiable
by their potentiality for shifting from the F position to the E position or from the
E position to the F position. They may also be dropped from a sentence without
affecting the sentence grammatically. Many kinds of adverbials may occur in the
F and E positions.

3.8.1. *Adverbial Noun Clusters*

One kind of sentence adverbial consists of a noun cluster. Such an adverbial may
also be called a TIME-EXPRESSION ADVERBIAL since the nucleus of its cluster will be a
noun lexeme expressing some kind of time, such as:

> *hôm nay* 'today' (lit. *day now*), *ngày nay* 'nowadays' (lit. *day now*), etc.;
> *thứ hai* 'Monday' (lit. *rank two*), *thứ ba* 'Tuesday' (lit. *rank three*), etc.;
> *tháng giêng* 'January' (lit. *month one*), *tháng hai* 'February' (lit. *month two*), etc.;
> *năm ngóai* 'last year' (lit. *year past*), *năm nay* 'this year' (lit. *year now*), etc.;
> *buổi sáng* 'morning' (lit. *moment* or *period morning*), *hồi trưa* 'noon' (lit. *moment noon*), etc.

These nouns may be preceded by indefinite numerals such as *mấy, vài* 'some', etc., and by definite numerals such as *một* 'one', *hai* 'two', etc.; they may be preceded or followed by ordinal numerals such as *thứ nhất* 'first' (lit. *rank one*), *thứ hai* 'second' (lit. *rank two*), etc.; and they may be followed by post-modifiers such as *này* 'this', *kia* 'there', etc. (the so-called demonstrators). The following is a list of some noun clusters commonly used as time-expression adverbials in the F or E sector:

(1) *Time Expressions for Present Time*

Hiện tại	Now
Hiện nay	Now
Hiện giờ	Now
Bây giờ	At present
Lúc này	This moment
Ngay lúc này	Right now, right this moment
Hồi này	This present period
Dạo này	This present period
Độ này	This present period
Ngày nay	Nowadays
Hôm nay	Today
Sáng hôm nay	This morning
Trưa hôm nay	This afternoon
Chiều hôm nay	This late afternoon
Tối hôm nay	This evening
Đêm hôm nay	Tonight
Tuần này	This week
Tháng này	This month
Năm nay	This year
Thế kỷ này	This century
Đời này	This generation
Đời bây giờ	This generation
etc.	

(2) *Time Expressions for Future Time*

Chốc nữa	A moment later
Lát nữa	A moment later
Tí nữa	A moment later
Mai sau	In the future
Sau này	In the future
Về sau	In the future
Về sau	In the future
Mai *OR* Ngày mai	Tomorrow
Sáng (ngày) mai	Tomorrow morning

Trưa (ngày) mai	Tomorrow afternoon
Chiều (ngày) mai	Tomorrow late afternoon
Tối (ngày) mai	Tomorrow evening
Đêm (ngày) mai	Tomorrow night
Ngày kia	Day after tomorrow
Sáng Ngày kia	The morning of the day after tomorrow
etc.	
Ngày kìa	Three days from now
Sáng ngày kìa	Three days from now in the morning
etc.	
Tuần sau	Next week
Tuần tới	Next week
Tháng sau	Next month
Tháng tới	Next month
Sang tháng	Next month
Năm sau	Next year
Năm tới	Next year
Sang năm	Next year
Thứ hai tới OR	
Thứ hai sau	Next Monday
etc.	
Hai tuần nữa	Two weeks from now
etc.	
Hai tháng nữa	Two months from now
etc.	
Ba năm nữa	Three years from now
etc.	
Thế kỷ tới OR	
Thế kỷ sau	Next century

(3) *Time Expressions for Past Time*

Khi nãy	Last moment or last time
Hồi nãy	Last moment or last time
Lúc Nãy	Last moment or last time
Hôm qua	Yesterday
Sáng hôm qua	Yesterday morning
Trưa hôm nay	Yesterday afternoon
Chiều hôm qua	Yesterday (late) afternoon
Tối hôm qua	Yesterday evening
Đêm hôm qua	Last night
Hôm kia	Day before yesterday

Sáng hôm kia etc.	The morning of the day before yesterday
Hôm kìa	Three days ago
Sáng hôm kìa etc.	Three days ago in the morning
Hôm nọ	The other day
Tháng trước	Last month
Tháng vừa qua	Last month
Tuần trước	Last week
Tuần vừa qua	Last week
Năm ngóai	Last year
Năm kia	The year before last
Năm kìa	Three years ago
Kỳ trước	Last time
Lần trước	Last time
Độ trước	Formerly
Thửơ (OR thủa) trước	Formerly
Trứớc kia	Formerly
Ngày xưa	Once upon a time
Xưa kia	Once upon a time
Thủa xưa	Once upon a time
Hồi xưa	Once upon a time
Bây giờ	Then, at that time
Đời bẩy giờ	Then, at that time
Lúc bây giờ	Then at that time
Lúc ẫy, OR Hồi ẫy, OR Dạo ẫy, OR Thủa ẫy	Then, at that time
Thế kỷ trứớc	Last century

(4) *Names of the week*

Thứ hai	Monday (lit. *rank two*)
Thứ ba	Tuesday (lit. *rank three*)
Thứ tư	Wednesday (lit. *rank four*)
Thứ năm	Thursday (lit. *rank five*)
Thứ sáu	Friday (lit. *rank six*)
Thứ bảy	Saturday (lit. *rank seven*)
Chủ nhật OR Chúa nhật	Sunday (lit. *God day*)

(5) *Names of the months*

Tháng giêng	January
Tháng hai	February (lit. *month two*)
Tháng ba	March (lit. *month three*)

Tháng tư	April (lit. *month four*)
Tháng năm	May (lit. *month five*)
Tháng sáu	June (lit. *month six*)
Tháng bảy	July (lit. *month seven*)
Tháng tám	August (lit. *month eight*)
Tháng chín	September (lit. *month nine*)
Tháng mười	October (lit. *month ten*)
Tháng một	November
Tháng chạp	December

The following examples show the use of these adverbials in the F and E sectors:

```
              F                 E
U: (15) a. Hôm qua tôi ăn cá.
        b.           Tôi ăn cá   hôm qua
K:                             |⟨hôm qua⟩|
                                  *      ←
                                  n    pod
```

Trans.: (15) a. *Yesterday* I ate fish.
          (*Lit.*: Day past I eat fish.)
       b. I ate fish *yesterday*.
          (*Lit.*: I eat fish day past.)

```
              F                       E
U: (16) a. Tháng tám này tôi về Việt Nam.
        b.           Tôi về Việt Nam   tháng tám này.
K:                                  |⟨tháng tám này⟩|
                                       *    ←   ←
                                       n   nu  pod¹³
```

Trans.: (16) a. *This August* I will go back to Vietnam.
          (*Lit.*: Month eight post-determiner I return Vietnam.)
       b. I will go back to Vietnam *this August*.
          (*Lit.*: I return Vietnam month eight post-determiner.)

3.8.2. *Adverbial Phrases*

Another kind of sentence adverbial is an adverbial phrase (i.e., a prepositional phrase) consisting of a group of words introduced by one of the members of a listable lexeme class called PREPOSITIONS. The following is an incomplete list of the prepositions:

Simple Prepositions

bằng	để	nhân	sau	xa

---

[13] For the explanation of the symbols, see the Introduction.

bên	đến	nhờ	trên	xuống
cách	giữa	nội	trong	
cạnh	hộ	ở	trước	
cho	khắp	qua	từ	
cùng	khỏi	quanh	tự	
cúôi	lên	ra	vào	
dứơi	ngoài	sang	về	

Complex Prepositions

chung quanh	ở cạnh	ở ngoài	nhân dịp
đàng sau	ở đàng	ở trên	ra khỏi
đàng trước	ở dưới	ở trong	ra ngoài
đôi với	ở gần	ở xa	xung quanh
ở bên	ở giữa	ngoài ra	

A preposition is distinguished by its position before a word or group of words which functions as its object. It is also distinguished by the fact that the preposition and its object together function as a single unit on the next higher level of the sentence. A preposition ceases to be a preposition when it follows a noun or noun cluster. In the following examples, the first *trong* and *trước* are prepositions, while the second *trong* and *trúóc* are not:

R: ⟨*trong* | nhà |⟩   K: |⟨nhà *trong*⟩|
             * ←

  r   n   n   m
  in   house   house in
  inside the house   the house at the back

R: ⟨*trúóc* | cửa |⟩   K: |⟨cửa *trúóc*⟩|
              * ←

  r   n   n   m
  before door   door front
  in front of the door   the front door

A word or group of words introduced by a preposition is called A PHRASE (OR A PREPOSITIONAL PHRASE). The following are examples of adverbial phrases in the F and E sectors:

      F   E
U: (17) a. *Ở nứớc ta* nhiều người học tiếng Anh.
   b.   Nhiều người học tiếng Anh *ở nứớc ta.*
R: ⟨ở | nứớc ta |⟩
    r

K: |⟨nước ta⟩|
               *   ←
             n   pN

Trans.: (17) a. *In our country* many people learn English.
             (*Lit.*: In country we many man study sound Britain.)
        b. Many people learn English *in our country*.
             (*Lit.*: Many man study sound Britain in country we.)

                  F   E
U: (18) a. *Trong tháng này* tin chiến sự có vẻ nghiêm trọng.
      b.   Tin chiến sự có vẻ nghiêm trọng *trong tháng này*.

R: ⟨ trong | tháng này | ⟩
           r

K: |⟨tháng này⟩|
            *   ←
            n   pod

Trans.: (18) a. *This month* the war news seems to be serious.
             (*Lit.*: In month post-determiner news war affair have appearance
             seem severe important (serious).)
        b. The war news seems to be serious *this month*.
             (*Lit.*: News war affair have appearance seem severe important
             (serious) in month post-determiner.)

A prepositional phrase may be part of a noun cluster. When that noun cluster functions in turn as the object of a preposition, the first phrase becomes part of the larger phrase. Thus a phrase may be included within another phrase, as in the following example:

                  F   E
U: (19) a. *Trên cái bàn trong buồng ăn* có ba quả táo.
      b.   Có ba quả táo *trên cái bàn trong buồng ăn*.

R: ⟨trên | cái bàn trong buồng ăn | ⟩
           r

K: |⟨cái bàn trong buồng ăn⟩|
             →   *   ←————
             prd n

R: ⟨ trong | buồng ăn | ⟩
                r

K: |⟨buồng ăn⟩|
                  *   ←
                n   v[14]

---

[14] For the explanation of the symbols, see the Introduction.

Trans.: (19) a. *On the table in the dining-room* there were three apples.

            (*Lit.*: On pre-determiner table in room eat exist three fruit apple.)

        b. There were three apples *on the table in the dining-room.*

            (*Lit.*: Exist three fruit apple on pre-determiner table in room eat.)

3.8.3. *Adverbial Included Clausids*

A third kind of adverbial that may occur in the F and E sectors is an adverbial included clausid. For example:

                  F   E

U: (20) a. *Nếu tôi có tiền* tôi sẽ mua cái nhà ấy.

        b.   Tôi sẽ mua cái nhà ấy *nếu tôi có tiền.*

Trans.: (20) a. *If I have money*, I will buy that house.

            (*Lit.*: If I have money I later time buy pre-determiner house post-determiner.)

        b. I will buy that house *if I have money.*

            (*Lit.*: I later time buy pre-determiner house post-determiner if I have money.)

If *nếu* is cut off from the construction *nếu tôi có tiền*, there will remain the word group *tôi có tiền*, which is similar in form to a major sentence since (1) it consists of a subject and of a predicatid that makes a predication about the subject, (2) its units occur in normal order, and (3) it is not included in any larger construction. However, this word group does not begin with a capital letter, nor does it end with a terminal punctuation mark. In Allen's analysis, this kind of construction is called a "clausid" or a "non-included clausid". As was mentioned in section 3.1., the term CLAUSID is used to show that the verb in the clausid is not time-oriented.

The word group *nếu tôi có tiền* thus consists of a clausid introduced by *nếu*, which is one of the members of a listable lexeme class called CLAUSID INTRODUCERS or CLAUSID INCLUDERS. Clausids introduced by clausid includers are INCLUDED CLAUSIDS. But clausids which are not introduced or which are introduced by members of other listable lexeme classes (such, for example, as the sentence linkers) are NON-INCLUDED CLAUSIDS. For example:

                L

U: (21) a. *Thật vậy*, bà Ba thích trẻ con lắm.

        b. *Nhưng*   ông Ba có thích trẻ con không?

Trans.: (21) a. *In fact*, Mrs. Ba liked children very much.

            (*Lit.*: Indeed Mrs. Ba like young child very.)

        b. *But* did Mr. Ba like children?

            (*Lit.*: But Mr. Ba emphatic particle like young child no?)

The following is a partial list of the adverbial-clausid includers:

Simple Adverbial-Clausid Includers

bởi	do	nhân	tại
để	gía	nhờ	tùy
dù	hễ	ngộ	theo
dẫu	khi	như	ví
dẫu	nêu	phỏng	vì

Complex Adverbial-Clausid Includers

bởi vì	gía thử	tuy là	theo như
cũng như	khi mà	tuy rằng	vì chưng
dẫu mà	mặc dẩu	từ khi	vì rằng
dù mà	mọi khi	tuy vẫn	vì lẽ rằng
dẫu cho	phỏng như	tuy mà	vì là
đang khi	phần vì	trứơc khi	ví bằng
dù rằng	nêu mà	trong khi	ví phỏng
gía như	nhược bằng	từ khi	ví thử
gía phỏng như	sau khi	trong lúc	ví mà
gỉa sử	sau khi mà	trong khi mà	ví thể
		trứơc khi mà	
		tại vì	

The following are examples of adverbial included clausids in the F and E sectors. (Non-included clausids on other than the sentence level will be labeled "H".)

```
                    F                              E
U: (22) a.  Trứơc khi tôi đi, tôi quét nhà cẩn thận.
        b.                  Tôi quét nhà cẩn thận trứơc khi tôi đi.
                    I
Cld:        ⟦trứơc khi │ tôi đi⟧
                         S  Pd
                              ←---
H:                      │ tôi │ đi
```

Trans.: (22) a. *Before I left*, I swept the house carefully.
            (*Lit.*: Before I go I sweep house careful.)
         b. I swept the house carefully *before I left*.
            (*Lit.*: I sweep house careful before I go.)

```
                    F                              E
U: (23) a.  Vì trời mưa, tôi không đi chợ được.
        b.                  Tôi không đi chợ được vì trời mưa.
                    I
Cld:        ⟦vì │ trời mưa⟧
                 S   Pd
                      ←----
H:              │ trời │ mưa
```

Trans.: (23) a. *Because it rained*, I could not go to the market.

   (*Lit.*: Because sky rain I no go market possible.)

   b. I could not go to the market *because it rained*.

   (*Lit.*: I no go market possible because sky rain.)

In the process of analysis, an included clausid is enclosed between barred square brackets, and the includer or includer position is cut off from the rest of the clausid by a vertical line. It is to be noted that the subject of the adverbial clausid in the F or E sector may or may not have the same referent as the subject of the sentence.

3.8.3.1. *Special Adverbial Clausid.* — One special clausid includer, *mà* 'if', occurs not at the beginning of its included clausid, but after the subject of its clausid. By its presence, *mà* signals the fact that the clausid in which it appears is an included clausid. (A clausid of this kind occurs only in the F position.) The position of *mà* in such clausids will be labeled I'. For example:

                    F
U: (24)   *Chị mà đi* thì tôi khổ.
                    I'
Cld: ⟦chị | mà | đi⟧
           S   Pd
H: ┌──────┐ ←---
           │ chị │   đi
           └──────┘

Trans.: (24)   *If you went away*, I would be unhappy.

   (*Lit.*: Older sister if go then I unhappy.)

                    F
U: (25)   Anh mà không giúp nó thì chương trình đó hỏng.
                      I'
Cld: ⟦anh | mà | không giúp nó⟧
           S   Pd
H: ┌──────┐ ←-------------
           │ anh │   không giúp nó
           └──────┘

Trans.: (25)   *If you did not help him*, the program would fail.

   (*Lit.*: Older brother if no help he then program post-determiner fail.)

When a *mà* clausid is shifted from the F position to the E position, the clausid includer *nếu* 'if' must be used to introduce the clausid, either in place of *mà* or added to *mà*. *Nếu* may occur in the clausid separately from *mà*, or together with *mà* as a compound includer. *Nếu*, *nếu mà*, and *nếu... mà* seem to be in free variation, although the most frequently used of the three is *nếu* alone. The following are examples of included clausids with *nếu* in the E position:

   U: (26) a. Tôi sẽ khổ *nếu chị đi*.

I
Cld: ⟦nếu | chị đi⟧
                           S   Pd

H: ┌──────┐
                           │ chị │ đi
                           └──────┘

b. Chương trình đó sẽ hỏng, *nếu anh mà không gíup nó*.

                              I   I'
Cld: ⟦nếu | anh | mà | không gíup nó⟧
                              S   Pd

H: ┌──────┐
                           │ anh │   không gíup nó
                           └──────┘

c. Tôi sẽ đánh anh, *nếu mà anh đánh nó*.

                              I
Cld: ⟦nếu mà | anh đánh nó⟧
                              S   Pd

H: ┌──────┐
                           │ anh │ đánh nó
                           └──────┘

Trans.: (26) a. I would be unhappy *if you went away*.
              (*Lit.*: I later time unhappy if older sister go.)
          b. The program would fail *if you did not help him*.
              (*Lit.*: Program post-determiner later time fail if older brother if no
               help he.)
          c. I will beat you *if you beat him*.
              (*Lit.*: I later time beat older brother if older brother beat he.)

3.8.3.2. *Elliptical Adverbial Included Clausids*. — An elliptical included clausid may
occur in either the F or E sector. The subject is omitted in such a clausid, but the
missing subject must be the same as the subject of the sentence. The following are
examples of such elliptical adverbial included clausids:

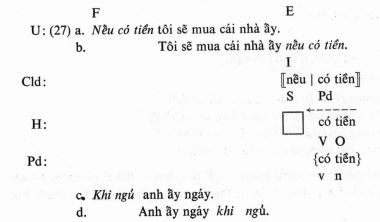

                F   E
U: (27) a. *Nếu có tiền* tôi sẽ mua cái nhà ấy.
       b.   Tôi sẽ mua cái nhà ấy *nếu có tiền*.
                                             I
Cld: ⟦nếu | có tiền⟧
                                         S   Pd
H: ┌──┐
                                       │ │ có tiền
                                       └──┘
                                         V O
Pd: {có tiền}
                                         v n

       c. *Khi ngủ* anh ấy ngáy.
       d.   Anh ấy ngáy *khi   ngủ*.

Cld: I
　　　　　　　⟦khi | ngủ⟧
　　　　　　　S　　Pd

H:
　　　　　　　◻　ngủ
　　　　　　　　　V

Pd:
　　　　　　　　{ngủ}
　　　　　　　　　v

Trans.: (27) a. *If (I) have money*, I will buy that house.
　　　　　　　　(*Lit.*: If have money I later time buy pre-determiner house post-determiner.)
　　　　　　b. I will buy that house *if (I) have money*.
　　　　　　　　(*Lit.*: I later time buy pre-determiner house if have money.)
　　　　　　c. *When (he) sleeps*, he snores.
　　　　　　　　(*Lit.*: When sleep older brother post-determiner snore.)
　　　　　　d. He snores *when (he) sleeps*.
　　　　　　　　(*Lit.*: Older brother post-determiner snore when sleep.)

The predicatid in elliptical clausids of this type may consist of any one or more of the many units that may occur on the predicatid nucleus level.

3.8.4. *Adverbial Predicatids*

A fourth kind of adverbial that may occur in the F sector is an adverbial predicatid. As was stated in section 3.2.2., a predicatid is a trunk with no subject. A predicatid occurring in the F sector usually refers to, or makes a predication about, the subject of the sentence. The following are examples of adverbial predicatids in the F sector:

　　　　　　　F　　　　　　S

U: (28) a. *Đọc xong thơ,)* | Lan | khóc rưng rức.
Pd:　　　　{đọc xong thơ}
　　　　　　F　　　　　　S

U:　　b. *Ăn xong cơm,)* | Lan | đi ngủ.
Pd:　　　　{ăn xong cơm}

Trans.: (28) a. *Having read the letter*, Lan cried pitifully.
　　　　　　　　(*Lit.*: Read complete letter Lan cry pitifully.)
　　　　　　b. *Having finished her meal*, Lan went to bed.
　　　　　　　　(*Lit.*: Eat complete rice Lan go sleep.)

When an adverbial predicatid shifts from the F position to the E position, an appropriate clausid includer is added to it, thus forming an elliptical clausid. For example:

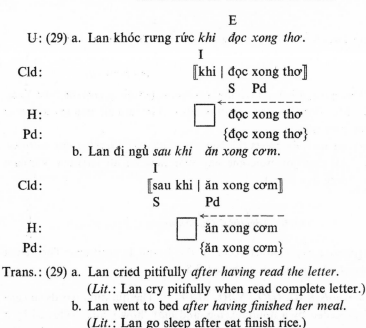

Trans.: (29) a. Lan cried pitifully *after having read the letter.*
              (*Lit.*: Lan cry pitifully when read complete letter.)
          b. Lan went to bed *after having finished her meal.*
              (*Lit.*: Lan go sleep after eat finish rice.)

The missing elements in the elliptical clausids *khi đọc xong thơ* and *sau khi ăn xong cơm* are their respective subjects — in both cases, *Lan.* When *Lan* is added to the elliptical clausids, they become full included clausids.

   When an elliptical clausid shifts from the E position to the F position, it may lose its clausid includer and become an adverbial predicatid, or it may retain the includer and remain an elliptical clausid in the F position.

3.8.5. *Adverbials of time and place*

The F and E sectors are potentially positions for more than single units. Two different kinds of adverbials can occur in these sectors. The first kind answers questions like *When?* or *On which day?* or *How often?* The second kind of adverbial answers the question word *Where?* These two kinds of adverbials may be referred to as adverbials of time and adverbials of place.

   The usual order for such adverbials in the F position is time-place, while their usual order in the E position is place-time.

   Adverbials of time and place occur in the F position more frequently than they do in the E position. They regularly occur in the F position in Yes-No questions. The following are examples of adverbials of time and place:

                 F_t F_p
U: (30) a. *Sáng hôm nay, trên toàn cõi Việt Nam,* mọi người vui vẻ đón mừng
          Năm Mới.

$$E_p$$
b. Mọi người vui vẻ đón mừng Năm Mới *trên toàn cõi Việt Nam*
$$E_t$$
sáng hôm nay.

Trans.: (30) a. *This morning, all over Vietnam*, everyone joyfully greets the New Year.
        (*Lit.*: Morning day now on all territory Vietnam all man joy welcome
        gay year new.)
      b. Everyone joyfully greets the New Year *all over Vietnam this morning.*
        (*Lit.*: All man joy welcome gay year new on all territory Vietnam
        morning day now.)

3.8.6. *Adverbial Questions*

Two kinds of interrogative expressions occur in the F and E positions. They elicit
the two kinds of adverbials discussed in section 3.8.5.

3.8.6.1. *The question words BAO, GIỜ, NÀO, MẤY.* — The question words *bao giờ*
'when', *nào* 'which' preceded by a noun lexeme, and *mấy* 'how many' followed by a
noun lexeme indicating the moment or time asked about, may occur in either the
F or E position. When such expressions occur in the F position, they ask about time
later than the time of asking, that is, about later time. On the other hand, when such
expressions occur in the E position, they ask about the time earlier than the time of
asking; that is, about earlier time. The following are examples of the use of such
expressions in both the F and E positions:

	F		E
Qn: (31) a.	*Hôm nào*	ông Ba đi?	
b.		Ông Ba đi	*hôm nào?*
c.	*Lúc mấy giờ*	thì ông Ba tới?	
d.		Ông Ba tới	*lúc mấy giờ?*
e.	*Bao giờ*	cô Lan về Việt Nam?	
f.		Cô Lan về Việt Nam	*bao giờ?*

Trans.: (31) a. *On what day* will Mr. Ba go?
        (*Lit.*: Day which Mr. Ba go?)
      b. *On what day* did Mr. Ba go?
        (*Lit.*: Mr. Ba go day which?)
      c. *At what time* will Mr. Ba come?
        (*Lit.*: Moment how many hour then Mr. Ba arrive?)
      d. *At what time* did Mr. Ba come?
        (*Lit.*: Mr. Ba arrive moment how many hour?)
      e. *When* will Miss Lan go back to Vietnam?
        (*Lit.*: When Miss Lan return Vietnam?)

f. *When* did Miss Lan go back to Vietnam?
   (*Lit.*: Miss Lan return Vietnam when?)

3.8.6.2. *The question word ĐÂU.* — The question word *đâu* (or *ở đâu*) 'where' may occur in either the F or E position, but it occurs more frequently in the latter. The following are examples of the use of *đâu* and *ở đâu* in the F and E positions, with possible answers:

                    F
Qn: (32) a. *Đâu*   có hiệu bánh ngon?
  U: b. *Ở phố Gia Long* có hiệu bánh ngon.
                    E
Qn: c. Mọi người đón mừng Năm Mới *ở đâu?*
  U: d. Mọi người đón mừng Năm Mới *ở Việt Nam.*
OR: e. *Ở Việt Nam* mọi người đón mừng Năm Mới.

Trans.: (32) a. *Where* is there a good bakery?
                (*Lit.*: Where exist shop cake delicious?)
             b. There is a good bakery in *Gia Long Street.*
                (*Lit.*: In street Gia Long exist shop cake delicious.)
             c. *Where* did people gayly greet the New Year?
                (*Lit.*: All man welcome gay year new where?)
        d., e. People gayly greeted the New Year *in Vietnam.*
                (*Lit.*: All man welcome gay year new in Vietnam.)

3.8.6.3. *Special cases.* — When the M_1 particle *cũng* 'also' occurs in the M_1 position, the question words *đâu* or *ở đâu* 'where', *bao giờ* 'when', *nào* 'which', and *mấy* 'how many' — if they occur in the F (but not the E) position — are no longer question words. They become instead indefinite adverbs of place or time, as in the following examples:

                F M_1
U: (33) a. *Ở đâu*   người ta *cũng* biết là ông Ba chăm học.
        b. *Bao giờ*   đèn điện *cũng* sáng hơn đèn dầu.
        c. *Hôm nào* ông Ba   *cũng* học hành chăm chỉ.
        d. *Mấy giờ* ông Ba   *cũng* tới chơi.

Trans.: (33) a. *Everywhere* people know that Mr. Ba is studious.
                (*Lit.*: Everywhere people also know that Mr. Ba studious.)
             b. Electric light is *always* brighter than oil light.
                (*Lit.*: When lamp electricity also bright more lamp oil.)
             c. Mr. Ba studies earnestly *every day.*
                (*Lit.*: Day whichever Mr. Ba also study studious.)
             d. *Whatever the time*, Mr. Ba will also come.
                (*Lit.*: How many hour Mr. Ba also arrive play.)

3.8.7. *The F and E sectors in Vietnamese as contrasted with the
F and E sectors in English*

Although clusters occur in the F and E positions in both English and Vietnamese, Vietnamese has only adverbial noun clusters, while English has both adverbial noun clusters and adverbial adverb clusters, as can be seen from the following examples:

F

Yesterday morning) Percy took coffee up to his mother before breakfast.

E

Percy took a cup of coffee up to his mother (*very carefully.*[15]

Again, although adverbial predicatids may occur in both the F and E positions in English, in Vietnamese they occur only in the F position. In order to shift to the E position, they have to be preceded by clausid includers — that is, they are changed to elliptical included clausids.

The types of question words used in the F and E positions in Vietnamese are similar to some of the WH question words used in English. But while in Vietnamese these question words occur in the F and E positions, the WH question words in English occur in the I or introductory position.

Finally, while the F and E positions in English are positions for adverbials of time, manner, and place, in Vietnamese they are positions for only adverbials of time and place.

3.9. COMPOUND SENTENCES

In section 3.8.3. it was stated that a word group like *tôi có tiền* met all the criteria for a major sentence except that it did not begin with a capital letter and end with a terminal punctuation mark. Such a word group was called a non-included clausid. Two, three, or even more non-included clausids may occur together and form what is called a "COMPOUND SENTENCE". The following are examples of compound sentences:

U: (35) a. Tôi có tiền rồi tôi tậu một cái xe hơi.
     b. Ông Ba ăn cơm rồi ông xuống phố.
     c. Ông Ba chơi đàn nhưng bà Ba hát.

Trans.: (35) a. I had money, then I bought a car.
         (*Lit.*: I have money then I buy one pre-determiner car.)
     b. Mr. Ba had his meal, then he went down town.
         (*Lit.*: Mr. Ba eat rice then Mr. descend street.)
     c. Mr. Ba played a musical instrument, but Mrs. Ba sang.
         (*Lit.*: Mr. Ba play musical instrument but Mrs. Ba sing.)

These compound sentences could have been written as separate sentences as follows:

[15] These examples are taken from Robert L. Allen, *A Modern Grammar of Written English* (New York, The Macmillan Company, in press).

U: (36) a. Tôi có tiền. Rồi tôi tậu một cái xe hơi.

        b. Ông Ba ăn cơm. Rồi ông xuống phố.

        c. Ông Ba chơi đàn. Nhưng bà Ba hát.

(Not all compound sentences can be written as two separate sentences in this way.)

    While the words *rồi* and *nhưng* in examples 36a, 36b, and 36c function as sentence linkers in the L position in their own sentences to link their sentences to the sentences preceding them, *rồi* and *nhưng* in examples 35a, 35b, and 35c only link one part of a sentence to another. *Rồi* and *nhưng* in examples 35a, 35b, and 35c belong to a class of listable lexemes called "COORDINATORS" (traditionally called coordinating conjunctions). Coordinators are used to join units of equal rank, not only on the sentence level but also on lower levels as well. The following is a partial list of sentence-level coordinators:

Sentence-Level Coordinators

cho	hay	khiến	nhưng
cũng như	hay là	khiến cho	nhưng mà
để	hoặc	là	ngõ hầu
để mà	hoặc là	mà	thành ra
để cho	kẻo	nên	thì
đến nỗi	kẻo mà	như	và

Sentence coordinators differ from adverbial clausid includers in that the clausids which they introduce cannot shift to the F position. In the following sentences, for example, *vì* is an adverbial includer but *mà* is a sentence coordinator:

U: (37) a. Tôi không về Saigon *vì trời mưa.*

        b. *Vì trời mưa* tôi không về Saigon.

        c. Tôi gọi *mà ông không quay lại.*

BUT NOT: **Mà ông không quay lại* tôi gọi.

        d. Anh phải nói rõ *cho họ hiểu.*

BUT NOT: **Cho họ hiểu* anh phải nói rõ.

Trans.: (37) a. I did not go back to Saigon *because it rained.*

          (*Lit.*: I no return Saigon because sky rain.)

        b. *Because it rained,* I did not go back to Saigon.

          (*Lit.*: Because sky rain I no return Saigon.)

        c. I called *but you did not turn back.*

          (*Lit.*: I call but Mr. no turn back.)

        d. You should speak clearly *so they can understana.*

          (*Lit.*: Older brother must speak clear so they understand.)

Many of the sentence-level coordinators are also used as coordinators on lower levels, to join units of the same kind. *Và* 'and', for example, may join the two parts of several different kinds of compound constructions, as in the following sentences:

U: (38) a. Ba mua ba quả cam *và* —

Và may join two non-included clausids in a compound sentence, as in —

b. Ba mua ba quả cam, *và* Lan mua ba quả táo.

Or it may join the two parts of a compound predicatid, as in —

c. Ba mua ba quả cam *và* cho Lan hai quả.

Or it may join the two parts of a compound noun cluster, as in —

d. Ba mua ba quả cam *và* hai quả táo.

Trans.: (38) a. Ba bought three oranges and —

(*Lit.*: Ba buy three fruit orange and —)

b. Ba bought three oranges and Lan bought three apples.

(*Lit.*: Ba buy three fruit orange and Lan buy three fruit apple.)

c. Ba bought three oranges and gave Lan two.

(*Lit.*: Ba buy three fruit orange and give Lan two fruit.)

d. Ba bought three oranges and two apples.

(*Lit.*: Ba buy three fruit orange and two fruit apple.)

When there are more than two units, commas are used to replace *và* 'and' except between the last two units, where both a comma and *và* are used. In the following example, the commas and *và* join the three noun clusters *ba quả cam* and *hai quả táo* and *một bó hoa*:

U: (39)   Sáng hôm qua, Ba mua *ba quả cam, hai quả táo, và một bó hoa.*

Trans.: (39)   Yesterday morning, Ba bought *three oranges, two apples, and a bunch of flowers.*

(*Lit.*: Morning day past Ba buy three fruit orange, two fruit apple, and one bunch flower.)

The following is a partial list of the coordinators used to join units on levels lower than the sentence level:

Lower-Level Coordinators

cho nên	đến nỗi	kẻo
cho đến nỗi	hay	mà
chứ đừng	hay là	ngõ hầu
chứ không	hoặc	như
cùng với	hoặc là	và
để	hơn là	với

The following two-part coordinators may be used to join units either on the sentence level or on lower levels:

cả... lẫn...	không những... mà còn...
đã... lại...	vừa... lại...
để... để...	vừa... vừa

The following are examples showing the use of some of these coordinators:

U: (40) a. Ba thích ăn cam *chứ không* thích ăn táo.

b. Ba biết tất cả mọi người *mà* không biết bà ấy.

c. Ba ăn cơm *với* cá.

d. Cô ấy buồn *mà* ốm.

e. Ba ăn *cả* cam *lẫn* táo.

f. Ba ăn hai quả cam *và* ba quả táo.

g. Ba *vừa* giỏi *vừa* chăm.

Trans.: (40) a. Ba liked to eat oranges *but* did *not* like to eat apples.

(*Lit.*: Ba like eat orange but not like eat apple.)

b. Ba knew every one *but* did not know that lady.

(*Lit.*: Ba know all man but no know Mrs. post-determiner.)

c. Ba ate rice *with* fish.

(*Lit.*: Ba eat rice with fish.)

d. She was sad *and* (*as a result*) sick.

(*Lit.*: Miss post-determiner sad and as a result sick.)

e. Ba ate *both* oranges and apples.

(*Lit.*: Ba eat all orange and apple.)

f. Ba ate two oranges *and* three apples.

(*Lit.*: Ba eat two fruit orange and three fruit apple.)

g. Ba was *both* intelligent *and* studious.

(*Lit.*: Ba both intelligent and studious.)

A GRAMMAR OF PRESENT-DAY WRITTEN VIETNAMESE:
THE SECTORS ON THE TRUNK LEVEL

4.1. THE I SECTOR

A sentence has been analyzed as consisting, on the sentence level, of a trunk and front and/or end adverbials. A position which precedes the trunk will be examined next. It will be called the I or INTRODUCTORY SECTOR. The I sector is the position for two kinds of words: question words and introducers.

4.1.1. *Interrogative expressions with SAO and GÌ*

The following interrogative expressions may occur in the I position to ask for units in the E or C position:

sao	why
tại sao	why
vì cớ gì	for what

The following are examples of questions with these question words, and of possible answers to them:

<pre>
                I
U: (1) a. <i>Sao</i> ông Ba không ăn cơm?
                                     E
       b.   Ông Ba không ăn cơm <i>vì ông không đói.</i>
                                      V C
       c.   Ông Ba không ăn cơm là <i>vì ông không đói.</i>
</pre>

Trans.: (1) a. *Why* didn't Mr. Ba have his meal?
            (*Lit.*: Why Mr. Ba no eat rice?)
         b. Mr. Ba did not have his meal *because he was not hungry.*
            (*Lit.*: Mr. Ba no eat rice because Mr. no hungry.)
         c. The reason that Mr. Ba did not have his meal was *because he was not hungry.*
            (*Lit.*: Mr. Ba no eat rice is because Mr. no hungry.)

I

U: (2) a. *Vì cớ gì* ông Ba không đi làm sáng hôm nay?

E

b. Ông Ba không đi làm sáng hôm nay *vì ông bị cảm?*

Trans.: (2) a. *Why* (for what reason) didn't Mr. Ba go to work this morning?

(*Lit.*: Because reason what Mr. Ba no go work morning day now?)

b. Mr. Ba did not go to work this morning *because he had a cold.*

(*Lit.*: Mr. Ba no go work morning day now is because Mr. passive cold.)

In the process of analysis, the interrogative expressions occurring in the I position are cut off from the trunk by a vertical line.

The addition of the particles

dù ... đi nữa 'whatever'

or *dù ... chăng nữa* 'whatever'

to *sao* 'why' or *gì* 'what' in the I position, and the addition of the M_1 particle *cũng* 'also' in the M_1 sector, change questions in which *sao* and *gì* occur into statements. For example:

	I	M_1	
Qn: (3) a.	*Sao*	ông Ba	không ăn cơm?
U: b.	*Dù sao đi nữa,*	ông Ba *cũng*	không ăn cơm.
Qn: c.	*Vì cớ gì*	| ông Ba	không đi làm sáng hôm nay?
U: d.	*Dù vì cớ gì đi nữa,*	| ông Ba *cũng*	không đi làm sáng hôm nay.

Trans.: (3) a. *Why* didn't Mr. Ba have his meal?

(*Lit.*: Why Mr. Ba no eat rice?)

b. *No matter what happened,* Mr. Ba was not willing to eat.

(*Lit.*: Whatever why Mr. Ba also no eat rice.)

c. *Why* (for what reason) didn't Mr. Ba go to work this morning?

(*Lit.*: Because reason what Mr. Ba no go work morning day now?)

d. *For whatever reason,* Mr. Ba would not go to work this morning.

(*Lit.*: Whatever because reason what Mr. Ba also no go work morning day now.)

4.1.2. *Introducers*

4.1.2.1. *Trunk Introducers.* — Members of the listable lexeme class of trunk introducers may sometimes be used in the I position to introduce the trunk. The following is a list of trunk introducers:

là	nhưng
mà	nhưng mà
nên	song
	thì

Là, *mà*, *nên*, and *thì* are used more frequently than the others. These introducers signal the beginning of the trunk, usually separating it from a preceding front adverbial included clausid. The selection of one of these introducers as opposed to another seems to be determined by the clausid includers of the included clausids in the F position. The following is a list of trunk introducers and appropriate clausid includers that may precede them in the F position:

là	*mà*	*nên*
hễ	nhân	bởi
nếu	nhờ	tại
mỗi khi	tại	vì
	tuy	bởi vì
	vì	tại vì
	bởi vì	
	mặc dầu	
	trong khi	

nhưng	*song*	*thì*	
tuy	tuy	dù	gía phỏng như
tuy là	tuy là	dầu	gỉa sử
tuy rằng	tuy rằng	dẫu	gỉa thử
		gía	khi mà
		hễ	phỏng như
		khi	nếu mà
		nếu	nhược bằng
		ngộ	sau khi
		dẫu mà	từ khi
		dù mà	trước khi
		dẫu cho	trong khi
		đang khi	trong lúc
		dù rằng	theo như
		gía như	ví mà

Unlike Vietnamese, English does not have such trunk introducers in the I position. The following are examples of the use of trunk introducers:

		F	I
U: (4)	a.	Hễ tôi có tiền	*là* tôi mua sách liền.
	b.	Vì anh mách thày gíao	*mà* Ba phải phạt.
	c.	Khi tôi đến	*thì* Ba đi rồi.
	d.	Bao giờ	*thì* Ba về Saigon?[1]

---

[1] The question word *bao giờ* 'when' may occur either in the F position or in the E position, as was stated in section 3.8.6.1., Chapter 3.

    e. Vì anh không cẩn thận *nên* kẻ trộm lấy mất ba cái xe đạp.

    f. Tuy Ba nói nhanh   *nhưng* tôi cũng vẫn hiểu được.

Trans.: (4) a. As soon as I have money, I will buy books.

        (*Lit.*: Whenever I have money then I buy book.)

      b. Because you reported him to the teacher, Ba was punished.

        (*Lit.*: Because older brother report teacher therefore Ba passive particle punish.)

     c. When I came, Ba had already gone.

        (*Lit.*: When I arrive then Ba go already.)

      d. When will Ba go back to Saigon?

        (*Lit.*: When then Ba return Saigon?)

      e. Because you were not careful, the thief stole three bicycles.

        (*Lit.*: Because older brother no careful therefore thief take three inanimate determiner bicycle.)

      f. Although Ba talked fast, I could still understand him.

        (*Lit.*: Although Ba speak fast but I still understand possible.)

These trunk introducers are also used to signal the beginning of the trunk when the subject of the front adverbial included clausid has the same referent as the subject of the sentence and the latter has been omitted. The omission of the subject of a sentence is less frequent than the omission of the subject of an adverbial included clausid, but is often found in informal conversational Vietnamese. The following are examples of sentences with trunk introducers whose subjects have been omitted:

                       I   S

U: (5) a. Hễ tôi có tiền   *là* ∅ mua sách liền.

      b. Vì Ba không học *mà* ∅ bị thày phạt.

      c. Vì tôi bị cảm   *nên* ∅ không đi Dalat được.

      d. Nếu ông ấy có tiền *thì* ∅ đã mua cái nhà đó.

      ∅ represents the missing subject unit.

Trans.: (5) a. As soon as I have money, (I) will buy books.

        (*Lit.*: Whenever I have money then buy book at once.)

      b. Because Ba did not learn his lesson, (he) was punished by the teacher.

        (*Lit.*: Because Ba no study lesson therefore passive particle teacher punish.)

      c. Because I had a cold, (I) could not go to Dalat.

        (*Lit.*: Because I passive particle cold therefore no go Dalat possible.)

      d. If he had had money, (he) would have bought that house.

        (*Lit.*: If Mr. post-modifier have money then earlier-time particle buy pre-determiner house post-determiner.)

4.1.2.2. *Clausid Introducers*. — As was stated in section 3.8.3., an included clausid without its clausid includer resembles a major sentence except for the fact that it does not begin with a capital letter and end with a terminal punctuation mark. The position for clausid introducers or clausid includers may be regarded as the same as the I position or position for trunk introducers. Since the main function of a clausid includer is to introduce the whole included clausid, the includer regularly occurs in the first position in the included clausid to signal the beginning of the clausid. For this reason, the front adverbial is usually shifted to the end position.

The following are examples of clausids with the front adverbials shifted to a position following the clausid includer or to the end of the included clausid:

Cld: (6) a. Vì tôi ốm   *hôm qua* ...

         b. Vì *hôm qua* tôi ốm ...

             I

         c. Vì   tôi ốm *hôm qua*

                  F   E

H: d.   tôi ốm *hôm qua*

         e. *hôm qua* tôi ốm

Trans.: (6) a., c. Because I was sick *yesterday* ...

                    (*Lit.*: Because I sick day past ...)

         b. Because *yesterday* I was sick ...

             (*Lit.*: Because day past I sick ...)

         d. I was sick *yesterday*

             (*Lit.*: I sick day past)

         e. *Yesterday* I was sick

             (*Lit.*: Day past I sick)

On re-examining the trunk introducer, it can be seen that, in sentences in which the front adverbial is an included clausid, a second adverbial unit may occur either in the end adverbial position or in the position following the trunk introducer. It therefore seems appropriate to refer to trunk introducers as 'trunk separators' whose primary function is to separate or mark off the trunk from a front adverbial included clausid. The following are examples with one front adverbial included clausid in the F position and another adverbial following the trunk introducer or occurring in the end adverbial position:

                I   F̃   E

U: (7) a. Vì tôi ốm *nên hôm qua* tôi không đi Dalat.

       b. Vì tôi ốm *nên*   tôi không đi Dalat *hôm qua*.

           F   I

       c. *Hôm qua*, vì tôi ốm *nên* tôi không đi Dalat.

Trans.: (7) a. Because I was sick (*therefore*) *yesterday* I did not go to Dalat.

                (*Lit.*: Because I sick therefore day past I no go Dalat.)

         b. Because I was sick I did not go to Dalat *yesterday*.

             (*Lit.*: Because I sick therefore I no go Dalat day past.)

    c. *Yesterday*, because I was sick, I did not go to Dalat.

      (*Lit.*: Day past because I sick therefore I no go Dalat.)

A time expression that belongs to the trunk rather than with the included clausid in the F position may be placed in either the shifted $\tilde{F}$ position, the E position, or the F position preceding the adverbial included clausid. A time expression may therefore occur in three different positions on the sentence level. If a time expression occurs after the adverbial included clausid, it may be regarded as part of the clausid. For example:

            F   I

U: (7) d. Vì tôi ốm *hôm qua nên* tôi không đi Dalat.

Trans.: (7) d. Because I was sick *yesterday*, I did not go to Dalat.

      (*Lit.*: Because I sick day past therefore I no go Dalat.)

If the adverbial included clausid contains a time expression, the time expression that belongs to the trunk usually occurs either in the shifted $\tilde{F}$ position or in the E position to distinguish it from the time expression that belongs to the included clausid in the F position. For example:

          F   I $\tilde{F}$ E

U: (8) a. Vì *hôm qua* tôi ốm *nên* hôm nay tôi không đi Dalat.

      b. Vì *hôm qua* tôi ốm *nên*   tôi không đi Dalat *hôm nay*.

or: c. Vì tôi ốm *hôm qua nên*   tôi không đi Dalat *hôm nay*.

Trans.: (8) a. Because (*yesterday*) I was sick (*therefore*) *today* I did not go to Dalat.

      (*Lit.*: Because day past I sick therefore day now I no go Dalat.)

      b. Because (*yesterday*) I was sick I did not go to Dalat *today*.

      (*Lit.*: Because day past I sick therefore I no go Dalat day now.)

      c. Because I was sick *yesterday* I did not go to Dalat *today*.

      (*Lit.*: Because I sick day past therefore I no go Dalat day now.)

If the front adverbial is an included clausid, it usually precedes an interrogative expression in the I position (or an interrogative expression plus the trunk introducer), instead of following them or occurring in the end adverbial position. For example:

                       I

U: (9) a. Nếu anh không ốm   *thì tại sao* anh không đi học?

      b. Nếu ông Ba không ốm *thì vì cớ gì* ông không đi làm?

Trans.: (9) a. If you were not sick, *why* didn't you go to school?

      (*Lit.*: If older brother no sick then why older brother no go study?)

      b. If Mr. Ba was not sick, *why* didn't he go to work?

      (*Lit.*: If Mr. Ba no sick then because reason what Mr. no go work?)

4.1.3. *The I Sector in Vietnamese as contrasted with the I Sector in English*

The I sector in an English sentence is the position for WH words and word groups, which may be used either as trunk introducers, or as the includers in included clauses;

it is also the position for other includers and for inverters. (See section 2.11.2., Chapter 2.) The I position in a Vietnamese sentence is the position for certain interrogative expressions which are roughly equivalent to the WH word *why*; it is also the position for trunk introducers or separators, and for clausid introducers or includers.

There are several differences between the use of the I position in Vietnamese, and the use of the I position in English. In the first place, Vietnamese does not have inverters; English, on the other hand, does not have separators like *là* and *mà* and *nên* and *thì*, which serve only to separate the trunk from a front adverbial included clausid. Again, while a trunk introducer in English precedes only the trunk proper, a trunk introducer in Vietnamese may also precede other front adverbials except front adverbial included clausids. The same is true of interrogative expressions occurring in the I position in Vietnamese. Clause (or clausid) includers occur in the I position in both Vietnamese and English.

4.2. THE SUBJECT SECTOR

As was stated in section 3.2.2., the second or trunk level consists of a subject and a predicatid. The subject of a sentence can be identified by inserting the interrogative expression *sao* 'why' or *tại sao* 'why' in the I position and the middle adverb *cũng* 'also' in the M_1 position: the word or words that occur between the interrogative expression and the middle adverb — and which cannot shift to the end adverbial position — will be the subject. For example:

	F	T	E
U: (10)	*Hôm qua*)	ông Ba về Saigon.	
		Ông Ba về Saigon (*hôm qua*.	
	I		
T:	*Tại sao*	ông Ba về Saigon?	
	I	M_1	
	Tại sao	ông Ba *cũng* về Saigon?	

Trans.: (10)   *Yesterday* Mr. Ba went back to Saigon.
(*Lit.*: Day past Mr. Ba return Saigon.)
Mr. Ba went back to Saigon *yesterday*.
(*Lit.*: Mr. Ba return Saigon day past.)
Why did Mr. Ba go back to Saigon?
(*Lit.*: Why Mr. Ba return Saigon?)
Why did Mr. Ba *also* go back to Saigon?
(*Lit.*: Why Mr. Ba also return Saigon?)

As *ông Ba* cannot shift to the end adverbial position, it must be the subject of the sentence.

                         F   S   Pd
                                          ←- - - - - -
U: (11)   Hôm qua | ông Ba | về Saigon.

Trans.: (11)   Yesterday Mr. Ba went back to Saigon.
                (*Lit.*: Day past Mr. Ba return Saigon.)

The procedure described above will usually identify the subject of a non-included clausid. The subject of an included clausid can be identified by first removing the clausid includer and then treating the remainder of the clausid as a non-included clausid. For example:

                                        E
U: (12)   Tôi quét nhà cẩn thận (*trước khi   tôi đi.*
                                        I
Cld: trước khi   tôi đi
H: tôi đi
                                        I
Qn: *Tại sao   tôi đi?*
                                        I   S M_1
Qn: *Tại sao* tôi *cũng* đi?

Trans.: (12)   I swept the house carefully *before I left.*
                (*Lit.*: I sweep house careful before I go.)
                before I left
                (*Lit.*: before I go)
                I left
                (*Lit.*: I go)
                Why did I leave?
                (*Lit.*: Why I go?)
                Why did I *also* leave?
                (*Lit.*: Why I also go?)

In a compound sentence, the subjects can be identified by examining each non-included clausid separately:

U: (13)   Hôm qua cô Ba quét nhà rồi cô đi chợ.
            F   T   +
H: hôm qua) cô Ba quét nhà
T: cô Ba quét nhà
        I
Qn: *Tại sao*   cô Ba quét nhà?
        I   S M_1
Qn: *Tại sao*   cô Ba *cũng* quét nhà?
                        H + T: cô đi chợ

I

Qn: *Tại sao* cô đi chợ?

I   S M₁

Qn: *Tại sao* cô *cũng* đi chợ?

Trans.: (13)   Yesterday Miss Ba swept the house carefully, and then she went to the market.

    (*Lit.*: Day past Miss Ba sweep house then Miss go market.)

    yesterday Miss Ba swept the house

    (*Lit.*: day past Miss Ba sweep house)

    Miss Ba swept house

    (*Lit.*: Miss Ba sweep house)

    Why did Miss Ba sweep the house?

    (*Lit.*: Why Miss Ba sweep house?)

    Why did Miss Ba *also* sweep the house?

    (*Lit.*: Why Miss Ba also sweep house?)

    she went to the market

    (*Lit.*: Miss go market)

    Why did she go to the market?

    (*Lit.*: Why Miss go market?)

    Why did she *also* go to the market?

    (*Lit.*: Why Miss also go market?)

Before considering the different kinds of constructions that may occur in the subject position, it is necessary to examine first two kinds of units which occur frequently in the subject position as well as in many other positions. These units are noun clusters and substitutes.

4.3. SUBSTITUTES

Substitutes belong to a listable lexeme class whose members are used to replace words, certain kinds of constructions, or even parts of constructions. Substitutes are used to refer to something or somebody already mentioned, or about to be mentioned, or to something or somebody in the presence of the speaker and the listener. For example:

U: (14) a. Tôi mua một cái áo màu xanh. *Nó* cũng không đẹp lắm.

      b. Tôi định *thể này*: ngày mai chúng ta sẽ đi xem hoa đào.

      c. *Đây* là chị tôi.

Trans.: (14) a. I bought a blue dress. *It* was not very beautiful.

        (*Lit.*: I buy one pre-determiner dress color blue. It also no beautiful very.)

      b. I have decided *this*: tomorrow we will go and see the cherry blossoms.

        (*Lit.*: I decide this: day tomorrow we go see flower cherry.)

c. *Here* is my sister.
   (*Lit.*: Here is older sister I.)

The so-called 'personal pronouns' in Vietnamese consist of the following:

1st person singular: *ta, tôi, tao, tớ, mình.*
2nd person singular: *mi, mày, người, mình.*
3rd person singular: *nó, y, hắn.*
1st person plural: *chúng ta, chúng tôi, chúng mình.*
2nd person plural: *chúng bay, chúng mày.*
3rd person plural: *chúng, chúng nó, họ.*
Reciprocal pronoun: *nhau.*

The pronoun *chúng ta* may be referred to as 'inclusive we' since it includes both the speaker and the listener, while the pronoun *chúng tôi* may be referred to as 'exclusive we' since it includes the speaker and other persons but not the person(s) spoken to. All the first- and second-person singular and plural pronouns above may be regarded as 'shifters'[2] rather than as substitutes since their meanings change with the context.

There are also a number of so-called 'honorific nouns of address' which are sometimes used as 'personal pronouns' in order to address persons appropriately according to their age, social status, and relationship to the speaker. These honorific nouns were originally used to signal relationships among the members of a family, but have been extended to include everyone. For instance, *ông* may mean either 'grandfather', 'Mr.', 'you', or 'I'. The following is a list of honorific nouns:

Anh Older brother, older male cousin, older male friend, friend, superior, younger subordinate, you, *or* I.
Ba Father, you, *or* I.
Bà Grandmother, Mrs., friend, female subordinate or superior, you, *or* I.
Bác Older uncle or aunt, male or female friend, subordinate, you, *or* I.
Cậu Father, younger maternal uncle, master, you, *or* I.
Cha Father, reverend father, you, *or* I.
Chàng He, *or* you. (Used only in literary writing.)
Cháu Nephew, niece, grandson, granddaughter, younger subordinate, you, *or* I.
Chị Older sister, older female cousin, older female friend, friend, younger subordinate, superior, you, *or* I.
Chú Younger paternal uncle, subordinate, you, *or* I.
Cô Younger paternal aunt, Miss, younger female friend, younger subordinate, superior, you, *or* I.

[2] See Otto Jespersen, *Language: Its Nature, Development and Origin* (London, George Allen & Unwin Ltd., 1922), p. 123; Roman Jakobson, *Shifters, Verbal Categories, and the Russian Verb* (Cambridge, Mass., Department of Slavic Languages and Literatures, Harvard University, 1957), p. 2; and Robert L. Allen, *A Modern Grammar of Written English* (New York, The Macmillan Company, in press), footnote 2, pp. 353-354.

Cổ	Very old superior, ancestor, *or* you.
Con	Son, daughter, younger subordinate, you, *or* I.
Cụ	Great-grandfather, great-grandmother, old superior, *or* you.
Dì	Younger maternal aunt, you, *or* I.
Đức	Venerable.
Em	Younger brother, younger sister, younger male or female friend, you, *or* I.
Già	Old man, you, *or* I.
Lão	Old man, you, *or* I.
Mẹ	Mother, you, *or* I.
Mợ	Mother, wife of younger maternal uncle, you, *or* I.
Nàng	She, *or* you. (Used only in literary writing.)
Ngài	Sir, you, *or* he.
Người	Sir, *or* he.
Ông	Grandfather, Mr., male subordinate or superior, friend, you, *or* I.
Thằng	He. (Used with a pejorative meaning.)
Thiếp	Concubine, *or* I. (Meaning 'I', *thiếp* is used only in literary writing.)
Thím	Wife of younger paternal uncle, you, *or* I.
Cụ cổ	Ancestor.
Cụ tổ	Ancestor.
etc.	

Except for the lexemes *thằng* and *đức*, all the honorifics listed above may be preceded by the plural particle *các*. *Thằng* 'he' is preceded by the plural particle *những*; *đức* (an honorific lexeme used to refer to God and to heroes such as *Đức Chúa Trời* '"Christian" God', or *Đức Thánh Khổng* 'the Venerable Confucius') is used without the plural particle.

With the exception of *ngài, mẹ, con, người, đức*, the honorifics listed above may be followed by one of the post-modifiers such as *này* 'this', *ấy* 'that', etc.

With the exception of *đức, thằng, chàng,* and *nàng*, all the honorifics may refer either to the speaker or to the listener, or to a third party (that is, they may refer to the first, second or third person), depending on the context. For example:

U: (15)   Chú đi Dalat rồi.
       uncle go Dalat already

may mean either:

       I have gone to Dalat already.
       You have gone to Dalat already.
or: Uncle has gone to Dalat already.

When used with the plural particle *các*, the honorifics refer to the second or third person plural. With one of the post-determiners *này, ấy*, etc., they refer to the third person. When preceded by *các* and followed by one of the post-determiners, an honorific becomes the third person plural substitute.

The honorifics are also used in compound lexemes such as:

ông bà 'grandparents', 'Mr. & Mrs.', *or* 'you'.
chị em 'sisters'.
anh chị em 'brothers and sisters'.

One honorific noun may follow another to function as its possessive modifier:

cậu	cháu		bà	cháu
father	grandchild		grandmother	grandchild
	my father			my grandmother

A 'personal pronoun' may also function as the modifier of an honorific:

mợ	tôi	cô	tôi
mother	I	aunt	I
	my mother		my aunt

An honorific noun may precede a proper noun, as in *bà Mai* 'Mrs. Mai', *cô Ngọc* 'Miss Ngoc', *mẹ cô Ngọc* 'Miss Ngoc's mother'. An honorific may also precede a noun cluster, as in

chị	hàng	rau
older sister	shop	vegetable
	a vegetable seller	

anh	thợ	giày
older brother	worker	shoe
	a shoemaker	

Sometimes the gender of an honorific noun is specified by means of a 'gender particle' or a word signaling a man or a woman or the like:

bác	gái	cụ	bà
elder aunt or	female	great-grandfather or	grandmother
elder uncle		great-grandmother	
	elder aunt		great-grandmother

When they function as substitutes, the 'personal pronouns' and the honorific nouns do not occur in the first sentence in a conversation but rather in sentences that follow other sentences in which the persons which they replace have been mentioned. Except for *nó* and *chúng*, the 'personal pronouns' and the honorifics when functioning as substitutes replace or represent only constructions or units referring to human beings. *Chúng* can refer to animals, and *nó* can sometimes refer to animals and things.

Ruth Crymes, in her "Some Systems of Substitution Correlations in Modern

American English", discusses two kinds of substitutes: 'primary' and 'secondary'.[3] Primary substitutes are listable lexemes which 'replace' constructions or words and WHICH DO NOT THEMSELVES OCCUR IN THE CONSTRUCTIONS OR UNITS WHICH THEY REPLACE. Secondary substitutes, on the other hand, 'represent' constructions: THEY THEMSELVES DO OCCUR IN THE CONSTRUCTIONS WHICH THEY REPRESENT. The English substitute *it*, for example, 'replaces' the construction *that red book* in the sentence *It is mine*, while *that* 'represents' the same construction in *That is mine* since *that* itself occurs as part of the construction represented. These same two kinds of substitutes are also to be found in Vietnamese.

4.3.1. *Primary Substitutes*

Words such as *đúng thế* 'right' and *thật không* 'really' are often used as primary substitutes for sentences. For example:

U: (16) a. *Hoa lại thăm bà Hai luôn. Đúng thế.*
          (or: Vâng, cô ấy lại thăm bà Hai luôn.)
      b. Tôi sắp về Việt Nam. *Thật không?*
          (or: *Thật không?* Chị sắp về Việt Nam à?)

Trans.: (16) a. *Hoa often comes to see Mrs. Hai. Right.*
              (*Lit.*: Hoa come visit Mrs. Hai often. Right.)
              or: Yes, she often comes to see Mrs. Hai.
              (*Lit.*: Yes, Miss post-determiner come visit Mrs. Hai often.)
          b. *I am going back to Vietnam. Really?*
              (*Lit.*: I later-time particle return Vietnam. Really?)
              or: *Really?* You are going back to Vietnam?
              (*Lit.*: Really? Older sister later-time particle return Vietnam question word.)

All the question words in Vietnamese are used as primary substitutes for words or constructions expected in the answers. They can occur in almost any sector in a Vietnamese sentence. For example:

U: (17) a. *Hoa* là con bà Ba. *Ai?* (Ai là con bà Ba? Or: Hoa là ai?)
      b. Aó Lan màu *xanh lá cây.* Aó Lan màu *gì?* Or: Aó Lan màu xanh *thế nào?*

Trans.: (17) a. *Hoa* is Mrs. Ba's child. *Who?* (Who is Mrs. Ba's child? Or: Who is Hoa?)
              (*Lit.*: Hoa is child Mrs. Ba. Who? (Who is child Mrs. Ba? Or: Hoa is who?))

---

[3] Ruth Crymes, "Some Systems of Substitution Correlations in Modern American English" (unpublished Ed.D. project report, Teachers College, Columbia University, New York, 1965).

    b. Lan's dress is *leaf green. What* color is Lan's dress? Or: *What kind of green* is Lan's dress?

        (*Lit.*: Dress Lan color green leaf tree. Dress Lan color what? Or: Dress Lan color green how?)

Those 'personal pronouns' which occur as substitutes may function as primary substitutes for non-introduced clausids or for noun clusters. For example:

    U: (18) a. Anh có trông thấy *thằng bé đứng ở ngoài sân không*?
                         Nó là con bà Hai đầy.
         b. *Những đứa trẻ* nghịch ồn quá.
           Chúng   nghịch ồn quá.

Trans.: (18) a. Do you see *the little boy who is standing in the courtyard? He* is Mrs. Hai's child.
          (*Lit.*: Older brother emphatic particle see boy little stand out courtyard no? He is child Mrs. Hai final particle.)
        b. *The children* played too noisily. *They* played too noisily.
          (*Lit.*: Plural particle child play noisy very. They play noisy very.)

The lexemes *vậy* and *thế* 'so' may be used as primary substitutes for included clausids. For example:

    U: (19) a. Chị Ba bảo *chị sắp đi Dalat*.
         b. Chị Ba nói *vậy* à?
         c. Tôi không hiểu sao chị ấy lại nói *thế*?

Trans.: (19) a. Ba said *she was going to Dalat*.
          (*Lit.*: Older sister Ba say older sister latertime particle go Dalat.)
        b. Did Ba say *so*?
          (*Lit.*: Older sister Ba say so question word.)
        c. I did not understand why she said *so*.
          (*Lit.*: I no understand why older sister post-modifier again say so?)

The verb *làm* 'do' plus a question word like *gì* 'what' may be considered a primary substitute for predicatids. For example:

    U: (20) a. Cô Ba *vừa mua một cái áo mới*.
         b. Cô Ba *làm gì*?
         c. Cô Ba *rán ba con gà*.
         d. Cô Ba *làm gì*?

Trans.: (20) a. Miss Ba *has just bought a new dress*.
          (*Lit.*: Miss Ba just buy one pre-determiner dress new.)
        b. *What did* Miss Ba *do*?
          (*Lit.*: Miss Ba do what?)

      c. Miss Ba *fried three chickens.*
         (*Lit.*: Miss Ba fry three pre-determiner chicken.)
      d. *What did* Miss Ba *do*?
         (*Lit.*: Miss Ba do what?)

The lexemes *như thể* 'like that', *như vậy* 'like this', and *thể này* 'as such' are used as primary substitutes for modifiers. For example:

  U: (21) a. Tôi có trông thấy một cái nhà *tròn.*
         b. Anh có trông thấy nhà *như vậy* à?
  or: c. Anh có trông thấy nhà *như thể* à?
         d. Nhà *thể này* mới đẹp.

Trans.: (21) a. I saw a *round* house.
         (*Lit.*: I emphatic particle see one pre-determiner house round.)
      b. Did you (really) see a house *like this*?
         (*Lit.*: Older brother emphatic particle see house like this question
           word?)
      c. Did you (really) see a house *like that*?
         (*Lit.*: Older brother emphatic particle see house like that question
           word.)
      d. *Such a* house is beautiful.
         (*Lit.*: House as such only beautiful.)

4.3.2. *Secondary Substitutes*

Unlike primary substitutes, lexemes which function as secondary substitutes may occur as parts of the constructions or units which they represent. As a result, they do not replace the whole construction in which they occur but only part of it. This sort of substitution may be referred to as 'elliptical substitution'. There are several kinds of secondary substitutes in Vietnamese.

    The pre-determiner *con* and the identifier *cái* may combine with a post-determiner to represent a noun cluster from which the nucleus noun has been omitted. For example:

  U: (22) a. *Con chó này* của Lan.
         b. *Con*   *này* của Lan.
         c. Tôi có *hai cái áo mưa*: *cái này* dài, *cái kia* ngắn.

Trans.: (22) a. *This dog* is Lan's.
         (*Lit.*: Animate pre-determiner dog this belong to Lan.)
      b. *This* is Lan's.
         (*Lit.*: Animate pre-determiner this belong to Lan.)
      c. I have *two raincoats*: *this* (*one*) is long, *that* (*one*) is short.

(*Lit.*: I have identifier particle dress rain: identifier particle this long, identifier particle that short.)

A secondary substitute may be formed by:

(1) an identifier or a pre-determiner representing a noun cluster:

U: (23) a. *Cái nhà cao nhất* là *cái* của cha tôi.
      b. *Con ngựa đen* là *con* của anh Ba.

Trans.: (23) a. The tallest building is *the* (*house that*) belongs to my father.
      (Lit.: Identifier particle house high first is identifier particle belong to father I.)
      b. The black horse is *the* (*horse that*) belongs to Ba.
      (*Lit.*: Animate pre-determiner particle horse black is animate pre-determiner belong to older brother Ba.)

(2) A numeral and a pre-determiner representing a whole noun cluster:

U: (24) Tôi mua *ba con chó*: *một con* trắng và *hai con* vàng.

Trans.: (24) I bought *three dogs*, *one* white and *two* yellow.
      (*Lit.*: I buy three animate pre-determiner particle dog: one animate pre-determiner particle white and two animate pre-determiner particle yellow.)

In the example above, *một con trắng* and *hai con vàng* substitute for *một con chó trắng* and *hai con chó vàng*.

Clausid introducers may represent clausids, as in the following example:

U: (25) Tôi làm cơm trước, rồi rửa bát *sau*.
      (I.e., sau khi tôi làm cơm.)

Trans.: (25) I prepared the meal first, then washed the dishes after(wards). (I.e., *after I had prepared the meal*.)
      (*Lit.*: I do rice before then wash bowl after. (I.e., after I do rice.)

4.3.3. *Differences between the uses of substitutes in English and Vietnamese*

Although such substitute words as the pro-nominals may, in English, replace constructions which refer to things and animals as well as to persons, the 'personal pronouns' in Vietnamese are used only as substitutes for constructions which refer to human beings.

Again, many of the substitutes in English are substitutes for TAGMEMES — that is, FOR CONSTRUCTIONS OCCURRING IN SPECIFIC POSITIONS. Pro-nominals, for example, replace nominals — and nominals are FUNCTIONAL units, that is, units occurring in certain positions only. The same noun cluster, for example, may function in a nominal sector in one sentence and thus be replaceable by a pro-nominal, but may function in an adverbial sector in another sentence and then take a pro-adverbial as its substitute. For example:

F	S	
	Last Saturday	was a very special day.
	It	was Percy's birthday.
Last Saturday	Percy	was a very happy boy.
Then	he	was twelve years old.[4]

In Vietnamese, however, substitutes are substitutes for CONSTRUCTIONS, not for tagmemes. A certain construction or unit will always have the same substitute no matter in what position it may occur in a sentence.

And finally the secondary substitutes in English always INTRODUCE the constructions which they represent (that is, the constructions which could occur in the positions occupied by the substitutes if there were no ellipsis). In Vietnamese, on the other hand, the secondary substitutes include not only those listable lexemes that introduce the constructions which they represent but also listable lexemes that may occur in the middle or at the end of the constructions which they represent.

4.4. NOUN CLUSTERS

According to Allen, a noun cluster is a construction which has a noun as its nucleus "preceded and/or followed by one or more adjectivals."[5] He then defines adjectivals as follows:

Any lexeme or construction occurring on the same level as the nucleus of a noun cluster ... is, by definition, a modifier of that nucleus. We will call any modifier of the nucleus of ... a noun cluster ... AN ADJECTIVAL.[6]

The following chart shows the order of occurrence of adjectivals within a noun cluster in Vietnamese:

1	2	3	4
A plural particle and/or a cardinal numeral	An identifier	A pre-determiner	The nucleus (or 'Head Word')

5	6	7	8
An adjunct	Modifiers of shape and/or color	An ordinal numeral cluster	A phrase

---

[4]   These examples are taken from Robert L. Allen, *A Modern Grammar of Written English* (New York, The Macmillan Company, in press), p. 394.
[5]   *Ibid.*, p. 397.
[6]   *Ibid.*, p. 432.

9	10	11
A possessive	An included clausid	A post-determiner

The different kinds of adjectivals will be discussed individually below. (Numbers will be used to refer to the positions indicated in the chart above.)

4.4.1. *Plural Particles and Cardinal Numerals*

Vietnamese noun clusters are usually 'unmarked' with regard to number. When it is necessary to specify plurality, however, plural particles or cardinal numerals may be used to 'mark' a noun cluster. When such particles or numerals occur in a noun cluster, they usually introduce the cluster. The following is a list of plural particles:

Simple Plural Particles

Cả	All.
Các	All (vague).
Chư	All (vague).
Chút	A few (occurring before uncountable nouns).
Dăm	A few (occurring before countable nouns).
Ít	A few (occurring before countable and uncountable nouns).
Khắp	Every(where).
Lắm	Many (occurring before countable and uncountable nouns).
Liệt	All (vague).
Mấy	Some (occurring before countable nouns).
Mỗi	Each (occurring before countable nouns).
Mọi	All.
Mươi	A few (occurring before countable nouns).
Nhiều	Many (occurring before countable and uncountable nouns).
Những	Many (occurring before countable nouns).
Nửa	Half.
Suốt	All.
Tí	A few.
Từng	Each.
Toàn	All.
Vài	Some (occurring before countable nouns).

Compound Plural Particles

Dăm ba	a few	*Mỗi một*	each one
Dăm bảy	a few	*Năm ba*	some, a few
Hết cả	all	*Năm bảy*	some, a few
Hết cả mọi	all	*Phần đông những*	most of
Hết các	all	*Phần nhiều*	most of

Hết thảy	all	*Phần nhiều những*	most of
Hết thảy các	all	*Suốt cả*	all
Hết thảy mọi	all	*Tất cả*	all
Hết thảy những	all	*Tất cả các*	all
Ít nhiều	some	*Tất cả những*	all
Khắp cả	all	*Tất cả mọi*	all
Khắp các	all	*Toàn thể*	all
Khắp mọi	all	*Toàn thể những*	all
		Vô số	plenty of

Những and *các* are the most commonly used plural particles. *Chư* and *liệt* are used only with Sino-Vietnamese nouns. While the plural particles such as *những*, *các*, *mấy*, *mọi*, etc., only occur before countable nouns, *lắm*, *nhiều*, *cả*, etc., may occur either before countable or uncountable nouns. The following are examples of noun clusters containing plural particles:

K : (26) a. |⟨mấy quả cam⟩|
    → * ←
    pl.p. n n
    some fruit orange
    some oranges

K : b. |⟨những con chim quý⟩|
    → → * ←
    pl.p. prd n m[7]
                bird precious
    precious birds

The cardinal numerals include all the numbers, such as *một* 'one', *hai* 'two', *sáu mươi* 'sixty', etc. All numbers which consist of more than one word function as single units on the noun cluster level. The following are examples of noun clusters containing cardinal numerals:

K : (27) a. |⟨chín cây chuối⟩|
    → * ←
    nu n n
    nine tree banana
    nine banana plants

K : b. |⟨ba mươi cái bàn⟩|
    ————→ *
    nu   prd n
    thirty   table
    thirty tables

In general, when a cardinal numeral occurs in a noun cluster, there is no need for a plural particle. But in special cases, when the speaker wishes to stress both the idea of plurality and also a specific number, he may use both a plural particle and a cardinal numeral, with the former preceding the latter, as in the following examples:

U : (28) a. Tất cả mười quả cam này đều tròn cả.
K : |⟨tất cả mười quả cam này⟩|
          → → * ← ←
          pl.p. nu n n pod

U :   b. Lan ăn   những sáu con tôm.

[7] For the explanation of the symbols, see the Introduction.

K: |⟨những sáu con tôm.⟩|

                  →   → →   *

                 pl.p.   nu prd n^8

Trans.: (28) a. All ten of these oranges are round.

           (*Lit.*: All ten fruit orange this all round all.)

        b. Lan ate six shrimps.

           (*Lit.*: Lan eat many six animate pre-determiner shrimp.)

Plural particles or cardinal numerals may combine with the question words *gì* 'what', *nào* 'which', and *đâu* 'where' to form interrogative noun clusters. For example:

U: (29) a. Hoa mua   *những gì?*

K: |⟨những gì⟩|

                 pl.p.   q

U: b. Hoa mua   *năm cái nào?*

K: |⟨năm cái nào⟩|

                 nu prd q

U: c. Hoa đi   *những đâu?*

K: |⟨những đâu⟩|

                 pl.p.   q

Trans.: (29) a. *What* did Hoa buy?

           (*Lit.*: Hoa buy many what?)

        b. *Which five* (*things*) did Hoa buy?

           (*Lit.*: Hoa buy five pre-determiner which?)

        c. *To what places* did Hoa go? (Cf. Where all did Hoa go?)

           (*Lit.*: Hoa go many where?)

4.4.2. *Pre-determiners*

There are only two pre-determiners in Vietnamese: *con*,[9] the pre-determiner for nouns referring to animate (living) things or animals (excluding human beings), and *cái*, the pre-determiner for nouns referring to inanimate things such as tables and houses.

The pre-determiner *con*[10] precedes the names of animals to suggest that these nouns are used as count nouns; its omission before these nouns suggests that the latter are used as mass nouns referring to the whole species. For example, when we say *con ngựa* 'horse', *con chim* 'bird', we are referring to some individual horse or bird. But

---

[8] For the explanation of the symbols, see the Introduction.

[9] In some exceptional cases, *con* is used as a pre-determiner before (non-living) nouns such as *con sông* (a river), *con đường* (a road), *con dấu* (a seal), *con dao* (a knife), *con quay* (a top - i.e., 'a child's toy'), *con thoi* (a shuttle), *con tem* (a stamp).

[10] *Con* is also used as a noun of address with the meaning of 'child' or 'children', or as a modifier with the meaning of 'little'.

when we say *ngựa* 'horse', *chim* 'bird', we are then referring to horses or birds as a species.

Like the pre-determiner *con*, the pre-determiner *cái* is used to suggest 'countability' or 'units' in the nouns that follow it. But it is noted that not all the nouns referring to inanimate things in Vietnamese need to be preceded by the pre-determiner *cái*. For example, the nouns *cây* 'tree', *tre* 'bamboo', and *cam* 'orange' do not need to be preceded by the predeterminer *cái*. Without *cái* they are actually mass nouns. To suggest the idea of 'countability' or 'units', these nouns are used in conjunction with other nouns of the same kind. For example:

K: (30) a. |⟨cây tre⟩|	K: b. |⟨quả cam⟩|
* ←	* ←
n n	n n
tree bamboo	fruit orange
a bamboo plant	an orange

The following are examples of nouns preceded by the pre-determiner *cái*:

K: (31) a. |⟨cái bàn⟩|	K: b. |⟨cái thuyền⟩|	K: c. |⟨cái bát⟩|
→ *	→ *	→ *
prd n	prd n	prd n
a table	a boat	a bowl

Some verbs or modifiers become nouns when they are preceded by the pre-determiner *cái*:

Examples with verbs:

die	weigh	row
|⟨cái chết⟩|	|⟨cái cân⟩|	|⟨cái chèo⟩|
→ *	→ *	→ *
prd n	prd n	prd n
death	balance	oar

Examples with modifiers:

beautiful	sad	gay
|⟨cái đẹp⟩|	|⟨cái buồn⟩|	|⟨cái vui⟩|
→ *	→ *	→ *
prd n	prd n	prd n
beauty	sadness	gaiety

Pre-determiners follow plural particles or cardinal numerals when the latter occur in noun clusters. For example:

K: (32) a. |⟨những con ngựa⟩| K: b. |⟨năm cái ghế⟩|

    →   →   *   →   →   *

    pl.p.   prd n   nu   prd n

    many   horse   five   chair

    horses   five chairs

Sometimes the omission of a pre-determiner may change the meaning of the nucleus noun in a cluster. For example:

K: (33) a. |⟨một cái nhà⟩| K: b. |⟨một nhà⟩|

    →   →   *   →   *

    nu   prd n   nu   n

    one   house   one house

    a house   a family

4.4.3. *The Identifier CÁI*

Allen states the function of the determiner *the* in contrast to that of *a* and *an* in a noun cluster in English as follows:

… the "definite" determiner *the* — is used to refer to an entity that has been or is about to be identified, in contrast to the "indefinite" determiners *a* and *an*, which are used to refer to entities that are unidentified (or at least not-as-yet identified).[11]

In this way, the determiner *the* is used to refer to an 'identified' person, place, or thing that both speaker or writer and listener or reader 'know about'.[12]

Similarly, the identifier *cái* in Vietnamese is used before the nucleus noun in a noun cluster to signal a person or thing that is about to be identified in that cluster. A noun that does not ordinarily require a pre-determiner may be preceded by the identifier *cái* when the speaker wishes to show what is about to be identified. For example:

            mặt trời   ông Ba

            face sky

            the sun   Mr. Ba

K: (34) a. |⟨cái mặt trời |⟨chiều hôm qua⟩|⟩|

         →   *   ←

         i   n   cluster

        (the face sky evening day past)

         the sun   yesterday evening

---

[11] Robert L. Allen, *A Modern Grammar of Written English* (New York, The Macmillan Company, in press), p. 492.

[12] *Ibid.*, p. 491.

b. |⟨cái ông Ba ⟨ở phố Gia Long⟩⟩|
   →   *   ←   ←——————
   i   n   n   phrase
   (the Mr. Ba in street Gia Long)
   the Mr. Ba on Gia Long Street

The identifier *cái*[13] is most commonly used in a noun cluster in which one of the post-determiners cannot be used — that is, a noun cluster in which a prepositional phrase, a possessive, or a clausid (either introduced or non-introduced) is used as an adjectival following the nucleus noun. For example:

K: (35) a. |⟨cái người thợ may ⟨ở phố Gia Long⟩⟩|
        →   *   ←——   ←——————————
        i   n   n   phrase
        (the person tailor   in street Gia Long)
        the tailor on Gia Long Street

K: b. |⟨cái   áo   trắng ⟨của   bà tôi⟩⟩|
        →   *   ←—— ←————
        i + prd n   m   possessive
        (the   dress white belonging to grandmother me)
        the white dress of my grandmother *or*:
        my grandmother's white dress

K: c. |⟨cái   nhà   ⟦tôi bán hôm qua⟧⟩|
        →   *   ←————————————
        i + prd n[14]   clausid
        (the   house I sell day past)
        the house I sold yesterday

But the identifier *cái* may also be used even when one of the post-determiners which are also used to identify does occur in the same noun cluster; in such a case, the *cái* seems to reinforce the function of identifying the nucleus noun performed by the post-determiner. For example:

K: (36) a. |⟨năm cái cây tre   này⟩|
        →   → * ←   ←
        nu i n n   pod
        (five the tree bamboo this)
        these five bamboo plants

[13] Besides being used as a pre-determiner and as an identifier, *cái* can also be used as a modifier with the meaning of 'large, big, main' (as in *đường cái* 'main road', *sông cái* 'main river'), or as part of a noun lexeme with the meaning of 'child' (as in *con cái* 'child' or 'children'), or as a gender particle with reference to *female* animals (as in *bò cái* 'cow'). Since it is assumed that the meaning of a given lexeme is determined by both its form and the position in which it occurs, it does not matter — for this analysis — whether these *cái*'s are all 'different' lexemes, or merely the same lexeme functioning in different positions.

[14] For the explanation of the symbols, see the Introduction.

K: b. |⟨cái con bò đen   ẫy⟩|
            →   →   *   ←   ←
            i   prd n   m   pod
           (the   cow black that)
           that black cow

Another function of the identifier *cái* is to make a free non-introduced clausid into an included or bound clausid. *Con chó gậm xương* 'A dog chews bones', for example, is a free sentence or clausid. With the addition of the identifier *cái*, it becomes an included clausid, that is, a clausid which cannot occur alone as a sentence. This type of included clausid usually occurs in the subject position in a sentence. For example:

U: (37) a. Cái *con chó gậm xương* là con Vện.
K: cái | con chó gậm xương
          i
                S   V   O
H: con chó gậm xương
               prd n   v   n

Trans.: (37) a. *The dog which gnawed bones* was Vện.
        (*Lit.*: The pre-determiner dog gnaw bone is pre-determiner Ven.)

U: (37) b. Cái *ông đang ăn cơm* là cậu của Hoa.
K: cái ông đang ăn cơm
          i
                S TR V O
H: ông đang ăn cơm

Trans.: (37) b. *The man who was eating his meal* was Hoa's father.
        (*Lit.*: The Mr. in the process of eat rice is father belonging to Hoa.)

It can be seen that in the examples above *cái* functions as the introducer of a clausid, and its included clausid then functions rather like the nucleus of a cluster with the identifier *cái* as its modifier. Such a cluster may be called a 'quasi-noun-cluster' since it is similar in form to a noun cluster but does not have a noun as its nucleus. The included clausid usually consists of a subject, a verb, and an object.

The following are examples of clausids functioning as the nuclei of quasi-noun-clusters:

K: (38) a. |⟨*cái thuyền đánh cá*⟩| = the fishing boat
            →   *
            i
                S   V   O
               thuyền đánh cá
               n   v   n
          (the boat beat fish)

K: (38) b. |⟨cái *thửa ruộng mới   cày*⟩| = the newly ploughed field
→ *
i

            S   TR   V
H: thửa ruộng mới   cày
            n   n   tr   v
        (the piece field   recent plough)

The quasi-noun-cluster cited above may in turn be modified by included clausids, prepositional phrases, or possessives. For example:

K: (39) a. |⟨cái *thuyền đánh cá* ⟦*mà Lan tả*⟧⟩|
        → *   ←————
        i   clausid
      (the boat   beat fish that Lan describe)
      the *fishing boat* that Lan described

      b. |⟨cái *thuyền đánh cá* ⟨*của*   *ông Ba*⟩⟩|
        → *   ←————
        i   possessive
      (the boat   beat fish belonging to Mr. Ba)
      the *fishing boat* of Mr. Ba

      c. |⟨cái *thửa ruộng mới   cày*   ⟨*trong Chợ Lớn*⟩⟩|
        → *   ←————
        i   phrase
      (the piece field   recent plough in   Chợ Lớn)
      the *newly ploughed field* in Chợ Lớn

Quasi-noun-clusters may also be used with post-determiners. But ambiguity may occur in such cases if the included clausid ends in a noun because the post-determiner may then be taken as going with the entire nucleus of the quasi-noun-cluster or else with only the noun immediately preceding the post-determiner. For instance, *cái người đánh cá này* (lit., 'the person beats fish this') could mean either 'the man who catches this kind of fish, not the other kind', or 'this man who catches fish, not that one'. But ambiguity does not occur when the included clausid functioning as the nucleus of the quasi-noun-cluster does not end in a noun. For example:

K: (39) d. |⟨cái *thửa ruộng mới   cày*   *này*⟩|
        → *   ←
        i   pod
      (the piece field   recent plough this)
      this newly ploughed field

When the identifier *cái* occurs in a noun cluster, it fills the slot between the slot for cardinal numerals or plural particles and the slot for pre-determiners. For example:

U: (40) a.   *Năm cái con gà mái* bé quá.

K: |⟨năm cái con gà mái⟩|

             →   →   →   *   ←

             nu   i   prd n gn[15]

U: b.   *Những cái con ngựa đen* chạy nhanh lắm.

K: |⟨những cái con ngựa đen⟩|

             →   → → → * ←

             pl.p. i   prd n   m

Trans.: (40) a. *The five hens* were too small.

     (*Lit.*: Five the pre-determiner chicken female small very.)

     b. *The black horses* ran very fast.

     (*Lit.*: Many the pre-determiner horse black run fast very.)

As can be seen from the examples given above, *cái*, when it functions as an identifier, occurs before the pre-determiner *con*. But the same does not hold true of *cái* when it functions as a pre-determiner. The identifier *cái* and the pre-determiner *cái* have the same form and occur in neighboring positions. Ambiguity may result, therefore, since only one *cái* can occur in a single noun cluster and it is sometimes difficult to determine which of the two *cái*'s a given *cái* is. There is no ambiguity in the case of nouns which are not used with the pre-determiner *cái*. *Cái* preceding such a noun must be the identifier *cái*. For example:

K: (41) a. |⟨cây tre⟩| K: b. |⟨quả chuối⟩|

             *   ←   *   ←

             n   n   n   n

             tree bamboo   fruit banana

             a bamboo plant   a banana

K: c. |⟨cái cây tre⟩| K: d. |⟨cái quả chuối⟩|

             → * ←   → * ←

             i   n   n   i   n   n

                tree bamboo   fruit banana

             the bamboo plant   the banana

But in the case of nouns which are used with the pre-determiner *cái* and which may or may not be used with the identifier *cái*, it is hard to determine which *cái* a given *cái* is. The simplest solution is to consider *cái* in these intermediate cases as performing two functions at the same time: that of identifier and that of pre-determiner. For example:

U: (42) a.   *Mấy cái   ví ấy* đẹp quá.

K: |⟨mấy cái   ví ấy⟩|

             →   →   * ←

             pl.p. i + prd n pod

[15] For the explanation of the symbols, see the Introduction.

U: b.   *Năm cái*   *nhà ông Ba mua* đẹp quá.

K: |⟨năm cái   nhà ⟦⟨ông Ba mua⟧⟩|

            →   →   *   ←————

            nu   i + prd n   clausid

Trans.: (42) a. *These bags* were very beautiful.

(*Lit.*: Some the pre-determiner bag that beautiful very.)

b. *The five houses* that Mr. Ba has bought are very beautiful.

(*Lit.*: Five the pre-determiner house Mr. Ba buy beautiful very.)

4.4.4. *The Nucleus Noun*

The position for the nucleus of a noun cluster is a position for the non-listable lexeme class of NOUNS. Nouns are defined as words which may be preceded by the pre-determiner *cái* or *con*, or by the identifier *cái*. For example:

K: |⟨cái quạt⟩| K: |⟨con chó⟩| K: |⟨cái cày⟩|

    →   *   →   *   →   *

    prd n   prd n   i   n

    fan   dog   tree

The position for the nucleus of a noun cluster may be filled by either a simple noun lexeme or a compound noun lexeme. The nucleus position in a quasi-noun-cluster is filled by a clausid. (See Section 4.4.3.)

When a noun functions alone in a position regularly filled by a noun cluster, the noun will be considered to be a special kind of noun cluster consisting of only a nucleus, with no modifiers. For example:

         S   V

U: (43) Chim bay.   Trans.: Birds fly.

              v

K: |⟨chim⟩|

          *

          n

          bird fly

4.4.5. *Adjunct Position*

The position following that of the nucleus noun in a noun cluster is the position for an adjunct. For example:

K: (44) a. |⟨một miếng bánh⟩| K: b. |⟨hoa   anh đào⟩|

            →   *   ←   *   ←————

            nu   n   n   n   n

            (one piece bread)   (flower cherry)

            one slice of bread   cherry blossoms

Vietnamese nouns are not marked for gender. *Bò* can mean either 'bull' or 'cow', *bác* can mean either 'uncle' or 'aunt'. When gender needs to be specified, a Vietnamese speaker uses one of several 'gender particles' — nouns denoting gender. The following are the gender particles:

(1) Gender particles for vegetables and animals:

male	*female*
đực	mái
trống	cái
sống	nái

(2) Gender particles for human beings:

male	*female*
đàn ông	đàn bà
trai	gái
ông	bà
nam	nữ

These nouns or gender particles occur in the adjunct position following the nucleus noun position. For example:

K: (45) a. |⟨cây đu đủ   cái⟩| K: b. |⟨người đàn ông⟩|
     *   ←— ←   *   ←——
     n n   gn   n   gn
     tree papaya female   person male
     a female papaya tree   a man

There are two gender particles, however, *nam* and *nữ*, which go only with Sino-Vietnamese nouns. These particles precede rather than follow the nouns they modify. For example:

K: (45) c. |⟨nam học   sinh⟩| K: d. |⟨nữ độc   gỉa⟩|
     →   *   → *
     gn   n   gn n
     a   male student   a   female reader

Nouns denoting religion, nationality, and the names of persons or places also occur in the noun adjunct position. The order of occurrence of these nouns is generally gender-religion-nationality. For example:

K: (46) a. |⟨người đàn bà Phật   giáo   Việt Nam⟩|
     *   ←—   ←———   ←———
     n   gn   n   n   n
     (person female Buddha religion Vietnam)
     the Vietnamese Buddhist women

K: b. |/đoàn |⟨nữ học sinh⟩| Công giáo Việt Nam\|
      |\ → *
      |\ * ←——————— ←———— ←————

      n   gn   n   n   n
      (group female student universal religion Vietnam)
      the Vietnamese Catholic girls' students' group

K: c. |⟨người đàn bà Pháp⟩| K: d. |⟨thành phô Nữu Ũ'ơc⟩|
    * ←— ←—   * ←———

    n   gn   n   n   n
    (person female France)   (city New York)
    a French woman   New York City

A verb may also occur in the adjunct position. When it does, it is usually preceded by one of the following nouns functioning as the nucleus of the cluster: *cách* 'way', *việc* 'job', *sự* 'fact' or 'concept', *đức* 'virtue', and *cuộc* 'event'. For example:

K: (47) a. |⟨cuộc bàu cử⟩| K: b. |⟨cách xêp đặt⟩|
      * ←—   * ←———

    n   v   n   v
    event elect   way organize
    the election   the organization

A noun cluster may function as a modifier of the nucleus noun of another noun cluster. For example:

K: (48) a. |/một đàn |⟨tám con chim⟩|\| = a flock of eight birds
      |\ → * ←—————————
      nu n   cluster
K: |⟨tám con chim⟩|
          → → *
          nu prd n
    (one flock eight bird)

K: b. |/một đoàn |⟨mười lăm cái xe⟩|\| = a group of fifteen cars
      → * ←—————————
      nu n   cluster
K: |⟨mười lăm cái xe⟩|
          —————→ → *
    (one group fifteen vehicle)

A noun cluster may also function as a modifier of another noun cluster. The two together may in turn be modified by still another cluster, and so on. For example:

K: (48) c.

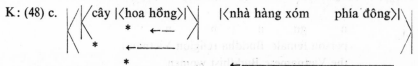

K: |/|⟨nhà hàng xóm⟩| |⟨phía đông⟩|\|
                                   |/   *   ←— /|
                                        *   ←————

K: |⟨nhà hàng xóm⟩|
                                        *   ←————

Trans.: (48) c. the rose plant of the neighbor on the east side
            (*Lit.*: tree flower rose house neighbor direction east).

4.4.6. *Modifiers*

The sixth position within a noun cluster is the position for the non-listable lexeme class of MODIFIERS. The term 'modifiers' is used here instead of 'adjectives' for the reason that the modifiers in Vietnamese occur not only after nouns in noun clusters and in the complement position, as in English, but also in the droppable position, and in the M_2 or middle adverb position. The following are examples of modifiers occurring in noun clusters:

K: (49) a. |⟨gạo trắng⟩| K: b. |⟨ngô vàng⟩|
            *   ←—   *   ←—
           n   m   n   m
           rice white   corn yellow
           white rice   yellow corn

Modifiers denoting colors are sometimes preceded by the noun *màu* 'color'. For example:

K: (49) c. |⟨áo trắng⟩| or: K: d. |/áo |⟨màu trắng⟩|\|
            *   ←— |/   *   ←— /|
                                           |/   *   ←————
           n   m   n   n   m
           dress white   dress color white
           white dress   white dress

The modifiers have their own modifiers, which will be called "MODI-MODIFIERS".[16] Modi-modifiers are of two kinds: pre-modi-modifiers and post-modi-modifiers. The following are lists of both kinds of modi-modifiers:

Pre-Modi-Modifiers

(1) of Vietnamese modifiers:

Cực	extremely	*Khá*	quite
Cực kỳ	extremely	*Rất*	very
Hơi	rather, a little	*Tuyệt*	extremely
Hơi hơi	fairly		

[16] This term is borrowed from Robert L. Allen, *A Modern Grammar of Written English* (New York, The Macmillan Company, in press).

(2) of Sino-Vietnamese modifiers:

Chí	very		*Thậm*	extremely
Đại	very		*Tồi*	extremely

Post-Modi-Modifiers

Biết bao	how much (used to express exclamation)
Biết bao nhiêu	how much (used to express exclamation)
Biết ngần nào	how much (used to express exclamation)
Hơn cả	most
Hơn hết cả	most
Lắm	very
Nhất	most
Quá	very
Quá lắm	too much
Thật	really
Tuyệt	extremely
Vô cùng	infinitely, indefinitely
Vô kể	innumerably
Vô sồ	innumerably

Special Post-Modi-Modifiers

(đẹp)	*ghê*	*terribly*	(beautiful)
(bẩn)	*khiếp*	*awfully*	(dirty)
(trong)	*leo lẻo*	*very*	(clear)
(đỏ)	*lòm*	*very*	(red)
(dài)	*lượt thượt*	*very*	(lengthy)
(tối)	*mù*	*blindly*	(dark)
(xanh)	*ngắt*	*very*	(green)
(đỏ)	*quệch*	*very*	(red)
(cũ)	*rích*	*very*	(old)
(xanh)	*rờn*	*very*	(green)
(đỏ)	*rực*	*very*	(red)
(buồn)	*tênh*	*very*	(sad)
(trong)	*veo*	*very*	(limpid)
(nghèo)	*xơ xác*	*very*	(poor)

Comparative Forms of Modifiers

modifiers	comparative forms	
...	*một cách...*	*...in a manner of...*
...	*bằng...*	*...equal to...*
...	*hơn...*	*...more...*
...	*kém...*	*...less...*
...	*ngang...*	*...equal to...*

...   *như*...   *...as...*
...   *thua*...   *...less...*
          càng...càng... *the more...the more...*

Modifiers tend to have only pre-modi-modifiers when they occur within a noun cluster, but take both pre-modi-modifiers and post-modi-modifiers when they occur in the complement position, or in the droppable position. The following are examples of modifiers preceded by pre-modi-modifiers in noun clusters:

K: (50) a. |/một người đàn bà |⟨rất đẹp⟩|\|

          nu n   gn   mm m
          (one person female very beautiful)
          a very beautiful woman

K: b. |/một người |⟨thật to lớn⟩|\|

          nu n   mm   m
          (one person   really big)
          a very big person

A modifier is sometimes used to modify another modifier, as in the following examples:

K: (51) a. |/mặt |⟨đỏ hồng hồng|⟩|\|

          n   m m
          (face   red pink)
          a reddish face

K: b. |/người |⟨hoàn toàn sung sướng⟩|\|

          n   mm   m
          (person perfect   happy)
          a perfectly happy person

A noun or a noun cluster may sometimes follow a modifier and modify it. For example:

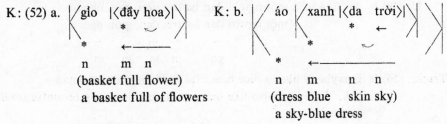

K: (52) a. |/gio |⟨đầy hoa⟩|\| K: b. |/ áo |/xanh |⟨da trời⟩|\|\|

          n   m n   n   m   n   n
          (basket full flower)   (dress blue   skin sky)
          a basket full of flowers   a sky-blue dress

A prepositional phrase may also follow a modifier and modify it. For example:

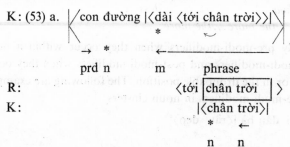

K: (53) a. |/con đường |⟨dài ⟨tới chân trời⟩⟩|\|

          prd n   m   phrase

R: ⟨tới | chân trời | ⟩

K: |⟨chân trời⟩|

                             n   n

Trans.: (53) a. a road stretching to the horizon
             (*Lit.*: pre-determiner road long until foot sky)

K: (53) b. |/người đàn bà |⟨đẹp   ⟨như tiên⟩⟩|\|

          n   gn   m   phrase

R: ⟨như | tiên | ⟩

                            r   n

          (person female   beautiful like fairy)
          a woman beautiful as a fairy

As can be seen from the examples given above, modifiers occurring in noun clusters tend to occur singly rather than in a series with one modifier following another. Two modifiers may occur consecutively, however, with a modifier denoting shape preceding a modifier denoting color, as in the following example:

K: (54) a. |⟨cái   bàn   vuông đen⟩|

           prd   n   m   m
           (table square black)
           a square black table

If more than two modifiers occur in a noun cluster, they must be separated from one another by commas. The following is an example of a noun cluster having more than two modifiers:

U: (54) b. Ai cũng mến một người đàn bà trẻ, đẹp, giỏi, ngoan.

                |⟨một người đàn bà trẻ, đẹp, giỏi, ngoan⟩|

                  nu n   gn   m   m   m   m

Trans.: (54) b. Everybody likes a nice beautiful brilliant young woman.
           (*Lit.*: Everyone also like one person female young beautiful brilliant nice.)

4.4.7. *Ordinal Numeral Clusters*

When a cardinal numeral occurs in the first position preceding the nucleus noun within a noun cluster, it functions as a cardinal numeral. When the same cardinal numeral occurs in the position following the nucleus noun after the position for modifiers, it becomes an ordinal numeral. In this position — that is, the seventh position within a noun cluster — the ordinal numeral does not generally occur alone but with the noun *thứ* 'rank' or *hạng* 'class' in an ordinal numeral cluster. For example:

K: (55) a. |⟨ba   lớp⟩| K: b. |⟨lớp ba⟩|
              →   *   *   ←
              nu   n   n   ord
              three class   class third
              three classes   third grade class

K: c. |⟨ba con chó trắng⟩| K: d. ⌐con chó   trắng |⟨thứ ba⟩|⌐
              → → *   ←—   →   *   ←—   ←——
              nu prd n   m   prd n   m   n   ord
              (three dog white)   (dog white rank   three)
              three white dogs   the third white dog

K: e. ⌐ba   tầm vải   đen |⟨hạng ba⟩|⌐
                                        *   ←
              →   *   ←   ←   ←——
              nu   n   n   m   n   ord
            (three piece material black class third)
            three pieces of third-class black material

There is another Sino-Vietnamese word, *đệ* 'rank', which is used less often than the nouns *thứ* 'rank' and *hạng* 'class', and which is used only with Sino-Vietnamese numerals. For example:

K: (56) a. ⌐lớp |⟨đệ   tứ⟩|⌐
                      *   ←
              *   ←——
              n   n   ord
            (class rank fourth)
            class fourth = ninth-grade class

In clusters containing such Sino-Vietnamese numerals, the word order of Chinese is sometimes used — that is, the ordinal numeral sometimes precedes the nucleus noun (which will also be a Sino-Vietnamese word). For example:

U: (56) b. Nguyễn Trãi là đệ nhất   công thần   của nhà Lê.

K: |⟨đệ nhất⟩| công thần ⟨của nhà Lê⟩
                         *   ←—
                         ———————→ *   ←—————
                         ord   n   phrase

Trans.: (56) b. Nguyễn Trãi was a first-rank loyal courtier of the Lê dynasty.
                (*Lit.*: Nguyễn Trãi was rank first loyal courtier belonging to house
                Lê.)

4.4.8. *Prepositional Phrases, Possessives, Included Clausids*

The three positions following the position for ordinal numeral clusters within a noun
cluster are the positions for a prepositional phrase, a possessive, and an included
clausid, with the prepositional phrase preceding the possessive, and the possessive
preceding the included clausid. The following are examples of noun clusters with
prepositional phrases, possessives, and included clausids:

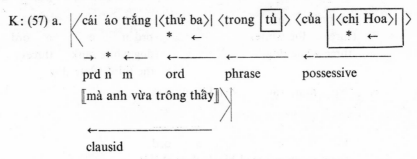

K: (57) a. cái áo trắng |⟨thứ ba⟩| ⟨trong [tủ]⟩ ⟨của |⟨chị Hoa⟩|⟩
                              *   ←   *   ←
           → *   ←—   ←———   ←———   ←———
           prd n m   ord   phrase   possessive
           [[mà anh vừa trông thấy]]
                ←————————————
                clausid

Trans.: (57) a. The third white dress of Hoa's that you have just seen in the closet
                (that is, the dress in the closet)
                (*Lit.*: pre-determiner dress white rank third in closet belonging to
                older sister Hoa that older brother just see)

K: (57) b. cây cam |⟨thứ một trăm⟩| ⟨ngoài [sân]⟩ ⟨của |⟨cô Mai⟩|⟩
                         *   ←————   * ←—
           *   ←   ←————————   ←————   ←————
           n   n   ord   phrase   possessive
           [[mà chị tưới nước tôi hôm qua]]
                ←——————————————
                clausid

Trans.: (57) b. Miss Mai's hundredth orange tree in the courtyard that you watered
                yesterday evening.
                (*Lit.*: tree orange rank hundredth out courtyard belonging to Miss
                Mai that older sister water (verb) water evening day past)

Lengthy noun clusters such as those in examples 57a and 57b are not commonly used in Vietnamese.

Prepositional phrases have already been described in Section 3.8.2., Chapter III. A prepositional phrase may function as an adjectival in a noun cluster to modify the nucleus noun. When it does, it fills the eighth position, as was shown in examples 57a and 57b.

Possession is shown in Vietnamese by adding a prepositional phrase made up of the preposition *của* 'belonging to' followed by a noun cluster, by one of the 'personal pronouns', or by one of the honorific nouns of address. A possessive unit may function as an adjectival in a noun cluster to modify the nucleus noun. When it does, it fills the ninth position, as was shown in examples 57a and 57b.

There is often a danger of ambiguity when a possessive following a noun at the end of a prepositional phrase may be taken to be a modifier of that noun rather than of the nucleus of the whole noun cluster. For instance, in the example 57a, the possessive unit *của chị Hoa* may be understood as part of the prepositional phrase *trong tủ* immediately preceding it rather than as an adjectival modifying the nucleus noun *áo*. As such, the example 57a may be analyzed as follows:

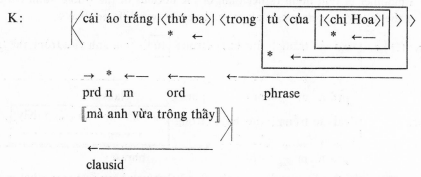

Trans.: The third white dress that you have just seen in Hoa's closet.
(*Lit.*: pre-determiner dress white rank third in closet belonging to older sister Hoa that older brother just see)

The *của* is sometimes omitted before a 'personal pronoun' or before an honorific noun of address when such omission does not cause ambiguity. For example:

K: (58) a. |⟨làng ⟨của tôi⟩⟩| or: K: b. |⟨làng   tôi⟩|
* ←——   * ←
n possessive   n   pN
r pN
(village belonging to me)   (village me)
my village   my village

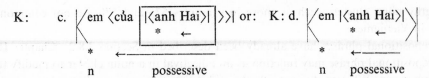

K: c. |⟋em ⟨của |⟨anh Hai⟩| ⟩⟩| or: K: d. |⟋em |⟨anh Hai⟩|⟍
                      *   ←   *   ←
        n   possessive   n   possessive

Trans.: (58) c. Hai's younger sibling
                 (*Lit.*: younger sibling belonging to older brother Hai)
             d. Hai's younger sibling
                 (*Lit.*: younger sibling older brother Hai)

Included clausids regularly function as adjectivals within noun clusters. Such clausids are introduced by the adjectival clausid includer *mà*. When an included clausid functions as an adjectival in a noun cluster to modify the nucleus noun, it fills the tenth position, as was shown in examples 57a and 57b.

There is a danger of ambiguity when a clausid follows a noun at the end of a prepositional phrase or at the end of a possessive unit, since the clausid may be taken to be a modifier of that noun rather than of the nucleus of the whole noun cluster. Each of the following examples may be analyzed in two different ways:

K: (59) a. |⟋cái áo trắng |⟨thứ ba⟩| ⟨trong [tủ] ⟩ ⟦mà anh vừa trông thấy⟧⟩
                                *   ←
            → * ←—   ←——   ←———   ←————————
            prd n m   ord   phrase   clausid

or: |⟋cái áo trắng |⟨thứ ba⟩| ⟨trong [tủ ⟦mà anh vừa trông thấy⟧] ⟩⟩
                                *   ←
            → * ←—   *   ←   ←————————————
            prd n m   ord   phrase

Trans.: (59) a. the third white dress in the closet that you have just seen (that is, the
                 dress that you have just seen)
         or: the third white dress in the closet that you have just seen (that is,
                 the closet that you have just seen)
                 (*Lit.*: pre-determiner dress white rank third in closet that older
                 brother just see)

K: (59) b.

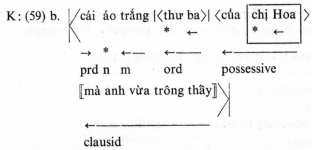

|⟋cái áo trắng |⟨thư ba⟩| ⟨của [chị Hoa] ⟩
                   *   ←   *   ←
→ * ←—   ←——   ←——
prd n m   ord   possessive
⟦mà anh vừa trông thấy⟧⟍

        ←————————
        clausid

or:
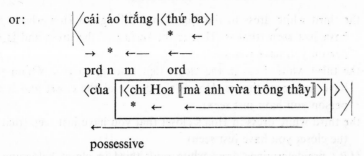

possessive

Trans.: (59) b. the third white dress of Hoa's that you have just seen
    or: the third white dress which belongs to Hoa whom you have just seen
              (*Lit.*: pre-determiner dress white rank third belonging to older sister
              Hoa that older brother just see)

The example 57a may also be analyzed as follows:

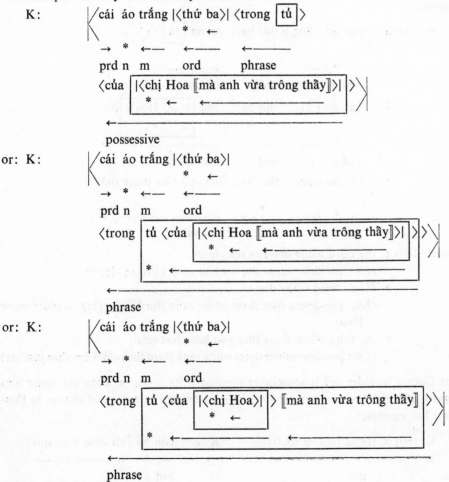

Trans.:   the third white dress in the closet that belongs to Hoa whom you
            have just seen (that is, Hoa is the owner of the dress and is the
            person you have just seen)

or: the third white dress in the closet that belongs to Hoa whom you
            have just seen (that is, Hoa is the owner of the closet and is the
            person you have just seen)

or: the third white dress in Hoa's closet that you have just seen (that is,
            the closet you have just seen)

            (*Lit.*: pre-determiner dress white rank third in closet belonging to
            older sister Hoa that older brother just see)

Ambiguity results from the fact that the possessive unit or the clausid is far removed from the nucleus noun of the whole cluster. Ambiguity may be avoided if only a prepositional phrase, a possessive, or a clausid occurs in a single noun cluster. For example:

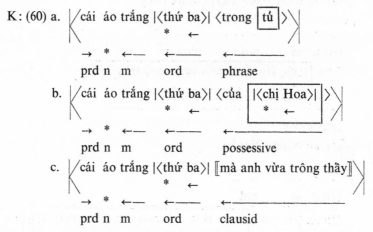

Trans.: (60) a. the third white dress in the closet
            (*Lit.*: pre-determiner dress white rank third in closet)
         b. Hoa's third white dress
            (*Lit.*: pre-determiner dress white rank third belonging to older sister
            Hoa)
         c. the third white dress that you have just seen
            (*Lit.*: pre-determiner dress white rank third that older brother just see)

The clausid includer *mà* is sometimes omitted if its omission does not cause ambiguity. (Cf. the frequent omission of the includer *that* in adjectival clauses in English.) For example:

K: (60) d. |⟨nhà ⟦chúng tôi ở⟧⟩| K: e. |⟨con bò ⟦tôi mua hôm qua⟧⟩|
          *   ←————   → *   ←————
          n   prd n

```
          S    V                    S   V   E
H:        chúng tôi ở      H:        tôi mua hôm qua
```

Trans.: (60) d. the house we live (in)
      (*Lit.*: house we live)
   e. the cow I bought yesterday
      (*Lit.*: pre-determiner cow I buy day past)

4.4.9. *Post-determiners*

The last position within a noun cluster is the position for post-determiners (i.e., the so-called 'demonstratives'). Post-determiners are used to identify the nucleus nouns of noun clusters. The following is a list of the most important post-determiners:

Ấy	that (indefinite)
Đây	this (here)
Đẩy	that (there, indefinite)
Đó	that (definite)
Khác	other
Kia	over there, beyond one unit of place or time
Kìa	over there, beyond two units of place or time
Kĩa	over there, beyond three units of time
Này	this
Nãy	that (a moment ago)
Nọ	that (the one I referred to, indefinite)
Rày	this (time)

The following are examples of noun clusters with post-determiners:

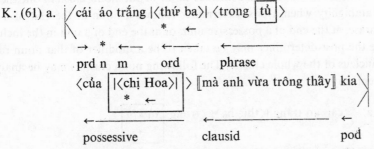

Trans.: (61) a. that third white dress in the closet that belongs to Hoa and that you
          have just seen
          (*Lit.*: pre-determiner dress white rank third in closet belonging to
          older sister Hoa that older brother just see over there)

K: b. | / cây cam |⟨thứ một trăm⟩| ⟨ngoài [sân] ⟩
                          *   *   ←———
             *   ←   ←———   ←——
             n   n   ord   phrase
             ⟨của | |⟨cô Mai⟩| | ⟩ ⟦mà chị tưới tôi hôm qua⟧ đó \ |
                          * ←
             ←————————   ←——————————   ←
             possessive   clausid   pod[17]

Trans.: (61) b. that hundredth orange tree in the courtyard of Miss Mai that you
               watered last evening
               (*Lit.*: tree orange rank hundredth out courtyard belonging to Miss
               Mai that older sister water (verb) evening day past that)

K: (61) c. | / tấm vải đen |⟨hạng nhất⟩| ⟦mà cô Mai vừa mua⟧ đó \ |
                               *   ←—
             *   ← ←   ←———   ←——————————   ←
             n   n m   ord   clausid   pod

Trans.: (61) c. that piece of first-class black material that Miss Mai has just bought
               (*Lit.*: piece material black class first that Miss Mai just buy that)

Lengthy noun clusters such as those in examples 61a and 61b are not commonly
used in Vietnamese.

If a post-determiner occurs in a noun cluster, it must occur as the last item; that
is, it must occur in the eleventh position within a noun cluster. Any lexeme or construction occurring after a post-determiner, therefore, cannot belong to the preceding
noun cluster.

If the adjectival immediately preceding a post-determiner in a noun cluster is any
unit from positions other than positions eight, nine, or ten, there is no ambiguity.
The post-determiner will modify the nucleus noun of the noun cluster. But there is
a danger of ambiguity when a post-determiner follows a noun at the end of a prepositional phrase, at the end of a possessive unit, or at the end of a unit in the included
clausid, since the post-determiner may be taken to be a modifier of that noun rather
than of the nucleus of the whole cluster. The following noun clusters may be analyzed
in two different ways:

K: (62) a. | / cái áo trắng |⟨thứ ba⟩| ⟨trong [tủ *kia*] ⟩ \ |
                              *   ←   *   ←
             →   *   ←—   ←——   ←——————
             prd n m   ord   phrase

[17] For the explanation of the symbols, see the Introduction.

or: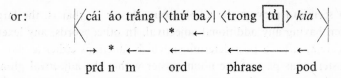

Trans.: (62) a. the third white dress in the closet *over there* (that is, in *that* closet)
or: *that* third white dress
    (*Lit.*: pre-determiner dress white rank third in closet over there)

K: (62) b.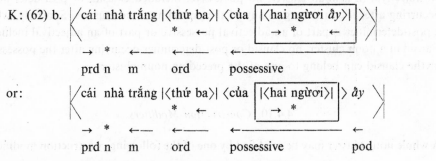

or:

Trans.: (62) b. the third white house of *those* two people
or: *that* third white house of the two people
    (*Lit.*: pre-determiner house white rank third belonging to two person that)

K: (62) c.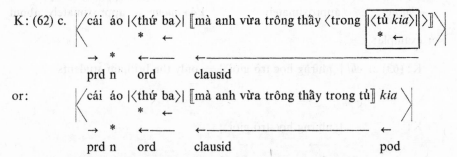

or:

Trans.: (62) c. the third white dress that you have just seen in *that* closet
or: *that* third white dress that you have just seen in the closet
    (*Lit.*: pre-determiner dress rank third that older brother just see in closet over there)

Post-determiners in noun clusters similar to those of examples 62a, 62b, and 62c above are generally considered part of the phrase, of the possessive, or the clausid, but are rarely considered part of the whole noun cluster.

There is, however, one particular characteristic of post-determiners that needs to be mentioned. When a post-determiner occurs as part of a prepositional phrase, of a possessive, or of a clausid which functions as an adjectival in a noun cluster, the post-determiner not only closes the noun cluster in which it occurs to any additional adjectival, but also seems to prevent the whole noun cluster — that is, the larger noun cluster — from having any additional adjectival. In other words, any lexeme or construction occurring after a post-determiner which functions either as part of the whole noun cluster or as part of the noun cluster within the adjectival phrase, the adjectival possessive, or the adjectival clausid cannot belong to any of the preceding noun clusters.

Therefore, if a post-determiner is part of the prepositional phrase functioning as an adjectival in a noun cluster, no possessive, included clausid, or post-determiner occurring after it can belong to any of the preceding noun clusters. Similarly, when a post-determiner is part of an adjectival possessive or part of an adjectival included clausid in a noun cluster, no clausid or post-determiner occurring after the possessive or the clausid can belong to any of the preceding noun clusters.

4.4.10. *Construction Modifiers*

A whole noun cluster may be modified by one of the following construction modifiers:

Chỉ	only	*Đúng*	exactly
Chính	just, exactly, there	*Ngay*	even, right
Cũng	same	*Độ chừng*	approximately, about
Độ	about	*Vào khoảng*	approximately, about
Chừng	approximately	*Vào quãng*	approximately, about

For example:

K: (63) a. *chỉ* |⟨những học trò giỏi⟩| = only the brilliant students

c

K: |⟨những học trò giỏi⟩|
         ⎯→   *   ←
         pl.p.   n   m
         (only many student brilliant)

K: b. *cùng* |⟨một tiếng⟩| = the same word

c

      |⟨một tiếng⟩|
       →   *
       nu   n
      (same one word)

The construction modifiers *ngay* 'even, right' and *chính* 'there, right, just, exactly' may also modify prepositional phrases. For example:

R: (63) c. *chính* ⟨trong | tủ sách |⟩

        ↵

       c

R: ⟨trong | tủ sách |⟩

        r

K: |⟨tủ sách⟩|

          * ←

         n n

Trans.: (63) c. right (exactly) in the bookcase
        (*Lit.*: exactly in chest book)

4.4.11. *Differences between noun clusters in English and in Vietnamese*

According to Allen, the positions for elements in a noun cluster in English are as follows: (1) determiners, (2) numerals (ordinal + cardinal), (3) descriptive adjectives (in the order: opinion + size + shape + color), (4) adjectivals of place of origin or nationality, (5) adjectival nouns (or noun adjuncts), (6) the nucleus noun, (7) adjectival phrases, (8) adjectival predicatids, and (9) adjectival clauses.[18]

The positions for elements in a noun cluster in Vietnamese are as follows: (1) numerals (plural particles and/or cardinal numerals), (2) identifiers, (3) pre-determiners, (4) the nucleus noun, (5) adjuncts (in the order: gender + religion + nationality), (6) modifiers (of shape and/or color), (7) ordinal numeral clusters, (8) phrases, (9) possessives, (10) included clausids, and (11) post-determiners.

Certain differences may be noted between English noun clusters and Vietnamese noun clusters:

While determiners occur only in the first position in a noun cluster in English, Vietnamese determiners are of two kinds: those which occur in the third position in a cluster (herein called 'pre-determiners'), and those in the last position — the eleventh position — in a cluster (herein called 'post-determiners'). Vietnamese has, in addition, a separate position for the identifier *cái*, which functions very much like the determiner *the* in English. (In both languages, the determiners may function as secondary substitutes.)

While numerals (both ordinal and cardinal) occur in the second position in a noun cluster in English, cardinal numerals in Vietnamese fill the first position, while ordinal numeral clusters occupy the seventh position. In addition, Vietnamese also has plural particles, which occur in the first position in a noun cluster when the plural reference of the cluster needs to be emphasized. (In English, plural reference is expressed obligatorily by the inflectional ending of the nucleus noun.)

[18]   Robert L. Allen, *A Modern Grammar of Written English* (New York, The Macmillan Company, in press), p. 433.

While the different kinds of adjectives occur in the third position in a noun cluster in English, the modifiers in Vietnamese (which correspond, by and large, to the adjectives in English) occur in the sixth position in a Vietnamese noun cluster. While adjectives in English may occur one after the other in a long series, modifiers in Vietnamese tend to occur singly or in groups of two. Furthermore, certain ideas which would be expressed by adjectives in the adjective position in English, are expressed by nouns in the noun adjunct position in Vietnamese.

The nucleus of a quasi-noun-cluster in English may be an adjective (as in *the poor in spirit*) or the *-ing* form of a verb (as in *the fishing in this lake*). The most common kind of nucleus in quasi-noun-clusters in Vietnamese, on the other hand, is a clausid, as in *cái thuyền đánh cá* 'the fishing boat' (*lit.*: 'the boat beat fish').

There is one striking similarity between English noun clusters and Vietnamese noun clusters. The last three positions in a noun cluster in English are positions for phrases, predicatids, and clauses respectively; similarly, the last four positions in a Vietnamese noun cluster are positions for phrases, possessives, included clausids, and post-determiners respectively. While the possessive case in English may be expressed by a prepositional phrase introduced by *of* in the phrase position, or by a noun or noun cluster with the possessive ending *'s* or *s'* or *'* in the determiner position, the possessive in Vietnamese is expressed by a special prepositional phrase introduced by *của* 'belonging to' occurring after the regular position for prepositional phrases. While phrases precede predicatids and clauses in English noun clusters, phrases also precede clausids in Vietnamese. Vietnamese noun clusters, however, have post-determiners in the last position which not only signal the ending of noun clusters in which they occur but also signal the ending of larger noun clusters if it happens that the noun clusters in which they appear are parts of adjectival phrases, of adjectival possessives, or of adjectival clausids.

4.5. CONSTRUCTION IN THE SUBJECT SECTOR

The position of the subject sector has been discussed in Section 4.2., but constructions or units that may fill the subject position have not been presented. The following are the kinds of constructions that fill the subject position in a Vietnamese sentence:

4.5.1. *Noun Clusters*

For example:

```
                    S
U: (64)     Ba con chó trắng đang gậm xương.
K:          |⟨ba con chó trắng⟩|
             →    →   *   ←
            nu  prd  n    m
```

Trans.: (64)   *Three white dogs* were gnawing bones.
(*Lit.*: Three pre-determiner dog white in the process of gnaw bone.)

4.5.2. *Substitutes*

These include:

(1) Primary Substitutes. For example:

          S
U: (65) a. *Mấy ngườời bạn Thái ở Nữu ướớc* cho tôi nhiều thứ.
     b. *Họ*   cho tôi nhiều thứ.

Trans.: (65) a. *Some Thai friends in New York* gave me many things.
          (*Lit.*: Some person friend Thailand in New York give me many thing.)
     b. *They* gave me many things.
          (*Lit.*: They give me many thing.)

(2) Secondary substitutes. For example:

          S
U: (66) a. *Con chó trắng* đang gậm xương.
     b. *Con ấy*   đang gậm xương.

Trans.: (66) a. *The white dog* was gnawing bones.
          (*Lit.*: Animate pre-determiner dog white in the process of gnaw bone.)
     b. *It* was gnawing bones.
          (*Lit.*: Animate pre-determiner that in the process of gnaw bone.)

4.5.3. *Predicatids*

For example:

          S
U: (67) a. *Hút thuốc trong giường* là rất nguy hiểm.
          V   O   C
Pd: {hút thuốc trong giường}

Trans.: (67) a. *Smoking in bed* is very dangerous.
          (*Lit.*: Smoke cigaret in bed is very dangerous.)

There is a special case of predicatids consisting of only verbids (like noun-clusters consisting only of nouns). This kind of predicatid may occur in the subject position.

For example:

          S
U: (67) b. *{Ăn cắp}* là một điều xấu xa.
          v

Trans.: (67) b. *Stealing* is a bad thing.

         (*Lit.*: Steal is one reason bad.)

The absence of any noun clusters that might function as subjects for the predicatids in examples 67a and 67b suggests that the facts stated apply to everyone in general, not to anyone in particular. This use of predicatids without subjects of their own is common in proverbs. For example:

            S

U: (67) c. *Uống nước* phải nhớ lấy nguồn.

Pd: {uống nước}

Trans.: (67) c. Those who *drink water* should remember the source.

         (*Lit.*: Drink water must remember source.)

4.5.4. *Non-Introduced Clausids*

Clausids occurring in the subject position of a Vietnamese sentence are not introduced by includers, as are nominal clauses in English. These clausids meet all the criteria for major sentences except that of terminal punctuation (and possibly, also, of capitalization). Such clausids may be referred to as 'contact' clausids or as non-introduced included clausids. For example:

           S

U: (68) a. *Con chó trắng đang gậm xương* là con Vện.

           S   TR V O

H: ⟦con chó trắng đang gậm xương⟧

           S

U: b. *Con chim có mỏ vàng* đang đậu trên cây.

           S   V   O

H: ⟦con chim có mỏ vàng⟧

Trans.: (68) a. *The white dog (which was) gnawing bones* was Ven.

         (*Lit.*: Pre-determiner dog white in the process of gnaw bone is pre-determiner Ven.)

       b. *A bird (that) has a yellow beak* is perching on the tree.

         (*Lit.*: Pre-determiner bird have beak yellow in the process of perch on tree.)

4.5.5. *Question Words*

The question word *ai* 'who' may occur alone in the subject position, or it may combine with other elements in a noun cluster occupying the subject position. The question words *gì* 'what', *nào* 'which', *bao nhiêu* 'how much' always combine with other elements in a noun cluster to fill the subject position. For example:

S

U: (69) a. *Bao nhiêu nhà trong phố* bị cháy?
    b. *Con gì*   đang ăn cỏ?
    c. *Người nào*   đi với ông Ba?
    d. *Ai*   có xe hơi?
    e. *Bò của ai*   đang ăn cỏ?

Trans.: (69) a. *How many houses in the street* were burned down?
      (*Lit.*: How many house in street passive particle burn?)
     b. *What animal* was eating grass?
      (*Lit.*: Animate pre-determiner what in the process of eat grass?)
     c. *Which man* went with Mr. Ba?
      (*Lit.*: Person which go with Mr. Ba?)
     d. *Who* has a car?
      (*Lit.*: Who have car?)
     e. *Whose cow* was eating grass?
      (*Lit.*: Cow belonging to who in the process of eat grass?)

However, when the lexeme *là* is added to the question word *bao nhiêu* in subject position, the sentence in which *bao nhiêu là* occurs becomes a statement rather than a question. *Bao nhiêu là* then functions as an indefinite numeral lexeme. (Cf. the use of the question word *what* + *-ever* in English to form the indefinite *whatever*.) For example:

S

U: (69) f. *Bao nhiêu là nhà trong phố* bị cháy.

Trans.: (69) f. *So many houses in the street* were burned.
      (*Lit.*: Many house in street passive particle burn.)

Sentences in which the question words *ai, gì, nào, bao nhiêu* occur in the subject position also become statements rather than questions if one of the emphatic lexemes *cả, hết*, etc., occurs in the D position, and/or if *cũng* occurs in the M_1 position, and/or if the negator *không* or *chẳng* is used before the question word *ai* or before an honorific noun. For example:

	S	M_1	D
Qn: (70) a.	*Ai*		có xe hơi?
U:	*Chẳng ai*		có xe hơi.
	Ai	*cũng*	có xe hơi *cả*.
Qn: b.	Bò của *ai*		ăn cỏ?
U:	Bò của *ai*	*cũng*	ăn cỏ *cả*.

Trans.: (70) a. *Who* has a car?
      (*Lit.*: Who have car?)
      Nobody has a car.

(*Lit.*: No person have car.)

Everyone has a car.

(*Lit.*: Person also have car emphatic particle.)

b. *Whose* cow eats grass?

(*Lit.*: Cow belonging to who eat grass?)

Everyone's cow also eats grass.

(*Lit.*: Cow belonging to everyone also eat grass emphatic particle.)

			S	M₁	D
Qn:	(70)	c.	Cô *nào*	hái hoa?	
U:			*Không* cô *nào*	hái hoa	*cả*.
Qn:		d.	Bài *nào*	khó?	
U:			Bài *nào*	*cũng* khó	*hết*.

Trans.: (70) c. *Which* lady picked flowers?

(*Lit.*: Lady which pick flower?)

None of the ladies picked flowers.

(*Lit.*: No lady whichever pick flower emphatic particle.)

d. *Which* lesson is difficult?

(*Lit.*: Lesson which difficult?)

Every lesson is difficult.

(*Lit.*: Lesson whichever also difficult emphatic particle.)

			S	M₁	D
Qn:	(70)	e.	Quả *gì*	xanh?	
U:			Quả *gì*	*cũng* xanh.	
Qn:		f.	*Bao nhiêu* nhà	bị cháy?	
U:			*Bao nhiêu* nhà	*cũng* bị cháy	*cả*.
			Bao nhiêu nhà	bị cháy	*hết*.

Trans.: (70) e. *What* fruit is green?

(*Lit.*: Fruit what green?)

Every fruit is green.

(*Lit.*: Whatever fruit also green.)

f. *How many* houses were burned down?

(*Lit.*: How many house passive particle burn?)

Many houses were all burned down.

(*Lit.*: Many house also passive particle burn emphatic particle.)

Every house was burned down.

(*Lit.*: Every house passive particle burn emphatic particle.)

As the examples suggest, question words are changed into indefinite determiners or indefinite numerals when they co-occur with the lexeme *cũng* occurring in the M₁ position, or with one of the emphatic lexemes occurring in the D position, or with one of the negators used before the question word *ai* or an honorific noun.

Non-introduced clausids containing one of the question words listed above would be full questions if they were to occur alone as free sentences. But since they occur as included clausids in the subject position of larger sentences, their question words also become indefinite determiners. (Cf. the use of question words like *who* and *what* with the affix *-ever* to introduce nominal clauses in English.) For example:

                S

U: (71) a. *Ai theo lệnh*   sẽ được thưởng.
              S V   O

H: ⟦ai theo lệnh⟧

      b. *Người nào tin họ*   sẽ mất hết tiền.
             S   V O

H: ⟦người nào tin họ⟧

Trans.: (71) a. *Whoever follows the order* will be rewarded.
            who follows the order
            (*Lit.*: Whoever follow order later time particle passive particle
               reward.)
       b. *Whoever believes them* will lose all their money.
          who believes them
          (*Lit.*: Person whichever believe they later-time particle lose all money.)

4.5.6. *Omission of the Subject*

The subject position in a Vietnamese sentence may be vacant under certain special circumstances:

(1) When the subject of an adverbial included clausid in the F sector has the same referent as the subject of the sentence, the subject of the sentence may be omitted. The trunk is then usually preceded by one of the lexemes *thì*, *là*, *mà*, and *nên*, occurring in the I position. This is a case of ellipsis of the subject since it may be restored from the immediate linguistic context. For example:

         F   I S

U: (72) a. Nếu *ông Ba* có tiền thì ∅ đã mua cái nhà đó.

Trans.: (72) a. If *Mr. Ba* had money, (he would) buy that house.
              (*Lit.*: If Mr. Ba have money then earlier-time particle buy the house
                that.)

∅ represents the missing unit. When the adverbial clausid in the F position shifts to the E position, the subject position of the sentence must be filled. However, the subject of the adverbial clausid may then be omitted. For example:

S   E

U: (72) b. *Ông Ba* đã mua cái nhà đó *nếu ông ấy có tiền.*

                or: nếu ∅   có tiền.

Trans.: (72) b. *Mr. Ba* would buy that house if (*he*) had money.

           (*Lit.*: Mr. Ba earlier-time particle buy the house that if Mr. that have money.)

(2) The verb *có* meaning 'exist' does not require a subject when it occurs in the verbal position of a sentence. The subject in such a case is not omitted by ellipsis (as in the case discussed above) but is absent altogether. The function of *có* here is similar to that of *there is* or *there are* in English. For example:

         F   S V

U: (73) a. Trong khi anh đi vắng ∅ *có* một người đến hỏi anh.

         V   E

      b. *Có* một người đến hỏi anh *trong khi anh đi vắng.*

         F   S V

      c. *Ở* ngoài vườn ∅ *có* mấy cây chuối.

                V   E

      d.   *Có* mấy cây chuối *ở ngoài vườn.*

Trans.: (73) a. While you were absent, someone came and asked for you.

           (*Lit.*: While older brother go absent exist one person come ask older brother.)

      b. Someone came and asked for you while you were absent.

           (*Lit.*: Exist one person come ask older brother while older brother go absent.)

      c. In the garden, there are some banana plants.

           (*Lit.*: Out garden exist some tree banana.)

      d. There are some banana plants in the garden.

           (*Lit.*: Exist some tree banana out garden.)

4.5.7. *Differences between fillers of the Subject position in English and Vietnamese*

The subject position in a major sentence in English is always filled. When there is no person or thing for the subject to refer to, English speakers make use of the 'fillers' *it* and *there* to fill the subject position, as in *It is five o'clock* and *There is no time to lose.* In Vietnamese, on the contrary, the subject position may be left vacant when no person or thing is being referred to; the subject may also be omitted by ellipsis when it has already been mentioned in a clausid in the front adverbial position. (In English this kind of ellipsis is not permitted.)

Vietnamese has no 'fillers' like the English *it* and *there* cited above. Again, prepositional phrases do not occur in the subject position in Vietnamese sentences, as they occasionally do in English sentences. (Included clauses do not occur in the subject position in Vietnamese sentences, either, since Vietnamese has no time-oriented clauses.) But with these exceptions, the kinds of constructions that fill the subject position in both languages are much the same.

A GRAMMAR OF PRESENT-DAY WRITTEN VIETNAMESE:
THE SECTORS ON THE PREDICATID LEVELS

5.1. THE M_1, M_2, AND D SECTORS

As was pointed out in section 3.2.3., a predicatid nucleus may function as the nucleus of a predicatid cluster, in which it is preceded and/or followed by modifiers called predicatid adverbials. Predicatid adverbials are different from sentence adverbials in that they cannot always shift from one position to another. The positions for predicatid adverbials are the M_1, the M_2, and the D sectors.

5.1.1. *The M_1 Sector*

The M_1 sector is the position for the following M_1 lexemes:

Còn	still	*Cũng còn*	still (emphatic)
Cũng	also	*Cũng lại*	again (emphatic)
Lại	again	*Cũng vẫn*	still (emphatic)
Vẫn	still	*Hãy còn*	still (emphatic)

The M_1 position immediately follows the subject position. Together with *sao* 'why' in the I position, *cũng* 'also' in the M_1 position helps to identify the subject: the subject is that unit which can occur between *sao* and *cũng*, and which cannot shift to other positions.

The M_1 lexemes modify the predicatids that follow them. For example:

```
          S        M₁      Pd
U: (1) a. Ông Ba cũng    trở dạy lúc sáu giờ sáng.
       b. Ông Ba lại     sắp về Việt Nam.
       c. Cô Hoa cũng còn là người Việt Nam.
```

Trans.: (1) a. Mr. Ba *also* got up at six o'clock in the morning.
   (*Lit.*: Mr. Ba also get up moment six hour morning.)
   b. Mr. Ba is going back to Vietnam *again*.
   (*Lit.*: Mr. Ba again later time particle return Vietnam.)

c. Miss Hoa is *still* a Vietnamese.

(*Lit.*: Miss Hoa still is person Vietnam.)

Cũng, however, seems also to modify elements occurring in the two preceding sectors — namely, the front adverbial and the subject — whenever these two sectors contain question words, as shown in section 3.8.6.3. and 4.5.5. in chapters III and IV. *Cũng* changes these question words into 'indefinite determiners' or 'indefinite pronouns' and thus changes the sentences in which they appear into statements. For example:

	F	S	M_1	Pd[1]
U: (2) a.	*Bao giờ*	ông Ba		về Việt Nam?
b.	*Bao giờ*	ông Ba	*cũng*	về Việt Nam.
c.		*Ai*		về Việt Nam?
d.		*Ai*	*cũng*	về Việt Nam cả.

Trans.: (2) a. *When* will Mr. Ba return to Vietnam?

(*Lit.*: When Mr. Ba return Vietnam?)

b. Mr. Ba *always* returns to Vietnam.

(*Lit.*: (*Bao giờ ... cũng* = always) Mr. Ba always return Vietnam.)

c. *Who* returned to Vietnam?

(*Lit.*: Who return Vietnam?)

d. *Everyone* returned to Vietnam.

(*Lit.*: Everyone return Vietnam emphatic particle.)

It may be that the M_1 position would be best analyzed as comprising two sub-positions: the first for *cũng* when it modifies the subject or a front adverbial in its sentence, that is, when the direction of modification of *cũng* is toward the subject and front adverbial; and the other for *cũng* meaning 'also', as well as for all the other M_1 lexemes. The direction of modification of the other M_1 lexemes (and of *cũng* 'also') is toward the predicatid. These two sub-positions may be represented as follows:

M_1	
1	2
←—	—→
cũng	cũng
	còn
	lại
	vẫn
	cũng còn
	cũng lại
	cũng vẫn
	hãy còn

---

[1] For the explanation of the symbols, see the Introduction.

Another way of analyzing these two different uses of *cũng* is to state that the valence holding between *bao giờ*, *ai*, etc., and *cũng* overrides *cũng*'s function as a pre-modifier of the predicatid and converts it into a post-modifier of the subject or front adverbial, instead.

Since the M_1 position is essentially an adverbial position, it is possible for adverbial units to shift to the M_1 sector from other sectors. Certain elements denoting time that would most commonly occur in the F position, for example, sometimes shift to the M_1 position. Such shifting seems to place greater emphasis on the subject, which then comes first in its sentence. If *cũng* also occurs, the shifted element precedes *cũng*. The following are examples of time adverbials shifted to the M_1 position:

	F	S	M_1	Pd
U: (3) a.	*Ngày mai*	ông Ba		mới về Saigon.
b.		Ông Ba	*ngày mai*	mới về Saigon.
c.	*Bây giờ*	tôi		chẳng muốn học hành gì nữa.
d.		Tôi	*bây giờ*	chẳng muốn học hành gì nữa.
e.	*Bao giờ*	tôi		cũng muốn về Việt Nam.
f.		Tôi	*bao giờ*	cũng muốn về Việt Nam.

Trans.: (3) a., b. Mr. Ba will not go back to Saigon until *tomorrow*.
(*Lit.*: Day tomorrow Mr. Ba until then return Saigon.)
c., d. *Now* I do not want to study any more.
(*Lit.*: Now I no want study what more.)
e., f. I *always* want to go back to Vietnam.
(*Lit.*: (*bao giờ* ... *cũng* = always) I always want return Vietnam.)

5.1.2. *The M_2 Sector*

The position for the second type of pre-modifiers in predicatid clusters comes between the 'TR' position and the 'Neg.' position — that is between the position for time-relationship particles and the position for the negative particles.

The M_2 position is the position for members of a listable lexeme class of MIDDLE ADVERBS, and also for members of the non-listable lexeme class of modifiers. (See section 4.4.6., chapter IV, above.) The following list includes most of the middle adverbs:

Simple Middle Adverbs

Ắt	of course, eventually	*Luôn*	often
Bỗng	suddenly	*Mải*	busily
Chỉ	only	*Mới*	just
Chính	really	*Năng*	often
Chót	regretfully	*Rặt*	all, totally
Chợt	suddenly	*Sực*	suddenly

Cứ	persistently	*Thoắt*	suddenly
Đều	all	*Thoặt*	at the beginning
Hay	often	*Thường*	often
Hơi	a little, a bit	*Toàn*	all, completely
Lại	again	*Vẫn*	still
Liên	right away,	*Vội*	hurriedly
	immediately	*Vụt*	suddenly

Complex Middle Adverbs

Chẳng còn	no longer	*Lần lượt*	gradually
Chẳng qua	only	*Lập tức*	immediately
Chẳng qua chỉ	only	*Luôn luôn*	often
Có lẽ	perhaps	*Một ngày một*	day by day
Ít khi	rarely	*Quyết nhiên*	certainly
Hết sức	wholeheartedly	*Vẫn còn*	still
		Vẫn cứ	persistently

The following are examples of sentences containing middle adverbs in the M_2 position:

           S M_2 Pd

U: (4) a. Ông Ba *chợt* {nghe thấy tiếng kêu}.

     b. Cô Lan *vội* {chạy ra cửa}.

     c. Chị Hoa *hay* {ăn kem}.

Trans.: (4) a. *Suddenly* Mr. Ba heard a cry.
          (*Lit.*: Mr. Ba suddenly hear sound cry.)
       b. Miss Lan *hurriedly* ran to the door.
          (*Lit.*: Miss Lan hurriedly run out door.)
       c. Hoa *often* eats ice-cream.
          (*Lit.*: Older sister Hoa often eat ice-cream.)

The other group of lexemes that may occur in the M_2 position are the modifiers. The following are examples of sentences containing modifiers in the M_2 position:

           S M_2 Pd

U: (5) a. Bà Ba   *thong thả* {ngồi xuống}.

     b. Bà   *vui vẻ*   {nói chuyện với chúng tôi}.

     c. Ông Ba *buồn rầu* {đi ra cửa}.

Trans.: (5) a. Mrs. Ba *slowly* sat down.
          (*Lit.*: Mrs. Ba slow sit down.)

     b. She *gaily* talked with us.
      (*Lit.*: Mrs. gay talk with us.)
     c. Mr. Ba *sadly* went to the door.
      (*Lit.*: Mr. Ba sad go out door.)

Most of the modifiers occurring in the M_2 position are 'descriptive' modifiers. Modifiers denoting colors, for example, do not seem to occur in the M_2 position. When modifiers occur in the M_2 position, they are rarely modified by any modi-modifier.

5.1.3. *The D Sector*

The D sector is the position for any unit which can be dropped but which cannot be shifted to the front position in its sentence. Such a 'droppable' unit functions as a post-modifier of the predicatid. Units that commonly occur in the D position include the following:

(1) CERTAIN 'DROPPABLE ADVERBS'. These include:

Cả	all	*Luôn*	often
Đã	earlier (first)	*Ngay*	immediately
Được	possibly	*Nữa*	more
Hoài	again and again	*Thôi*	only
Lắm	much		

The following are examples of sentences containing adverbs in the D position:

                 D
U: (6) a. Cô Lan muốn ăn cơm *nữa.*
    b. Tôi ăn ba bát cơm   *thôi.*
    c. Ông Ba đi Dalat   *luôn.*

Trans.: (6) a. Miss Lan wanted to eat *more* rice.
      (*Lit.*: Miss Lan want eat rice more.)
    b. I ate *only* three bowls of rice.
      (*Lit.*: I eat three bowl rice only.)
    c. Mr. Ba *often* went to Dalat.
      (*Lit.*: Mr. Ba go Dalat often.)

(2) THE MODIFIERS. But modifiers never occur alone in the D position: they always occur in clusters with modi-modifiers, or else they function as adjectivals in noun clusters consisting of numeral *một* 'one', the nucleus noun *cách* 'manner', and a modifier functioning as an adjectival. Modifiers may also occur in the D position in prepositional phrases consisting of the preposition *với* 'with' followed by a noun cluster made up of the numeral *một* 'one', the nucleus noun *vẻ* 'air' or 'appearance', and a modifier functioning as an adjectival. The following are examples of sentences containing modifiers in the D position:

D

U: (7) a. Ông Ba nói tiếng Anh   *rất nhanh*

K: |⟨rất nhanh⟩|

                                  ⌣   *

                                 mm m

 b. Ông Ba đi ra cửa   *một cách buồn rầu.*

K: |⟨một cách buồn rầu⟩|

                        →   *   ←———

                       nu   n   m

 c. Ông Ba đi ra cửa   *với   một vẻ buồn rầu.*

R: ⟨với | một vẻ buồn rầu |⟩

                        r

K: |⟨một vẻ buồn rầu⟩|

                            →   *   ←———

                           nu   n   m

Trans.: (7) a. Mr. Ba speaks English *very fast.*

  (*Lit.*: Mr. Ba speak sound England very fast.)

 b. Mr. Ba went *sadly* to the door.

  (*Lit.*: Mr. Ba go out door one manner sad.)

 c. Mr. Ba went to the door with a sad appearance.

  (*Lit.*: Mr. Ba go out door with one appearance sad.)

(3) PREPOSITIONAL PHRASES. Phrases introduced by prepositions may occur in the D position. For example:

D

U: (8) a. Tôi ăn cơm   *ở ngoai sân.*

R: ⟨ở ngoài | sân |⟩

             r   n

D

 b. Tôi để một quyển sách ở trên bàn   *cạnh một cái mũ.*

R: ⟨cạnh | một cái mũ |⟩

                        r

K: |⟨một cái mũ⟩|

                            →   →   *

                           nu prd n

Trans.: (8) a. I had my meal *in the courtyard.*

  (*Lit.*: I eat rice outside courtyard.)

 b. I put a book on the table *next to the hat.*

  (*Lit.*: I put one book book on table next to one pre-determiner hat.)

It is usually the preceding verbid that determines whether or not a given unit can be dropped — that is, whether or not it is filling the D sector. In sentence 8b, only one complement is required by the verbid *để*. Therefore, if the prepositional phrase *ở trên bàn* is shifted to a position after the prepositional phrase *cạnh một cái mũ*, it can be dropped from the sentence. That is to say, *ở trên bàn* will no longer be in the C position but in the D position, and *cạnh một cái mũ* will then occur in the C position and will no longer be droppable. Of the two prepositional phrases in sentence 8b, only one can be dropped; both cannot be dropped at the same time without making the sentence ungrammatical.

The following are examples of sentences whose final units cannot be dropped without making the sentences ungrammatical because of the kind of verbid occurring in the sentences:

	S	V	O	C²
U: (9) a.	Bà Ba	đổ	gạo	*vào nồi*.
But not:	*Bà Ba	đổ	gạo.	
b.	Tôi	để	quyển sách	*lên bàn*.
But not:	*Tôi	để	quyển sách.	

Trans.: (9) a. Mrs. Ba poured rice *into the saucepan*.
(*Lit.*: Mrs. Ba pour rice in saucepan.)
b. I put the book *on the table*.
(*Lit.*: I put book book on table.)

(4) THE INTERROGATIVE LEXEMES *thể nào* 'how', *ở đâu* 'where', *xong* 'completely', *chưa* '(not) yet?'. These lexemes, which convert the sentences in which they occur into questions, also occur in the D position. For example:

		D
Qn: (10) a.	Ông Ba nói tiếng Anh	*thể nào*?
b.	Bà Ba mua cam	*ở đâu*?
c.	Ông Ba về Việt Nam	*chưa*?
d.	Ông Ba làm bài	*xong chưa*?

Trans.: (10) a. *How* did Mr. Ba speak English?
(*Lit.*: Mr. Ba speak sound England how?)
b. *Where* did Mrs. Ba buy the oranges?
(*Lit.*: Mrs. Ba buy orange where?)
c. Has Mr. Ba gone back to Vietnam *yet*?
(*Lit.*: Mr. Ba return Vietnam (not) yet?)
d. Has Mr. Ba finished his homework *yet*?
(*Lit.*: Mr. Ba do lesson completely (not) yet?)

The lexemes *rồi* 'already' and *xong rồi* 'completely already' may be used in the D position to answer questions signaled by *chưa*. For example:

---

² For the explanation of the symbols, see the Introduction.

D

Qn: (11) a. Ông Ba về Việt Nam *chưa?*
U: b. Ông Ba về Việt Nam *rồi.*
Qn: c. Ông Ba làm bài   *xong chưa?*
U: d. Ông Ba làm bài   *xong rồi.*

Trans.: (11) a. Has Mr Ba gone back to Vietnam *yet?*
                 (*Lit.*: Mr. Ba return Vietnam (not) yet?)
             b. Mr. Ba has *already* gone back to Vietnam.
                 (*Lit.*: Mr. Ba return Vietnam already.)
             c. Has Mr. Ba finished his homework *yet?*
                 (*Lit.*: Mr. Ba do lesson completely (not) yet?)
             d. Mr. Ba has *already* finished his homework.
                 (*Lit.*: Mr. Ba do lesson completely already.)

(5) THE EMPHATIC LEXEMES *cả, đâu, hết, hết cả, làm gì, sốt,* and *sốt cả.* These emphatic lexemes are used in the D position for the following reasons:

  (a) To change questions with question words in the subject position into statements referring to the WHOLE of something, or to ALL of certain items referred to. The same kind of reference may result when the emphatic lexemes are added to statement sentences. For example:

D

Qn: (12) a. *Bao nhiêu*   cam bị thối?
U: b. *Bao nhiêu*   cam bị thối *cả.*
         c. Quả cam này   bị thối.
         d. Quả cam này   bị thối *hết.*

Trans.: (12) a. How many oranges were spoiled?
                 (*Lit.*: How many orange passive particle spoil?)
             b. *All* the oranges were spoiled.
                 (*Lit.*: How many orange passive particle spoil emphatic particle.)
             c. This orange was spoiled.
                 (*Lit.*: Fruit orange this passive particle spoil.)
             d. This orange is *all* spoiled.
                 (*Lit.*: Fruit orange this passive particle spoil emphatic particle.)

In example 12c the orange may be partly spoiled, but in example 12d the emphatic lexeme *hết* makes clear that the orange was all spoiled.

  (b) To help clarify ambiguous sentences. An emphatic lexeme added to a negative sentence containing a question word in the object position marks the sentence clearly as being a statement rather than a question. In writing, a question is marked by a question mark at the end of the sentence. In speech, the same group of words may be a statement or a question depending on the intonation: if the intonation rises at the end, the word group will be a question; if the intonation falls, it will be a statement.

But the presence of an emphatic lexeme in the D position will show unequivocally that the question words in sentences like the following are 'indefinite pronouns' or 'indefinite determiners' and that the sentences are therefore to be taken as statements. For example:

		Neg.	D
Qn: (13)	a.	Ông Ba *không* mua con *gì*?	
U:	b.	Ông Ba *không* mua con *gì*	*cả*.
Qn:	c.	Ông Ba *không* gặp người *nào*?	
U:	d.	Ông Ba *không* gặp người *nào*	*hết*.
Qn:	e.	Ông Ba *không* gặp *ai*?	
U:	f.	Ông Ba *không* gặp *ai*	*hết*.
Qn:	g.	Ông Ba *không* đi *đâu*?	
U:	h.	Ông Ba *không* đi *đâu*	*cả*.

Trans.: (13) a. *What* animal did*n't* Mr. Ba buy?
               (*Lit.*: Mr. Ba no buy pre-determiner what?)
             b. Mr. Ba did not buy *any* animal *at all*.
               (*Lit.*: Mr. Ba no buy pre-determiner any emphatic particle.)
             c. *Whom* did*n't* Mr. Ba meet?
               (*Lit.*: Mr. Ba no meet person which?)
             d. Mr. Ba did *not* meet *any* person *at all*.
               (*Lit.*: Mr. Ba no meet person any emphatic particle.)
             e. *Whom* did*n't* Mr. Ba meet?
               (*Lit.*: Mr. Ba no meet who?)
             f. Mr. Ba did *not* meet *anyone at all*.
               (*Lit.*: Mr. Ba no meet who emphatic particle.)
             g. *Where* did*n't* Mr. Ba go?
               (*Lit.*: Mr. Ba no go where?)
             h. Mr. Ba did *not* go *anywhere at all*.
               (*Lit.*: Mr. Ba no go anywhere emphatic particle.)

5.1.4. *Similarities and differences between the D and M sectors in English and Vietnamese*

The D position in Vietnamese is similar to that in English in many ways. In both languages, it functions as a position for post-modifiers of the predicatid (and, in English, also of the predicate). In both languages, units occurring in the D position can be dropped without affecting the grammaticality of the sentence, but such units cannot be shifted to the front position. In both languages, it is the preceding verb or verbid that determines whether a following unit can be dropped or not. Adverbs, adverb clusters, and prepositional phrases are the kinds of units that seem to occur most frequently in the D position in English, while adverbs, modifier clusters, stereotyped noun clusters, emphatic lexemes, prepositional phrases, and question words all occur in the D position in Vietnamese.

The M sector in an English sentence occurs between the X and the V positions (see section 2.13., above). This is the position for middle adverbs and also for middle adverb clusters which function as pre-modifiers of predicates and predicatids. For example:

Mrs. Zobel has (*almost*) *always* had an extra supply of eggs on hand.[3]

There is also a shifted M̃ position in English between the subject position and the X position (see section 2.13., above). The same kinds of units occur in both the M and shifted M̃ positions. For example:

Mrs. Zobel (*almost*) *always* has had an extra supply of eggs on hand.

In a Vietnamese sentence, however, there is no shifted M̃ position. But there are, instead, two different M positions, which have here been called the M_1 and M_2 positions. As in English, the M positions in Vietnamese occur between the subject and the verbal unit, and function as pre-modifiers of the predicatid.

The M_2 position in Vietnamese is a position for middle adverbs, but adverb clusters do not occur in this position, as they do in English. Modifiers may also occur in the M_2 position, although in English adjectives do not occur in either the M or the shifted M̃ position.

While the same kinds of units occur in either the M or shifted M̃ positions in English, units that regularly fill the M_2 position in Vietnamese do not occur in the M_1 position. The M_1 position is a position for a special group of M_1 lexemes, especially for the M_1 lexeme *cũng*, and for shifted elements from the F position. See section 5.1.1., above.)

5.2. THE VERBAL SECTOR

As was stated in section 3.2.4., above, there are four main positions on the fourth or predicatid nucleus level in a Vietnamese sentence. These are the verbal position, the object position, the particle position, and the complement position.

The verbal position is a position not only for verbs alone, but also for verb clusters. (As in English, VERBS in Vietnamese belong to a non-listable lexeme class.) In English they may be identified by their potentiality for taking -*ing*, -*s*, and -(*e*)*d* — or, in irregular verbs, corresponding morphological changes; in Vietnamese, verbs may be identified as that class of words which occur in the verbal sector and which may always be preceded by one of the auxiliaries. (Verbs may also be preceded by certain

[3] This example is taken from Robert L. Allen, *A Modern Grammar of Written English* (New York, The Macmillan Company, in press), p. 467.

nouns such as *cách* 'way', *việc* 'work', *sự* 'fact', etc. See section 4.4.5., above.) A verb always functions as the nucleus of a verb cluster; it may be modified by any one member of a listable lexeme class called AUXILIARIES. (A verb cluster consisting of only a verb with no auxiliaries will be treated as a special case, where the cluster contains a nucleus but no modifiers.)

Auxiliaries in Vietnamese include the following items:

Có thể	can
Dám	dare
Hãy	must, should
Nên	should
Phải	must

The auxiliary *hãy* is used only in commands or imperative sentences. For example:

<pre>
                          V
U: (14) a. Các con <i>hãy học hành</i> chăm chỉ.
K: hãy học hành
                         aux. v.
        b.   <i>Hãy ăn đi</i>   đã.
                         aux. v.
</pre>

Trans.: (14) a. You *should study* industriously.
              (*Lit.*: Plural particle child should study industrious.)
          b. *Eat* first (before you do something).
              (*Lit.*: Must eat first.)

Commands or requests may also be formed without either *hãy* or a subject — that is, by a predicatid beginning (generally) with a verb. Such sentences may be considered to make up one group or type of minor sentences. For example:

<pre>
            V   C   O
Pd: (15) a. <i>Rót</i> cho tôi chén nước chè.
                  O   Z
         b. <i>Học</i> bài đi.
</pre>

Trans.: (15) a. *Pour* me a cup of tea.
              (*Lit.*: Pour for me cup water tea.)
          b. *Study* your lesson.
              (*Lit.*: Study lesson final particle.)

The following are examples of verb clusters containing auxiliaries other than *hãy*:

<pre>
                          V
U: (16) a. Chúng ta <i>nên học</i> tiếng Nhật.
K: nên học
                         aux. v
</pre>

    b. Ông Ba   *phải về*   Saigon.

              phải về

              aux. v

    c. Cô Lan   *có thể nói*   tiếng Anh rất nhanh.

              có thể nói

              aux.   v

Trans.: (16) a. We *should study* Japanese.

         (*Lit.*: We should study sound Japan.)

       b. Mr. Ba *must go back* to Saigon.

         (*Lit.*: Mr. Ba must return Saigon.)

       c. Miss Lan *can speak* English very fast.

         (*Lit.*: Miss Lan can speak sound England very fast.)

A Vietnamese verb, having only one invariable form, does not by itself express time, mode or aspect. Time is expressed by the context, by time-expression particles, by time-relationship particles, or by a combination of such items. In the following three sentences, the verb *ăn* 'eat' remains the same although the time differs from one sentence to another:

U: (17) a. *Hôm qua* tôi *ăn* cam.

     b. *Hôm nay* tôi *ăn* cam.

     c. *Ngày mai* tôi ăn cam.

Trans.: (17) a. *Yesterday* I *ate* oranges.

         (*Lit.*: Day past I eat orange.)

       b. *Today* I *eat* oranges.

         (*Lit.*: Day now I eat orange.)

       c. *Tomorrow* I *will eat* oranges.

         (*Lit.*: Day tomorrow I eat orange.)

Since a Vietnamese verb does not express time, it may more properly be called a verbid where 'verbid' means 'non-finite verb form'. The cluster formed by a verbid and an auxiliary would then more properly be called a verbid cluster.[4] Verbids and verbid cluster will be referred to as such in the following sections.

Since time-relationship particles and passive particles may occur in a Vietnamese sentence with or without an accompanying verbid, they do not really form part of a verbid cluster, although they may be thought of as being loosely joined to a verbid cluster when such a cluster occurs. They are here analyzed, however, as filling positions different from the verbal position.

There are a number of lexemes which express different meanings and which combine with verbids to form what may be called 'two-word verbids', corresponding to

---

[4] For a more detailed discussion of time and time-relationship in Vietnamese, see Dào Thị Họi, "Representation of Time and Time-Relationship in English and Vietnamese" (unpublished doctoral project report, Teachers College, Columbia University, New York City, N.Y., 1965).

the combinations of verb and particle commonly referred to as 'two-word verbs' in English. The following are a few such lexemes:

Đến	at	*Qua*	over, across, through
Đi	go	*Ra*	out
Hẳn	definitely	*Thấy*	find
Hết	totally	*Theo*	follow
Lại	back	*Thuần*	purely
Lên	up	*Tới*	at
Mất	disappear	*Vào*	in
Nổi	capable of	*Về*	back
Phải	undergo, endure	*Xong*	completely
		Xuồng	down

The following are examples of sentences containing 'two-word verbids':

$$\text{V}$$

U: (18) a. Ông Ba *nghe thấy* người ta kêu.

　　 b. Cô Lan *xem qua* mấy quyển truyện.

　　 c. Con ma *biến mất*.

Trans.: (18) a. Mr. Ba *heard* people crying.

　　　　　(*Lit.*: Mr. Ba hear people cry.)

　　　 b. Miss Lan *looked through* some novels.

　　　　　(*Lit.*: Miss Lan look through some book story.)

　　　 c. The ghost *disappeared*.

　　　　　(*Lit.*: Pre-determiner ghost diappear.)

Most of the verbids occurring in such two-word verbids do not occur separately from the lexemes with which they are combined. A few do, however; the lexemes with which they are combined then occur in the B position, as in the following examples:

V	O	B

Pd: (19) a. *Mở* cửa *ra.*

　　 b. *Đóng* cửa *vào.*

　　 c. *Nâng* cái bàn *lên.*

Trans.: (19) a. *Open* the door.

　　　　　(*Lit.*: Open door out.)

　　　 b. *Shut* the door.

　　　　　(*Lit.*: Shut door in.)

　　　 c. *Lift off* the table.

　　　　　(*Lit.*: Lift off pre-determiner table up.)

Certain types of Vietnamese sentences do not require verbids. For instance, verbids regularly do not occur in sentences in which the complement is a modifier or modifier cluster referring to the subject. For example:

```
                S              V    C
U: (20) a. Tôi              nghèo.
                                 m
        b. Quyển sách ây    khá hay.
   K:                       |⟨khá hay⟩|
                               ⌣   *
                            mm  m
```

Trans.: (20) a. I (am) *poor.*
          (*Lit.*: I poor.)
        b. That book (is) *quite interesting.*
          (*Lit.*: Book book that quite interesting.)

However, ambiguity may result if the subject is not clearly separated from a modifier in the complement position. The unit *hoa đẹp*, for example, may be either a noun cluster with the noun *hoa* 'flower' as its nucleus and the modifier *đẹp* 'beautiful' as an adjectival modifying the nucleus *hoa*; or it may be a sentence with the noun *hoa* in the subject position and the modifier *đẹp* in the complement position. But if a post-determiner such as *ây* is added to the noun *hoa* to mark the end of the noun cluster — e.g., *hoa ây* — there will no longer be any ambiguity since the borderline between the subject and the complement is now clearly marked.

The special 'subject-complement separator' *thì* is frequently used to mark the borderline between a subject and a complement. For example:

```
            S          C   S         C
U: (21) a. Gần mực thì đen, gần đèn thì rạng.
```

Trans.: (21) a. (What is) near ink (becomes) black, (what is) near a lamp (becomes) bright.
         (*Lit.*: Near ink then black, near lamp then bright.)

In this sentence, the two prepositional phrases *gần mực* and *gần đèn* occur in the subject positions in their respective clausids, while the modifiers *đen* and *rạng* fill the two complement positions. The entire sentence *Gần mực thì đen, gần đèn thì rạng* is thus made up of two clausids linked together by a comma. The 'subject-complement separator' *thì* marks the boundary between the subject and the complement in each clausid. Without the *thì*, the modifiers *đen* and *rạng* would become part of the objects of the prepositions *gần* and *gần* — that is, they would become part of the noun clusters *mực đen* 'black ink' and *đèn rạng* '(a) bright lamp', with *đen* and *rạng* functioning as adjectivals modifying the nucleus nouns *mực* and *đèn*.

Again, verbids regularly do not occur in passive sentences in which the agent or performer of the action is named. For example:

```
        S   Pass. V O
U: (21) b. Tôi được   thày giáo cho ba quyển sách.
```

Trans.: (21) b. I was given three books by the teacher.

　　　　　　　(*Lit.*: I passive particle teacher give three book book.)

When a verbid does occur in a sentence, it determines the kind of unit that may or may not follow it. Vietnamese verbids are of three kinds: transitive, intransitive, and transitive/intransitive. By 'transitive verbids' are meant verbids that must be followed by objects; by 'intransitive verbids' are meant verbids that cannot be used with objects; and by 'transitive/intransitive verbids' are meant verbids that are used sometimes with, sometimes without, objects. For example, the verbid *học* 'study' is a 'transitive/intransitive verbid' since it may be used either with an object, as in the first example below, or else without any object, as in the second example:

　　　　　　　　S　　V　　O　　　　C
U: (22) a. Tôi *học* tiếng Anh.
　　　 b. Tôi *học*　　　　　ở trong nhà.
Trans.: (22) a. I *studied* English.
　　　　　　　(*Lit.*: I study sound England.)
　　　　　 b. I studied inside the house.
　　　　　　　(*Lit.*: I study in house.)

5.2.1. *Similarities and differences between verb(id)-clusters in English and Vietnamese*

While every verb in English has six different forms (see section 2.8.1., above), every Vietnamese verbid has one and only one form. Again, an English verb may show time, while a Vietnamese verbid never does.

Two or more auxiliaries may co-occur in a verb or verbid cluster in English; the next preceding auxiliary or X word then determines the form of the nucleus verbid.[5] A verbid cluster in Vietnamese, however, consists only of one auxiliary and a verbid, and both have invariable forms.

In both English and Vietnamese, it is the type of verb or verbid that determines the kind(s) of units (object and/or complement(s)) that follow it.[6]

5.3. THE 'TR' SECTOR, THE 'NEG.' SECTOR, AND THE 'PASS.' SECTOR

5.3.1. *The 'TR' Sector*

The 'TR' sector — that is, the position for time-relationship particles — falls between the M_1 and the M_2 sectors.

---

[5]   Robert L. Allen, *A Modern Grammar of Written English* (New York, The Macmillan Company, in press), pp. 476, 481.

[6]   *Ibid.*, p. 470.

Since a Vietnamese verbid does not show time, a Vietnamese sentence is not time-oriented, although it may show time-relationship (i.e., same time, earlier time, or later time) with reference to a specified time or with reference to another event.[7] Such time-relationship is shown by means of certain listable lexemes called TIME-RELATIONSHIP PARTICLES. The following is a list of these particles:

Chưa	not yet
Đã	earlier time-relationship
Đang (dương)	overlapping time-relationship, in the process of
Mới	immediate earlier time-relationship
Sắp	immediate later time-relationship
Sẽ	later time-relationship
Vừa	immediate earlier time-relationship
Đã đang	earlier overlapping time-relationship
Đã sắp	(past) later time-relationship
Sắp sửa	immediate later time-relationship
Sẽ đang	later overlapping time-relationship
Vừa mới	immediate earlier time-relationship

The following examples show the use of such time-relationship particles with verbids:

                    TR   V
U: (23) a. Ông Ba *sẽ   về* Việt Nam.
       b. Cô Lan *đã   đọc* quyển truyện đó.
       c. Tôi   *đang viết* thơ.

Trans.: (23) a. Mr. Ba *will return* to Vietnam.
              (*Lit.*: Mr. Ba later time-relationship particle return Vietnam.)
          b. Miss Lan *has read* that novel.
              (*Lit.*: Miss Lan earlier time-relationship particle read book story that.)
          c. I *am writing* a letter.
              (*Lit.*: I in the process of write letter.)

A time-relationship particle may also be used without a verbid when the complement in a sentence is either a modifier or a modifier cluster, as in the following examples:

                    TR   C
U: (24) a. Cây tre này *sẽ   cao* lắm.
       b. Chuỗi   *đang ngon.*
       c. Con chó này *đã   già*   rồi.

Trans.: (24) a. This bamboo plant *will be very tall.*
              (*Lit.*: Tree bamboo this later time-relationship particle high very.)

---

[7] For a more detailed discussion of time-relationship in Vietnamese, see Đào Thị Hợi, "Representation of Time and Time-Relationship in English and Vietnamese" (unpublished doctoral project report, Teachers College, Columbia University, New York City, N.Y., 1965).

    b. Bananas *are delicious at this time.*

       (*Lit.*: Banana in the process of delicious.)

    c. This dog *is* already *old.*

       (*Lit.*: Pre-determiner dog this earlier time-relationship particle old already.)

The time-relationship particle *chưa* 'not yet' expresses both the idea of negation and the idea of something not yet achieved at a certain time mentioned in the sentence or identified by the context. *Chưa* may therefore be considered as filling not only the 'TR' position but also the position for negative particles. For example:

TR + Neg.

U: (25) a. Ông Ba *chưa*   về Việt Nam.

     b. Cô Lan *chưa*   viết thư.

Trans.: (25) a. Mr. Ba has *not* returned to Vietnam *yet.*

       (*Lit.*: Mr. Ba not yet return Vietnam.)

     b. Miss Lan has *not* written any letter *yet.*

       (*Lit.*: Miss Lan not yet write letter.)

5.3.2. *The 'Neg.' Sector*

The 'Neg.' sector is the position for members of the listable lexeme class of NEGATORS. This position follows the M_2 sector and precedes the 'Pass.' sector. The following is a list of the negators:

Simple Negators

Chả	*no* (This is not a very polite negative particle. It is used only in informal speech.)
Chẳng	(emphatic) *no*
Chớ	(prohibitive) *no*
Chưa	*not yet*
Đừng	(prohibitive) *no*
Không	*no*

Complex Negators

Chẳng bao giờ	(emphatic) *never*
Chẳng hề	(emphatic) *never*
Chưa bao giờ	(have) *never*
Đừng bao giờ	(prohibitive) *never*
Không bao giờ	*never*
Không phải	*not* (used before equative verbid *là*)

The following are examples of sentences containing negative particles:

U: (26) a. Ông Ba *không*   về Việt Nam.

        b. Cô Hoa *chẳng bao giờ* ăn chuối.

Trans.: (26) a. Mr. Ba did *not* go back to Vietnam.

            (*Lit.*: Mr. Ba no return Vietnam.)

        b. Miss Hoa *never* eats bananas.

            (*Lit.*: Miss Hoa never eat banana.)

Chớ and *dừng* are used to signal negative commands or requests — that is, prohibitions — while *không phải* is the negator used with the equative verbid *là* in statements. For example:

		Neg.	V
U: (27)	a.	Con	*dừng*	*thức* khuya quá.
	b.	Con	*chớ*	*ăn* nhiều chuối quá.

                    Neg.   V

        c. Ông Ba *không phải là* ngừời Mỹ.

        d. Cô Lan *không phải là* con bà Hai.

Trans.: (27) a. You should *not* stay up too late.

            (*Lit.*: Child no stay awake late at night very.)

        b. You should *not* eat too many bananas.

            (*Lit.*: Child no eat many banana very.)

        c. Mr. Ba *is not* an American.

            (*Lit.*: Mr. Ba not is person America.)

        d. Miss Lan *is not* Mrs. Hai's child.

            (*Lit.*: Miss Lan not is child Mrs. Hai.)

In addition to the negators mentioned above, the 'Neg.' sector is the position for two emphatic lexemes: *có phải* and *có*. The emphatic lexeme *có phải* is used with the equative verbid *là* in affirmative yes-no questions. For example:

                   Neg.   V   Q

Qn: (28) a. Ông Ba *có phải là* ngừời Mỹ   *không*?

        b. Cô Lan *có phải là* con bà Hai *không*?

Trans.: (28) a. *Is* Mr. Ba an American?

            (*Lit.*: Mr. Ba emphatic lexeme is person American no?)

        b. *Is* Miss Lan Mrs. Hai's child?

            (*Lit.*: Miss Lan emphatic lexeme is child Mrs. Hai no?)

The emphatic lexeme *có* is used in emphatic non-negative sentences (both yes-no questions and statements, and after the negator *không* in emphatic negative statements). For example:

      U: (29) a. Ông Ba *có*   xem quyển truyện ẩy.

             b. Cô Lan *có*   gập bà Hai ở Nữu Ứớc.

                Neg.   Q

          c. Cô Lan *không có* gập bà Hai ở Nữu Ú'ợc.

Qn: d. Ông Ba *có*   xem quyển truyện ầy   *không?*

          e. Cô Lan *có*   gập bà Hai ở Nữu Ú'ợc *không?*

Trans.: (29) a. Mr. Ba *did* read that novel.

              (*Lit.*: Mr. Ba emphatic lexeme read book story that.)

          b. Miss Lan *did* meet Mrs. Hai in New York.

              (*Lit.*: Miss Lan emphatic lexeme meet Mrs. Hai at New York.)

          c. Miss Lan *did not* meet Mrs. Hai in New York.

              (*Lit.*: Miss Lan no emphatic lexeme meet Mrs. Hai at New York.)

          d. *Did* Mr. Ba read that novel?

              (*Lit.*: Mr. Ba emphatic lexeme read book story that no?)

          e. *Did* Miss Lan meet Mrs. Hai in New York?

              (*Lit.*: Miss Lan emphatic lexeme meet Mrs. Hai at New York no?)

Affirmative yes-no questions are formed with the question word *không* 'no' in the Q sector, while negative yes-no questions are formed with the question word *à* in the Q sector (see sections 6.1.2. and 6.1.3.).

    The emphatic lexeme *có* may also occur in yes-no questions in the complement position before a modifier or a modifier cluster as a construction modifier. For example:

                                  C   Q[8]

Qn: (30) a. Ông Ba nói tiếng Anh *có* khá   *không?*

     K: *có* |⟨khá⟩|

                              ⌣

                            c   m

          b. Ông Ba ngủ   *có* ngon lắm *không?*

     K: *có* |⟨ngon lắm⟩|

                              ⌣

                            c

     K: |⟨ngon lắm⟩|

                            *   ⌣

                          m   mm

Trans.: (30) a. *Did* Mr. Ba speak English well?

              (*Lit.*: Mr. Ba speak sound England emphatic and construction modifier particle well no?)

          b. *Did* Mr. Ba have a very good sleep?

              (*Lit.*: Mr. Ba sleep emphatic and construction modifier particle good (delicious) very no?)

The emphatic lexeme *có* is not used in sentences containing either the verbid *có* 'have'

---

[8] For the explanation of the symbols, see the Introduction.

or the equative verbid *là* in the verbal sector, or in sentences containing one of the time-relationship particles.

Chưa and *không* are the most widely used negators in Vietnamese. As was stated in section 5.3.1., *chưa* occurs in both the 'TR' position and the 'Neg.' position since it expresses both the idea of negation and the idea of 'earlier' time-relationship. *Không*, however, fills only the 'Neg.' sector when it functions as a negative particle. For example:

TR + Neg.

U: (31) a. Tôi   *chưa*   thổi cơm.

              Neg.

     b. Tôi   *không*   thổi cơm.

     c. Ông Ba *không*   gặp cô Lan.

Trans.: (31) a. I *have not* cooked rice *yet*.

          (*Lit.*: I not yet cook rice.)

     b. I *did not* cook rice.

          (*Lit.*: I no cook rice.)

     c. Mr. Ba *did not* meet Miss Lan.

          (*Lit.*: Mr. Ba no meet Miss Lan.)

Negative sentences with question words in the object position may be either statements or questions. In writing, the difference is signaled by the final punctuation. In speech, the difference is signaled by the intonation: rising intonation signals questions, falling intonation signals statements. For example:

O

Qn: (32) a.   Ông Ba không gặp *ai*?

     b. or: Ông Ba không gặp *ai*.

Trans.: (32) a. *Who* didn't Mr. Ba meet?

          (*Lit.*: Mr. Ba no meet who?)

     b. Mr. Ba did not meet anyone.

          (*Lit.*: Mr. Ba no meet anyone.)

In addition to the final punctuation or intonation, a writer or speaker may reinforce the fact that a given sentence is to be taken as a statement by the addition of one of the emphatic lexemes listed in section 5.1.3., above. For example:

D

U: (32) c. Ông Ba không gặp ai *cả*.

Trans.: (32) c. Mr. Ba did not meet anyone *at all*.

          (*Lit.*: Mr. Ba no meet anyone emphatic lexeme.)

When an emphatic lexeme is added in the D position, a question word in the object position becomes an indefinite determiner or indefinite pronoun.

5.3.3. *The 'Pass.' Sector*

The 'Pass.' sector — i.e., the position for the two passive particles *bị* and *được* —
precedes the verbal sector. *Bị* and *được* are used to signal the fact that the subjects
of their sentences do not actively engage in the events expressed by the verbids, but
rather suffer or bear passively the results of some action on the part of some known
or unknown performer. *Bị* suggests unfortunate or unhappy results, while *được*
suggests fortunate or happy results.

When the performer of the action is unknown or is intentionally not mentioned,
the sentence pattern is *S + Pass. + V* or *S + Pass. + V + C*. For example:

	S	Pass.	V	C
U: (33) a.	Học trò giỏi	*được*	thưởng.	
b.	Ông Ba	*được*	hoan hô.	
c.	Ông Ba	*bị*	đổi	ra Huê.

Trans.: (33) a. The brilliant students *were* rewarded.
        (*Lit.*: Student brilliant passive particle reward.)
      b. Mr. Ba *was* cheered.
        (*Lit.*: Mr. Ba passive particle cheer.)
      c. Mr. Ba *was* transferred to Huê.
        (*Lit.*: Mr. Ba passive particle transfer out Huê.)

When a speaker wishes to indicate the performer of the action, however, he does so
by leaving the verbal sector vacant and by adding an active clausid in the object
sector. (The verbid omitted from the verbal sector appears as the verbid in the clausid.)
For example:

	S	Pass.	O
U: (34) a.	Học trò giỏi	*được*	⟦*thày giáo khen*⟧
			S V
H:			⟦thày giáo khen⟧
b.	Ông Ba	*bị*	⟦*chính phủ đổi ra Huê*⟧
			S V C
H:			⟦chính phủ đổi ra Huê⟧

Trans.: (34) a. The brilliant students *were praised by the teacher.*
        ⟦the teacher praised⟧
        (*Lit.*: Student brilliant passive particle teacher praise.)
      b. Mr. Ba *was transferred to Huê by the government.*
        ⟦the government transferred to Huê⟧
        (*Lit.*: Mr. Ba passive particle government transfer out Huê.)

When passive sentences like these are changed to their active form, the units in the
clausid (in the object sector) will shift to the subject and verbal sectors, while the

subject in the passive sentence will become the object in the active sentence. For example:

           S   Pass. O

U: (35) a. Học trò giỏi *được thày giáo khen.*
           S   V   O

    b. *Thày giáo khen* học trò giỏi.
           S   Pass. O

    c. Ông Ba *bị   chính phủ đổi ra Huê.*
           S   V   O   C

    d. *Chính phủ đổi* ông Ba *ra Huê.*

Trans.: (35) a. The brilliant students *were praised by the teacher.*
          (*Lit.*: Student brilliant passive particle teacher praise.)
    b. *The teacher praised* the brilliant students.
          (*Lit.*: Teacher praise student brilliant.)
    c. Mr. Ba *was transferred to Huê by the government.*
          (*Lit.*: Mr. Ba passive particle government transfer out Huê.)
    d. *The government transferred* Mr. Ba *to Huê.*
          (*Lit.*: Government transfer Mr. Ba out Huê.)

It is not always 'natural', however, to make the object in an active sentence the subject in a passive sentence. For example, it is possible to say:

           S   V   O

U: (35) c. Ông Ba mua *ba quyển sách.*

But it would not sound natural to say:

           S   Pass.

    Ba quyển sách được ông Ba mua.

Trans.: (35) c. Mr. Ba bought *three books.*
          (*Three books* were bought by Mr. Ba.)
          (*Lit.*: Mr. Ba buy three book book.
          Three book book passive particle Mr. Ba buy.)

Moreover, the object is not the only unit in an active sentence which may become the subject of the corresponding passive sentence. When a sentence contains a complement consisting of a prepositional phrase made up of the preposition *cho* 'for' and a noun or a noun cluster, that noun or noun cluster may become the subject of a passive sentence. The clausid which will then fill the object position in the passive sentence will consist of a subject, an object, and — in the shifted C̃ position — an elliptical prepositional phrase consisting of the preposition *cho.* For example:

    Active voice:
        S   V   O   C
U: (36) a. Bà Hai mua một cái đồng hồ ⟨*cho cô Lan*⟩.

Passive voice:

S   Pass.   O

b. Cô Lan được ⟦*bà Hai mua   cho   một cái đồng hồ*⟧.
            S   V   C   O
            ⟦bà Hai mua ⟨cho ∅⟩ một cái đồng hồ⟧
S   Pass. V   C

But not: *Một cái đồng hồ được mua cho cô Lan.

Trans.: (36) a. Mrs. Hai bought a watch for Miss Lan.
              (*Lit.*: Mrs. Hai buy one pre-determiner particle watch for Miss Lan.)
          b. Miss Lan was bought a watch by Mrs. Hai.
              (*Lit.*: Miss Lan passive particle Mrs. Hai buy for one pre-determiner
              particle watch.)
              (A watch was bought for Miss Lan.)
              (*Lit.*: One pre-determiner particle watch passive particle buy for
              Miss Lan.)

The preposition *cho* 'for' in the last example may be thought of as introducing the elliptical prepositional phrase *cho* (*cô Lan*) because the missing element *cô Lan* may be supplied from the same sentence. The symbol ∅ in the clausid in example 36b represents the omitted element *cô Lan*. The elliptical phrase *cho* ∅ is similar to the elliptical phrase *on* ∅ in the following English sentence:

Percy cannot be depended *on*.[9] (= on ∅).

In this sentence, the preposition *on* may be said to introduce the elliptical phrase *on* (*Percy*) from which the missing element *Percy* may also be supplied from the sentence itself.

In example 36 above, it was not possible to make the object in the active sentence the subject of the passive sentence. This may have been because of lexical incompatibility. In attempting to find out whether the object in an active sentence could 'always' become the subject in a passive sentence, this writer deliberately used the following two 'non-sense' sentences, which she changed from the active to the passive:

Active voice:
            S   V   O
U: (1)   Cái ti ti bang *cái ta ta*.

Passive voice:
            S   Pass.   O
U: *Cái ta ta* được/bị ⟦cái ti ti bang⟧.
                            S   V
H: ⟦cái ti ti bang⟧

⁹ Robert L. Allen, *A Modern Grammar of Written English* (New York, The Macmillan Company, in press), p. 284.

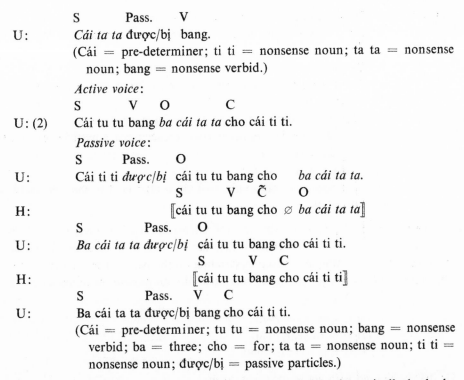

       S   Pass. V

U: *Cái ta ta* được/bị bang.

       (Cái = pre-determiner; ti ti = nonsense noun; ta ta = nonsense
       noun; bang = nonsense verbid.)

       Active voice:

       S   V O   C

U: (2)   Cái tu tu bang *ba cái ta ta* cho cái ti ti.

       Passive voice:

       S   Pass.   O

U: Cái ti ti *được/bị* cái tu tu bang cho   *ba cái ta ta.*

             S   V C̃   O

H: ⟦cái tu tu bang cho ∅ *ba cái ta ta*⟧

       S   Pass.   O

U: *Ba cái ta ta được/bị* cái tu tu bang cho cái ti ti.

             S   V   C

H: ⟦cái tu tu bang cho cái ti ti⟧

       S   Pass. V   C

U: Ba cái ta ta được/bị bang cho cái ti ti.

       (Cái = pre-determiner; tu tu = nonsense noun; bang = nonsense
       verbid; ba = three; cho = for; ta ta = nonsense noun; ti ti =
       nonsense noun; được/bị = passive particles.)

An examination of these nonsense sentences suggested that theoretically both the
object and the complement units in an active sentence may be made the subject of
a passive sentence. It may be that passive sentences which sound unnatural in Vietnamese do so because of lexical incompatibility. In the following active sentence, for
example, both the object and the complement may be made the subject of corresponding passive sentences:

       Active Voice:

       S   V O   C

U: (37) a. Chính phủ xây *một cái cầu cho dân chúng*.

       Passive voice:

       S   Pass. O

U: b. *Dân chúng* được ⟦chính phủ xây *cho* một cái cầu⟧.

             S   V C̃   O

H: ⟦chính phủ xây *cho* ∅ một cái cầu⟧

       S   Pass. O

U: c. *Một cái cầu* được ⟦chính phủ xây cho *dân chúng*⟧.

             S   V   C

H: ⟦chính phủ xây cho *dân chúng*⟧

       S   Pass. V C

U: d. *Một cái cầu* được xây *cho dân chúng*.

Trans.: (37) a. The government built *a bridge for the people*.
    (*Lit.*: Government build one pre-determiner particle bridge for
       people.)
  b. *The people* were built a bridge by the government.
    (*Lit.*: People passive particle government build for one pre-determiner
       particle bridge.)
  c. *A bridge* was built *for the people* by the government.
    (*Lit.*: One pre-determiner particle bridge passive particle government
       build for people.)
  d. *A bridge* was built *for the people*.
    (*Lit.*: One pre-determiner particle bridge passive particle build for
       people.)

Passive sentences with *bị* and *được* are not extensively used in Vietnamese. In fact, there are many verbids in Vietnamese which may be used with either passive or active meaning without causing any misunderstanding on the part of the listener or reader. The verbid *sinh* 'born', for example, may be used with passive meaning, as in:

      S   V   C
      Hoà sinh   năm 1940.
      (Hòa born year 1940)
      Hòa was born in 1940.

Or it may be used with active meaning, as in:

      S   V   O   C
      Bà Ba   sinh Hoà năm 1940.
      (Mrs. Ba born Hòa year 1940)
      Mrs. Ba gave birth to Hòa in 1940.

5.3.4. *Similarities and differences between the X sector in English
and the 'TR.', 'Neg.' and 'Pass.' sectors in Vietnamese*

While the X sector in English is the position for the X words, which carry both the time-orientation and time-relationship morphemes for the sentences in which they occur,[10] the 'TR' sector in Vietnamese is the position not for time-orientation particles (which do not exist in Vietnamese) but only for the time-relationship particles.

Again, while the English negator *not* (or its variant *n't*) cannot occur alone but must be 'carried' by an X word, the negators in Vietnamese can occur alone in the 'Neg.' position, a position which is distinct from the 'TR' position. Unlike English, Vietnamese has not one but many negators. Moreover, while the English negator

---

[10]   Robert L. Allen, *A Modern Grammar of Written English* (New York, The Macmillan Company, in press), p. 305.

not (or *n't*) has no effect upon the status of a sentence as question or statement, the negators in Vietnamese do, at least in speech.

The X words in English also have the function of carrying the emphatic stress in emphatic sentences (see section 2.9., above). This stress cannot occur separate from one of the X words. In Vietnamese, however, emphasis is signaled by the use of the emphatic lexeme *có*, which can occur alone (in the 'Neg.' position). In addition, Vietnamese also has an 'Em.' position, to which any unit that needs to be stressed can be shifted (see section 6.2.).

While passive sentences in English are expressed by means of passive verb clusters — that is, by some form of *BE* followed by the so-called 'past participle' of a verb[11] — passive sentences in Vietnamese are signaled by means of the separate passive lexemes *bị* and *được*, which are placed in the 'Pass.' position. These passive lexemes may be used with or without sentence verbids, as described in section 5.3.3.

In every English sentence there is, in addition to the X position, a shifted X̃ position, which is regularly filled by an X word in a 'Yes-No question' (see section 2.9., above). But with the exception of the lexeme *có phải* (in the 'Neg.' sector) which is used in Yes-No questions with the equative verbid *là* and also with the emphatic lexeme *có*, no time-relationship particle or negator or passive lexeme is used (in its own or a shifted position) to signal questions in Vietnamese. Affirmative Yes-No questions in Vietnamese are signaled by means of the question word *không* 'no', and negative Yes-No questions in Vietnamese are signaled by means of the question word *à* placed in the Q position. (See sections 6.1.2. and 6.1.3.).

While in English X words filling the X position or the shifted X̃ position perform all the functions mentioned above, in Vietnamese most of these functions are performed by different lexemes occurring in either the 'TR', the 'Neg.', or the 'Pass.' positions.

Units which follow the verbal sector in a sentence AND WHICH CANNOT BE DROPPED also form part of the predicatid nucleus. These units are required by the verbid: that is, their occurrence is forced by the type of verbid that precedes them. Such units may therefore be called 'verb (or verbid) complements'.[12] There are three such kinds of 'complements' in Vietnamese; they fill the object sector, the complement sector, and the particle sector respectively. Each of these will be discussed in turn.

5.4. THE 'O' SECTOR

The O or object sector is the position for a unit following (and required by) the verb. An object is distinguished from a complement by the fact that an object does not have the same referent as the subject of its sentence except when the reflexive *nhau*

---

[11] Robert L. Allen, *A Modern Grammar of Written English* (New York, The Macmillan Company, in press), p. 496.

[12] See Robert L. Allen, *A Modern Grammar of Written English* (New York, The Macmillan Company, in press), p. 536.

'selves' is used in the object sector, or when one of the so-called 'personal pronouns' (see section 4.3.) is used both in the subject and object sectors of the same sentence. For example:

		S		O
U: (38)	a.	*Ông Ba và ông Tư*	đánh	*nhau.*
	b.	*Lan và Hoa*	cãi	*nhau.*
	c.	*Chúng nó*	làm hại	*nhau.*
	d.	*Nó*	tự mắng	*nó.*
	e.	*Tôi*	làm hại	*tôi.*

Trans.: (38) a. *Mr. Ba and Mr. Tư* fought *each other.*
(*Lit.*: Mr. Ba and Mr. Tu fight selves.)
b. *Lan and Hoa* quarreled.
(*Lit.*: Lan and Hoa quarrel selves.)
c. *They* harmed *themselves.*
(*Lit.*: They do harm selves.)
d. *He* reproached *himself.*
(*Lit.*: He reproach he.)
e. *I* harmed *myself.*
(*Lit.*: I do harm I.)

			O
U: (39)	a.	Ông Ba mua	*ba quyển truyện.*
			C
	b.	Ông Ba là	*thày giáo của Hoa.*

Trans.: (39) a. Mr. Ba bought *three novels.*
(*Lit.*: Mr. Ba buy three book story.)
b. Mr. Ba was *Hoa's teacher.*
(*Lit.*: Mr. Ba is teacher belonging to Hoa.)

While *ông Ba* and *thày giáo của Hoa* in example 39b have the same referent, *ông Ba* and *ba quyển truyện* in example 39a do not. *Ba quyển truyện* in 39a is therefore in the object sector, while *thày giáo của Hoa* in 39b is in the complement sector. Generally, complements which have the same referent as the subjects of their sentences are preceded by the verbid *là* 'is/are', which functions as a 'linking' verbid.

However, not all complements have the same referents as their subjects. The names of places, for instance, do not when they occur alone or in prepositional phrases. For example:

			C
U: (39)	c.	Ông Ba về	*Saigon.*
	d.	Ông Ba đi	*ra Huê.*
R:			⟨ra │Huê│⟩
			r n

Trans.: (39) c. Mr. Ba returned *to Saigon*.

        (*Lit.*: Mr. Ba return Saigon.)

      d. Mr. Ba went *to Huê*.

        (*Lit.*: Mr. Ba go out Hue.)

Saigon and *ra Huê* are in the complement position in sentences 39c and 39d, but they do not have the same referent as *ông Ba*.

The following constructions or units may occur in the object position:

(a) NOUN CLUSTERS. Almost any noun cluster may occur in the object position of a sentence in Vietnamese. For example:

                              O

U: (40) a. Hôm qua ông Ba gập   *mẩy người bạn cũ.*

K: |⟨mẩy người bạn cũ⟩|

                        →   *   ← ←

                        pl.p. n   n   m

                    O

      b. Bà Ba ăn   *ba quả chuồi.*

K: |⟨ba quả chuồi⟩|

                  → * ←—

                  nu·n   n

Trans.: (40) a. Yesterday Mr. Ba met *some old friends*.

        (*Lit.*: Day past Mr. Ba meet some person friend old.)

      b. Mrs. Ba ate *three bananas*.

        (*Lit.*: Mrs. Ba eat three fruit banana.)

The noun cluster in the object position of an active sentence may sometimes become the subject in a passive sentence. For example:

        Active voice:

                    O

U: (41) a. Con mèo vồ   *con chuột.*

        Passive voice:

        S   Pass. O

      b. *Con chuột*   bị   con mèo vồ.

Trans.: (41) a. The cat caught *the mouse*.

        (*Lit.*: Pre-determiner cat catch pre-determiner mouse.)

      b. *The mouse* was caught by the cat.

        (*Lit.*: Pre-determiner mouse passive particle pre-determiner cat

          caught.)

(b) SUBSTITUTES. Both primary and secondary substitutes may also occur in the object position. For example:

(1) Primary substitutes:

O

U: (42)   (Hôm qua ông Ba gập *mẩy người bạn cũ*.)
       a. Hôm qua ông Ba gập *họ*.
         (Tôi trông thẩy   *mẩy đứa trẻ*   ờ trong vườn.)
       b. Tôi trông thẩy   *chúng nó*   ờ trong vườn.

Trans.: (42)   (Yesterday Mr. Ba met *some old friends*.)
         (*Lit.*: Day past Mr. Ba meet some person friend old.)
       a. Yesterday Mr. Ba met *them*.
         (*Lit.*: Day past Mr. Ba meet they.)
         (I saw *some children* in the garden.)
         (*Lit.*: I see some child in garden.)
       b. I saw *them* in the garden.
         (*Lit.*: I see they in garden.)

(2) Secondary substitutes:

U: (43)   (Bà Ba ăn *ba quả chuổi*.)
       a. Bà Ba ăn *ba*.
or: b. Bà Ba ăn *ba quả*.
         (Cô Lan trông thẩy *mẩy con chó trắng* ờ trong vườn.)
       c. Cô Lan trông thẩy *mẩy con*   ờ trong vườn.

Trans.: (43)   (Mrs. Ba ate *three bananas*.)
         (*Lit.*: Mrs. Ba eat three fruit banana.)
       a. Mrs. Ba ate *three*.
         (*Lit.*: Mrs. Ba eat three.)
       b. *Mrs. Ba ate *three fruits*.
         (*Lit.*: Mrs. Ba eat three fruit.)
         (Miss Lan saw several white dogs in the garden.)
         (*Lit.*: Miss Lan see several pre-determiner dog white in garden.)
       c. Miss Lan saw *several* in the garden.
         (*Lit.*: Miss Lan see several pre-determiner in garden.)

(c) CLAUSIDS. Clausids that may occur in the object position are of two kinds: non-introduced clausids and included clausids. Non-introduced clausids are similar to those described in section 4.5.4. They meet all the criteria for major sentences except that of an initial capital letter and that of terminal punctuation. This kind of clausid may also be referred to as a 'contact' clausid or a non-introduced included clausid. For example:

O

U: (44) a. Ông Ba biết   *chúng tôi không có tiền*.
                S   Neg. V O
H: ⟦chúng tôi không có tiền.⟧

    b. Mọi người bàu *anh Hai làm trưởng lớp.*
                          S   V C

H: ⟦anh Hai làm trưởng lớp⟧

Trans.: (44) a. Mr. Ba knew (that) *we did not have money.*
              (*Lit.*: Mr. Ba know we no have money.)
          b. Everybody elected *Hai president of the class.*
              (*Lit.*: All person elect older brother Hai do head class.)

The subject and verbal in a non-introduced clausid in the object position of a passive sentence may become the subject and verbal in the corresponding active sentence. For example:

          Passive voice:
          S   Pass. O
U: (45) a. Học trò giỏi được *thầy giáo khen.*

          Active voice:
          S   V
          b. *Thầy giáo khen* học trò giỏi.

Trans.: (45) a. The brilliant students were praised *by the teacher.*
              (*Lit.*: Student brilliant passive particle teacher praise.)
          b. *The teacher praised* the brilliant students.
              (*Lit.*: Teacher praise student brilliant.)

Included clausids occurring in the object position are introduced by one or the other of the two clausid introducers *rằng* and *là.* Clausids introduced by *rằng* or *là* are generally preceded by verbids such as:

Bảo	to tell	*Ngờ*	to suspect
Biết	to know	*Ngỡ*	to assume
Chắc	to assume, to be sure	*Nói*	to speak
Chép	to record	*Quyết*	to guarantee
Cho	to presume	*Tiếc*	to regret
Ở	to live, to dwell	*Tin*	to believe
Hứa	to promise	*Tưởng*	to assume, to imagine,
Mong	to expect, to hope		to think
Muốn	to want	*Ước*	to wish
Nghĩ	to think	*Xét*	to note, to remark

The following are examples of included clausids occurring in the object sector:

                S   V   O
U: (46) a. Tôi mong *rằng anh sẽ thành công.*
                         I
Cld: ⟦rằng | anh sẽ thành công⟧

```
                                 S    TR V
         H:                 ⟦      anh sẽ   thành công⟧
                         S      V       O
         b. Cô Lan tưởng  là  ông Ba mới mua quyển sách này.
                         I
         Cld:            ⟦⟦là | ông Ba mới mua quyển sách này⟧⟧
                             S     TR V  O
         H:                 ⟦  ông Ba mới mua quyển sách này⟧⟧
```

Trans.: (46) a. I hope *that you will succeed.*

(*Lit.*: I hope that older brother later time-relationship particle succeed.)

b. Miss Lan thought *that Mr. Ba had just bought this book.*

(*Lit.*: Miss Lan think that Mr. Ba just buy book book this.)

There is one particular case in which a clausid introduced by the clausid includer *rằng* seems to function as an appositive or adjectival clausid following a noun, instead of as an included clausid in the object sector. For example:

```
              S       V     C
U: (47) a.  Ông Ba ra đi  với  hy vọng  rằng mọi việc sẽ thành công.
    R:                   ⟨với  ┌──────────────────────────────┐
                               │ hy vọng rằng  mọi việc sẽ thành công  │  ⟩
                         r     └──────────────────────────────┘
    K:                        |⟨hy vọng ⟦rằng   mọi việc sẽ thành công⟧⟧⟩|
                             *          ←─────────────────────────
                             n
                                          I
    Cld:                                 ⟦rằng | mọi việc sẽ thành công⟧
                                              S    TR V
    H:                                       ⟦   mọi việc sẽ thành công⟧
```

Trans.: (47) a. Mr. Ba went away with the hope *that everything would be successful.*

(*Lit.*: Mr. Ba go away with hope that all work later time-relationship particle succeed.)

The clausid introducers *rằng* and *là* may sometimes be omitted, as may the clause introducer *that* in English. For example:

U: (47) b. Tôi tưởng *là chị học ở Nữu Ước.*

or: c. Tôi tưởng ∅ *chị học ở Nữu Ước.*

Trans.: (47) b. I thought *that you studied in New York.*

(*Lit.*: I think that older sister study in New York.)

c. I thought *you studied in New York.*

(*Lit.*: I think older sister study in New York.)

(d) 'INCLUDED' QUESTIONS. Certain kinds of questions may also occur in the object position. These may be called 'included' questions since they are included in larger sentences, or else 'indirect questions' since they do not ask directly. (Unlike the word order in indirect questions in English, however, the order of units in an indirect question in Vietnamese remains just as it would be in the corresponding direct question.) For example:

U: (48) a. Tôi không biết *cô Lan đi đâu?*
                          S   V C
Qn: ⟦cô Lan đi đâu⟧
       b. Ông Ba hỏi *bao giờ cô Lan ăn cơm?*
                      F   S   V   O
Qn: ⟦bao giờ cô Lan ăn cơm⟧
       c. Tôi không biết *cô Lan đã đi chưa?*
                          S   TR V D
Qn: ⟦cô Lan đã đi chưa⟧
       d. Cô Lan hỏi *sao ông Ba không đến?*
                      I   S   Neg. V
Qn: ⟦sao ông Ba không đến⟧
       e. Ông Ba hỏi *tôi có   ăn cam không?*
                      S Neg. V O   Q
Qn: ⟦tôi có   ăn cam không⟧

Trans.: (48) a. I did not know *where Miss Lan went.*
                (*Lit.*: I no know Miss Lan go where?)
        b. Mr. Ba asked *when Miss Lan had her meal.*
                (*Lit.*: Mr. Ba ask when Miss Lan eat rice?)
        c. I did not know *whether Miss Lan had gone yet or not.*
                (*Lit.*: I no know Miss Lan earlier time-relationship particle go not
                   yet?)
        d. Miss Lan asked *why Mr. Ba did not come.*
                (*Lit.*: Miss Lan ask why Mr. Ba no arrive?)
        e. Mr. Ba asked *whether I would eat oranges.*
                (*Lit.*: Mr. Ba ask I emphatic particle eat orange no?)

While English indirect questions regularly end with a period, Vietnamese indirect questions may end either with a period or a question mark.

(e) QUESTION WORDS. Question words may occur in the object position, either alone or as a part of larger units filling the object sector. For example:

Qn: (49) a. Ông Ba gập *ai?*
         b. Ông Ba mua *con bò cuả ai?*
         c. Ông Ba gập *người nào?*
         d. Ông Ba học *gì?*

e. Ông Ba mua *cái gì?*

f. Ông Ba nói *sao?*

g. Ông Ba mua *mấy cái bút?*

h. Ông Ba trồng *bao nhiêu cây cam?*

i. Ông Ba uống *bao nhiêu nước?*

Trans.: (49) a. *Who* did Mr. Ba meet?
(*Lit.*: Mr. Ba meet who?)

b. *Whose cow* did Mr. Ba buy?
(*Lit.*: Mr. Ba buy pre-determiner cow belonging to who?)

c. *Which man* did Mr. Ba meet?
(*Lit.*: Mr. Ba meet person which?)

d. *What* did Mr. Ba study?
(*Lit.*: Mr. Ba study what?)

e. *What* did Mr. Ba buy?
(*Lit.*: Mr. Ba buy pre-determiner what?)

f. *What* did Mr. Ba say?
(*Lit.*: Mr. Ba say what?)

g. *How many pens* did Mr. Ba buy?
(*Lit.*: Mr. Ba buy how many pre-determiner pen?)

h. *How many orange trees* did Mr. Ba plant?
(*Lit.*: Mr. Ba plant how many tree orange?)

i. *How much water* did Mr. Ba drink?
(*Lit.*: Mr. Ba drink how much water?)

The addition of the lexeme *là* to the question word *bao nhiêu* 'how many' changes the sentence in which it occurs into a statement; *bao nhiêu* and *là* together then function as an indefinite numeral. The addition of the indefinite lexeme *bất cứ* 'whatever' before any question word except *sao, mấy,* or *bao nhiêu,* or before a construction in the object sector that contains a question word, also changes a question into a statement. For example:

Qn: (50)   (Ông Ba có *bao nhiêu cam?*)

U: a. Ông Ba có *bao nhiêu là cam.*

Qn: (Ông Ba sẽ làm *việc gì?*)

U: b. Ông Ba sẽ làm *bất cứ việc gì.*

Trans.: (50)   (*How many oranges* did Mr. Ba have?)
(*Lit.*: Mr. Ba have how many orange?)

a. Mr. Ba has *too many oranges.*
(*Lit.*: Mr. Ba have too many orange.)
(*What kind of work* will Mr. Ba do?)
(*Lit.*: Mr. Ba later time-relationship particle work what?)

b. Mr. Ba will do *any kind of work.*
(*Lit.*: Mr. Ba later time-relationship particle whatever work any.)

All the examples given so far have involved only questions with no negators. However, as was pointed out in section 5.3.2., sentences with negators which contain question words in the object position may be taken either as statements or questions. This ambiguity can be resolved in speech by the intonation, in writing by the addition of emphatic lexemes in the D position. These emphatic lexemes make it clear that the sentences in which they occur are to be taken as statements. For example:

D

U: (51) a. Ông Ba không gặp ai   *cả.*
b. Ông Ba chưa định sao   *hêt.*
c. Ông Ba không bao giờ học gì *hêt cả.*

Trans.: (51) a. Mr. Ba did not meet anyone *at all.*
(*Lit.*: Mr. Ba no meet who at all.)
b. Mr. Ba has not decided anything *yet.*
(*Lit.*: Mr. Ba not yet decide whatever at all.)
c. Mr. Ba never learned anything *at all.*
(*Lit.*: Mr. Ba never learn whatever at all.)

With the addition of the emphatic lexemes in the D position, the question words in the object position become indefinite determiners.

5.4.1. *Similarities and differences between objects in English and Vietnamese*

English makes a distinction between nominal positions — that is, positions for constructions which may be replaced by pro-nominals — and non-nominal positions. As the object position in an English sentence is a nominal position, any construction occurring in the object position will be a nominal (and can be replaced by a pro-nominal — but not by another kind of substitute). Vietnamese, however, does not make any distinction between nominal and non-nominal positions: every construction-type in Vietnamese has its own kind of substitute regardless of where it occurs in a sentence, as was shown in section 4.3.3.

The filler *it* is regularly used in the object position in English to replace an object unit (predicatid or clause) which is then postponed to the PP position,[13] as in *I think it very strange that they didn't tell me.* In Vietnamese, however, there is no filler corresponding to *it* and no sector for postponed subjects or objects. Subjects and objects cannot be 'postponed' to the ends of sentences in Vietnamese.

Again, in Vietnamese question words asking about objects regularly occur in the object position in questions, while the equivalent question words in English occur in the I position in their questions (and usually force a shift of the X word to the shifted X̃ position).

Included or indirect questions occurring in the object position in Vietnamese

[13]   Robert L. Allen, *A Modern Grammar of Written English* (New York, The Macmillan Company, in press), pp. 416, 544.

sentences have the same word order as free non-included questions. Indirect questions in English, however, usually do not have the same word order as the corresponding direct questions: the X word in a direct question is shifted to the shifted X̃ position, while indirect questions follow the same order as statements. For example:

I   X̃ S V

Why | did you order such a large meal?

I

I asked you ⟦*why* | you ordered such a large meal].[14]

While in English a question mark is used after a direct question and a period after an indirect question, in Vietnamese a question mark may be used after both direct and indirect questions.

5.5. THE C AND SHIFTED Č SECTORS

Several different kinds of constructions may occur in the complement position in Vietnamese. Some complements — such as nouns or noun clusters, and even included clausids — regularly have the same referents as the subjects of the sentences in which they occur. Others, however, do not. Each type of complement will be discussed in turn.

(a) NOUN CLUSTERS. Nouns and noun clusters frequently occur in the complement position. Such nouns and noun clusters usually have the same referents as the subjects of the sentences in which they occur. For example:

```
U: (52) a. Mực là    một con chó đen.
K:                 |⟨một con chó đen⟩|
                     →   →   *   ←
                     nu  prd n   m
        b. Lan là    một giống hoa đẹp.
K:                 |⟨một giống hoa đẹp⟩|
                     →   *   ←   ←
                     nu  n   n   m
```

Trans.: (52) a. Mực is *a black dog.*
        (*Lit.*: Muc is one pre-determiner dog black.)
       b. The orchid is *a beautiful species of flower.*
        (*Lit.*: Orchid is one species flower beautiful.)

The verbid *là* is an equative or linking verbid relating the subject to the complement. When the verbid *là* is used in the verbal position, the unit occurring after it must be a complement referring to the unit in the subject position.

(b) MODIFIERS AND MODIFIER CLUSTERS. Modifiers and modifier clusters also occur

[14] *Ibid.*, p. 325.

in the complement position. They may be linked to the subject with or without an intervening verbid. For example:

(1) With a verbid:

                              V   C

U: (53) a. Ông Ba *nói   chậm.*
        b. Hai   *ăn   nhanh   như   chớp.*
    K: |⟨nhanh ⟨như | chớp |⟩⟩|
                                               ⌣

                              *

                              m

    R: ⟨như | chớp |⟩
                                    r   n

(2) With no verbid:

                          Neg.   C

        c. Tôi   *nghèo.*
        d. Ông Ba *không   tốt   như   ông Hai.*
    K: |⟨tốt ⟨như | ông Hai |⟩⟩|
                                               ⌣

                              *

                              m

    R: ⟨như | ông Hai |⟩
                                    r

    K: |⟨ông Hai⟩|
                                           *   ←
                                         n   n

Trans.: (53) a. Mr. Ba *spoke slowly.*
             (*Lit.*: Mr. Ba speak slow.)
         b. Hai *ate (as) fast as lightning.*
             (*Lit.*: Hai eat fast as lightning.)
         c. I am *poor.*
             (*Lit.*: I poor.)
         d. Mr. Ba is not *(as) good as Mr. Hai.*
             (*Lit.*: Mr. Ba no good like Mr. Hai.)

Ambiguity may arise if there is no clear-cut boundary line between the subject and complement units, especially if the subject unit is a noun cluster. If no other sector occurs between the subject and complement units, the complement modifier may be taken to be part of the noun cluster. For instance, the unit *hoa đẹp* may be taken as either a noun cluster or a sentence since there is no clear marking of a boundary line between *hoa* 'flower' and *đẹp* 'beautiful'. *Đẹp* may be an adjectival modifying the nucleus noun *hoa* in the noun cluster *hoa đẹp* 'beautiful flower', or it may be a modifier in the complement position following the subject *hoa* in the sentence *Hoa đẹp* 'The flower is beautiful'. Ambiguity may be avoided if the end of the subject is clearly marked, or if there are one or more other sectors occurring between the subject and the complement sectors. For example:

$$\text{S} \qquad\quad \text{M}_1 \quad \text{C}$$

U: (54) a. Nhà này   *rộng.*

   b. Cây cam cũng *khá cao.*

Trans.: (54) a. This house is *large.*

   (*Lit.*: House this large.)

   b. The orange tree was also *quite high.*

   (*Lit.*: Tree orange also quite high.)

In the following sentence, the modifier *trắng* 'white' can be analyzed either as part of the noun cluster occurring in the object position, or as a complement occurring in the complement position, because the object unit may occur without it and because it can be shifted to the shifted complement position:

$$\text{S} \qquad\qquad \text{V} \quad\quad \text{O}$$

U: (55) a. Chúng tôi sơn *cái xe đạp trắng.*

$$\text{S} \qquad\qquad \text{V} \quad \tilde{\text{C}} \quad \text{O} \qquad\quad \text{C}$$

or: b. Chúng tôi sơn   *cái xe đạp   trắng.*

   c. Chúng tôi sơn *trắng cái xe đạp.*

Trans.: (55) a. We painted *the white bicycle.*

   (*Lit.*: We paint pre-determiner bicycle white.)

   b. We painted *the bicycle white.*

   (Lit.: We paint pre-determiner bicycle white.)

   c. *We painted *white the bicycle.*

   (*Lit.*: We paint white pre-determiner bicycle.)

If the verbid *sơn* 'paint' in example 55a above were replaced by the verbid *mua* 'buy', *trắng* would then be part of the noun cluster in the object position, not a complement in the complement position, because it would not be shiftable to the shifted $\tilde{\text{C}}$ position. For example:

$$\text{S} \qquad\quad \text{V} \qquad\qquad \text{O}$$

U: (56) a. Chúng tôi *mua*   *cái xe đạp trắng.*

But not: b. *Chúng tôi *mua trắng cái xe đạp.*

Trans.: (56) a. We *bought a white bicycle.*

   (*Lit.*: We buy pre-determiner bicycle white.)

   b. *We *bought white* a bicycle.*

   (*Lit.*: We buy white pre-determiner bicycle.)

As was pointed out in section 5.3.2., the emphatic lexeme *có*, which normally occurs in the 'Neg.' position, may also occur as a construction modifier before a modifier or modifier cluster in the complement position in a yes-no question. It then shows that the emphasis in the question is on the modifier or the modifier cluster. For example:

$$
\begin{array}{lllll}
& \text{S} & \text{V} & \text{O} & \text{C} & \text{Q}
\end{array}
$$

Qn: (56) c. Ông Ba nói tiếng Anh *có   khá*   không?

K: có |⟨khá⟩|

                                        c   m

d. Ông Ba ngủ   *có   ngon lắm*   không?

                            có |⟨ngon lắm⟩|

                                  *
                            c   m   mm

Trans.: (56) c. Does Mr. Ba speak English *well*?

   (*Lit.*: Mr. Ba speak sound England emphatic particle well question word?)

d. Did Mr. Ba have a *good* sleep?

   (*Lit.*: Mr. Ba sleep emphatic particle good (delicious) very question word?)

(c) VERBIDS. Verbids may occur in the complement position, as in the following examples:

$$
\begin{array}{lllll}
& \text{S} & \text{TR} & \text{M}_2\ \text{V} & \text{C}
\end{array}
$$

U: (57) a. Chúng tôi   đi   *câu*.

b. Bà Ba   đang   học *đan*.

c. Anh Hai   chỉ thích *ngủ*.

Trans.: (57) a. We went *fishing*.

   (*Lit.*: We go fish.)

b. Mrs. Ba was learning *to knit*.

   (*Lit.*: Mrs. Ba in the process of study knit.)

c. Hai only likes *to sleep*.

   (*Lit.*: Older brother Hai only like sleep.)

(d) PREDICATIDS. Predicatids may also occur in the complement position. They refer to the subjects of the sentences in which they occur. For example:

$$
\begin{array}{lll}
& \text{S} & \text{V} & \text{C}
\end{array}
$$

U: (58) a. Tôi thích *chơi đàn dương cầm*.

                          V   O

Pd: {chơi đàn dương cầm}

                    S   V C

b. Ông Ba đi *câu cá*.

                          V   O

Pd: {câu cá}

Trans.: (58) a. I like *to play the piano*.

　　　　　(*Lit.*: I like play musical instrument piano.)

　　　　b. Mr. Ba went *fishing*.

　　　　　(*Lit.*: Mr. Ba go fish (verbid) fish (noun).)

Predicatids regularly occur as complement units in passive sentences. When such sentences are changed to their active form, the predicatids become parts of clausids in the object position. For example:

　　　　　Passive voice:
　　　　　S　　Pass. V　　C
U: (59) a. Anh Ba được bàu　*làm trưởng lớp*.

　　　　　　　　　　　　　　V　　C
Pd:　　　　　　　　　　　　{làm trưởng lớp}

　　　　　Active voice:
　　　　　S　　V　　O
　　　　b. Cả lớp bàu　*anh Ba làm trưởng lớp*.

　　　　　　　　　　　S　　V　　C
H:　　　　　　　　　　⟦anh Ba làm trưởng lớp⟧

Trans.: (59) a. Ba was elected *president of the class*.

　　　　　(*Lit.*: Older brother Ba passive particle do head class.)

　　　　b. The whole class elected *Ba president of the class*.

　　　　　(*Lit.*: All class elect older brother Ba do head class.)

The English sentence corresponding to example 59b would be *The whole class elected Ba president of the class*, with *Ba* filling the object position and *president of the class* filling the complement position. Such a combination of object and complement is called a 'contracted clausid' by Allen, who considers such clausids as "deriving from full clauses from which some form of 'BE' has been omitted" — that is, from which the time-orientation of the clause has been left out.[15] The complement in such a sentence refers to the object rather than to the subject. For example:

　　　　S　　　　　V　　O　　　　C
　　　The whole class elected ⟦*Ba ← president of the class*.⟧

A predicatid in the complement position in a Vietnamese sentence sometimes begins with a time-relationship particle, and may even have a clausid as its object. For example:

　　　　　S　　V　　C
U: (60) a. Ông Ba nói *đã đi Huê̂ rồi*.

　　　　　　TR V C　　D
Pd:　　　　　{đã đi Huê̂ rồi}

---

[15]   Robert L. Allen, *A Modern Grammar of Written English* (New York, The Macmillan Company, in press), pp. 593a, 594.

```
                 S      V      C
b. Thày giáo hứa  sẽ   đưa  chúng tôi đi xem vườn bách thảo.
                 TR V      O
Pd:                       {sẽ  đưa  chúng tôi đi xem vườn bách thảo}
                          S      V      O
H:                        [[chúng tôi đi xem vườn bách thảo]]
```

Trans.: (60) a. Mr. Ba said (*that*) *he had gone to Huê already.*
           (*Lit.*: Mr. Ba say earlier time-relationship particle go Huê already.)
        b. The teacher promised (*that*) *he would take us to see the botanical*
            garden.
           (*Lit.*: Teacher promise later time-relationship particle take we go see
            garden one hundred plant (tree).)

Such predicatids could be analyzed, instead, as forming elliptical non-introduced clausids since their missing subjects may be supplied from the sentences in which they occur. Examples 60a and 60b, for example, might be represented as follows:

```
                   S      V    C
U: (60) c. Ông Ba nói  ø  đã  đi Huê rồi.
                   S  TR V  C  D
H:                     [[ø đã  đi Huê rồi]]
                   S      V    C
d. Thày giáo hứa  ø  sẽ  đưa chúng tôi đi xem vườn bách thảo.
                  S TR V   O
H:                    [[ø sẽ  đưa chúng tôi đi xem vườn bách thảo]]
```

Trans.: (60) c. *Mr. Ba* said (*that*) *he had gone to Huê already.*
         (*Lit.*: Mr. Ba say earlier time-relationship particle go Huê already.)
        d. *The teacher* promised (*that*) *he would take us to see the botanical*
            garden.
           (*Lit.*: Teacher promise later time-relationship particle take we go see
            garden one hundred plant (tree).)

(e) CLAUSIDS. Two kinds of clausids may occur in the complement position. These are non-introduced clausids (or contact clausids) and included clausids.

  (1) Non-Introduced Clausids. Non-introduced clausids functioning in the complement position usually have the same referents as the subjects of the sentences in which they occur, and they are usually preceded by the equative (or linking) verbid *là*. For example:

```
                 S  V  C
U: (61) a. Ba là ngươi đang đứng ở trong vườn.
                 S   TR  V  C
H:               [[ngươi đang đứng ở trong vườn]]
```

```
                        S      V   C
          b. Sự thật là  các anh không biêt hát.
                        S      Neg.  V   C
H:                      ⟦các anh không biêt hát⟧
```

Trans.: (61) a. Ba is *the person (who) is standing in the garden.*
          (*Lit.*: Ba is person in the process of stand in garden.)
      b. The truth is *(that) you do not know how to sing.*
          (*Lit.*: Truth is plural particle older brother no know sing.)

(2) Included Clausids. An included clausid occurring in the complement position is generally introduced by some such introducer as the following:

Cho	so that	*Là*	that
Để	in order to	*Như*	like, as
Để cho	in order to	*Như là*	like, as
Đến nỗi	so that, such that	*Như thể*	similar to, the same as

The following are examples of included clausids in the complement position:

```
                     S   V    C
U: (62) a. Tôi làm  như  tôi đã hứa với anh.
                         I
Cld:                ⟦như | tôi đã hứa với anh⟧
                         S  TR V   C
H:                  ⟦      tôi đã hứa với anh⟧
        b. Ông Ba nói  là ông sắp về Việt Nam.
                         I
Cld:                ⟦là ông sắp về Việt Nam⟧
                         S  TR V  C
H:                  ⟦    ông sắp về Việt Nam⟧
                              C
        c. Anh Ba hăng hái hoạt động  đến nỗi anh sụt mất năm cân.
                                          I
Cld:                             ⟦đến nỗi anh sụt mất năm cân⟧
                                           S   V   O
H:                               ⟦        anh sụt mất năm cân⟧
```

Trans.: (62) a. I did *as I had promised you.*
          (*Lit.*: I do as I earlier time-relationship particle promise with older brother.)
      b. Mr. Ba said *that he was going back to Vietnam.*
          (*Lit.*: Mr. Ba speak that Mr. later time-relationship particle return Vietnam.)

c. Ba worked (*so*) enthusiastically *that he lost five kilograms.*
    (*Lit.*: Older brother Ba enthusiastic work such that older brother lose
    five kilogram.)

Clausids introduced by the clausid includers above may also occur in the object
position when their subjects do not have the same referent as the subjects of the
sentences in which they occur. For example:

```
                S    V    O
U: (62) d. Tôi làm  như  ông bảo.
                               I
Cld:                      ⟦như | ông bảo⟧
                               S    V
H:                        ⟦    ông bảo⟧
```

Trans.: (62) d. I did *as you said.*
              (*Lit.*: I do as Mr. say.)

(3) Elliptical included clausids. The subject of a clausid in the complement position
is sometimes omitted. An omitted subject must have the same referent as the subject
of the sentence. For example:

```
           S┌············································┐    C
U: (62) e. Tôi về Việt Nam  như    ∅ đã dự định.
                                    I
Cld:                        ⟦như | ∅ đã dự định⟧
                                   S  TR V
H:                          ⟦     ∅ đã dự định⟧
```

Trans.: (62) e. I went back to Vietnam *as I had planned.*
              (*Lit.*: I return Vietnam as earlier time-relationship particle decide.)

(f) TWO-COMPLEMENT UNITS. One sometimes finds two units in the complement sector.
The complement sector may thus be said to have two sub-positions, which may be
referred to as the C_1 position and the C_2 position. In an English sentence, as Allen has
pointed out, "every construction has been built up from its nucleus or core outward"
and, in a predicate or predicatid, it is the verb which determines whether a following
unit may be dropped or not.[16] Therefore, the closer a unit is to the verb, the more
tightly it is felt to be bound to the verb. The same thing may be said about units that
follow the verbid on the predicatid nucleus level in a Vietnamese sentence. Those
units which are closer to the verbid seem to be more important to the sentence in
which they occur than those which are farther from the verbid. A unit that at first
appears to be a complement in the C_2 position can sometimes be dropped without
affecting its sentence grammatically. Such a unit may thus be considered either as a

[16]   Robert L. Allen, *A Modern Grammar of Written English* (New York, The Macmillan Company,
in press), p. 471.

C_2 unit or as a D unit. The order of C_1 units and C_2/D units is generally one of the following:

(1) modifier + prepositional phrase
(2) modifier/modifier cluster + included clausid
(3) prepositional phrase + included clausid
(4) prepositional phrase + elliptical included clausid
(5) modifier/modifier cluster + elliptical included clausid
(6) two prepositional phrases

The following are examples of sentences containing units in the C_1 and C_2/D positions in the order mentioned above:

			C_1	C_2/D
U: (63)	a.	(1) Ba	nói	âm ĩ	ở trong nhà.
	b.	Ông Ba chạy	thật nhanh	ra cửa.
	c.	(2) Ông Ba nói	rõ	cho họ hiểu.
	d.	Ông Ba nói	thật rõ	cho họ hiểu.
	e.	(3) Cô Lan nói	với bà Hai	là cô sắp thi.
	f.	(4) Ông Ba vaò	Saigon	như ∅ đã dự định.
	g.	(5) Ông Ba tiêu	nhiều quá	đến nỗi ∅ mất hết tiền.
	h.	(6) Tôi	học	ở trong lớp với các bạn tôi.

Trans.: (63) a. Ba spoke *noisily in the house.*
   (*Lit.*: Ba speak noisy in house.)
   b. Mr. Ba ran *very quickly to the door.*
   (*Lit.*: Mr. Ba run real fast out door.)
   c. Mr. Ba spoke *clearly so that they could understand.*
   (*Lit.*: Mr. Ba speak clear so that they understand.)
   d. Mr. Ba spoke *very clearly so that they could understand.*
   (*Lit.*: Mr. Ba speak real clear so that they understand.)
   e. Miss Lan told *Mrs. Hai that she was going to have an examination.*
   (*Lit.*: Miss Lan speak with Mrs. Hai that Miss later time-relationship particle have an examination.)
   f. Mr. Ba went *to Saigon as had been decided.*
   (*Lit.*: Mr. Ba enter Saigon as earlier time-relationship particle decide.)
   g. Mr. Ba spend *so much that he ran short of money.*
   (*Lit.*: Mr. Ba spend much very such that lose all money.)
   h. I studied *in class with my friends.*
   (*Lit.*: I study in class with plural particle friend I.)

The symbol '∅' represents the missing subjects of the elliptical clausids.

The modifier cluster *thật nhanh* in example 63b may also follow the prepositional phrase *ra cửa*:

U: (63) i. Ông Ba chạy *ra cửa thật nhanh.*

Trans.: (63) i. Mr. Ba ran *to the door very quickly.*

             (*Lit.*: Mr. Ba run out door real fast.)

If the modi-modifier *thật* is omitted, however, the modifier *nhanh* may occur only in the C_1 position, not in the position following the prepositional phrase. The modifier clusters in examples 63c, 63d, and 63g cannot be shifted to a position following the included clausids. The modifier clusters in examples 63c and 63d would become part of the included clausids in the C_2 position if they were shifted to a position following the clausids. It appears, therefore, that the order of units in the C_1 and C_2/D positions is fairly fixed.

    (g) PREPOSITIONAL PHRASES. Prepositional phrases frequently occur in the complement position. The following are examples of prepositional phrases used in the complement position:

                               C

U: (64) a. Chim hót *trong lồng.*

R: ⟨trong ⟨lồng⟩⟩

                    r   n

        b. Chúng tôi chơi *trong một sân rộng.*

R: ⟨trong ⟨một sân rộng⟩⟩

                              r

K: |⟨một sân rộng⟩|

                         →   *   ←

                      nu   n   m

Trans.: (64) a. Birds chirped *in the cage.*

              (*Lit.*: Bird chirp in cage.)

        b. We played *in a large courtyard.*

              (*Lit.*: We play in one courtyard large.)

Possessives with *của* 'belonging to', which have been considered to be a special kind of prepositional phrase (see section 4.4.8.), may also occur in the complement position. The equative or linking verbid *là* is optional when the end of the subject unit is clearly indicated, especially if the subject is a noun cluster. For example:

                                C

U: (64) c. Cái áo này (là) *của tôi.*

        d. Nhà kia   (là) *của ông Ba.*

Trans.: (64) c. This dress is *mine.*

              (*Lit.*: Pre-determiner dress this is belonging to I.)

        d. That house is *Mr. Ba's.*

              (*Lit.*: House there is belonging to Mr. Ba.)

If *là* is omitted when the end of a subject cluster is not clearly marked — that is, when the cluster may take a possessive phrase as an adjectival — ambiguity results. For example:

U: (65) a.   *cái áo   của tôi*

|⟨cái áo⟩| ⟨của tôi⟩ 'This dress is mine.'

→   *

or: |⟨cái áo   của tôi⟩| 'this dress of mine'

→   *   ←————

          prd n   r   pN

b.   *nhà   của ông Ba*

|⟨nhà⟩| ⟨của ông Ba⟩ 'That house is Mr. Ba's.'

or: |⟨nhà   của ông Ba⟩| 'the house of Mr. Ba's'

          *   ←————

Trans.: (65) a. (*Lit.*: pre-determiner dress belonging to I)
b. (*Lit.*: house belonging to Mr. Ba)

But when *là* occurs in the verbal position, there is no ambiguity. For example:

                    V C

U: (66) a. Cái áo   *là* của tôi.
b. Cái nhà *là* của ông Ba.

Trans.: (66) a. The dress *is* mine.
(*Lit.*: Pre-determiner dress is belonging to I.)
b. The house *is* Mr. Ba's.
(*Lit.*: Pre-determiner house is belonging to Mr. Ba.)

The names of places, such as countries, cities, towns, and the like, may occur in the C position, either alone or preceded by a preposition. For example:

          C   C

U: (67) a. Tôi đi *Mỹ*   or: Tôi đi *sang Mỹ.*
b. Tôi ra *Huê.*   or: Tôi ra *ngoài Huê.*

Trans.: (67) a. I went *to America.*
(*Lit.*: I go America.
or: I go over America.)
b. I went out *to Huê.*
(*Lit.*: I go Huê.
or: I go out Huê.)

When two prepositional phrases in the complement position are preceded by the verbid *đi* 'go' in the verbal position, the preposition of the first prepositional phrase may be omitted:

U: (68) a. Tôi đi *tàu thủy vào Saigon.*
b. Tôi đi *Saigon   bằng tàu thủy.*

Trans.: (68) a. I went *by boat to Saigon*.
            (*Lit.*: I go boat in Saigon.)
        b. I went *to Saigon by boat*.
            (*Lit.*: I go Saigon by boat.)

Pro-phrases may also occur in the complement position. For example:

   U: (68) c. Gia đình ông Ba *ở đây*.
         d. Cô Lan đang học   *đó*.

Trans.: (68) c. Mr. Ba's family lives *here*.
            (*Lit.*: Family Mr. Ba live here.)
        d. Miss Lan was studying *there*.
            (*Lit.*: Miss Lan in the process of study there.)

(h) QUESTION WORDS. Question words may occur in the complement position either alone or as parts of larger constructions. The following examples show question words being used as complements or as parts of complements:

C

   Qn: (69) a. Ông Ba đi   *đâu*?
         b. Ông Ba đi   với người *nào*?
         c. Tên ông là   *gì*?
         d. Ông Ba nói chuyện với *ai*?

Trans.: (69) a. *Where* did Mr. Ba go?
            (*Lit.*: Mr. Ba go where?)
        b. *Whom* did Mr. Ba go with?
            (*Lit.*: Mr. Ba go with person which?)
         c. *What* is your name?
            (*Lit.*: Name Mr. is what?)
        d. *Whom* did Mr. Ba talk to?
            (*Lit.*: Mr. Ba talk with who?)

The addition of negators to the complements in such questions does not turn the sentences into statements. The addition of negators merely turns questions with question-word complements into negative questions. For example:

Neg.

   Qn: (70) a. Ông Ba *không* đi *đâu*?
         b. Ông Ba *không* đi với người *nào*?
         c. Anh   *không* đưa quyển sách cho *ai*?

Trans.: (70) a. *Where* did*n't* Mr. Ba go?
            (*Lit.*: Mr. Ba no go where?)
        b. With *whom* did*n't* Mr. Ba go?
            (*Lit.*: Mr. Ba no go with person which?)

c. *Whom* did*n't* you give the book to?

   (*Lit.*: Older brother no give book book to who?)

However, the addition both of negators and of emphatic lexemes (in the D position — see section 5.1.3.) to questions with question-word complements, does turn them into statements; the question words then become indefinite determiners or indefinite pronouns. For example:

$$\text{D}$$

U: (71) a. Ông Ba *không* đi *đâu cả.*

$$\text{D}$$

b. Ông Ba *không* đi với người *nào hết.*

Trans.: (71) a. Mr. Ba did *not* go *anywhere at all.*

   (*Lit.*: Mr. Ba no go anywhere at all.)

b. Mr. Ba did not go with *anyone at all.*

   (*Lit.*: Mr. Ba no go with person any at all.)

(i) THE SHIFTED C̃ SECTOR. When both the object position and the complement position are filled, the object unit precedes the complement unit. For example:

$$\text{O} \qquad\qquad \text{C}$$

U: (72) a. Bà Ba mua *một cái áo cho cô Lan.*

b. Bà Ba viết *ba cái thơ về nhà.*

Trans.: (72) a. Mrs. Ba bought *a dress for Miss Lan.*

   (*Lit.*: Mrs. Ba buy one pre-determiner dress for Miss Lan.)

b. Mrs. Ba wrote *three letters home.*

   (*Lit.*: Mrs. Ba write three pre-determiner letter toward house.)

There is also a shifted complement position, C̃, which precedes the object position, to which certain kinds of complements can be shifted. Such shifted complements are similar to the so-called 'indirect objects' in English. For example:

$$\text{C̃} \qquad\qquad \text{O}$$

U: (73) c. Bà Ba mua *cho cô Lan một cái áo.*

d. Bà Ba viết *cho cô Lan ba cái thơ.*

Trans.: (73) c. Mrs. Ba bought *Miss Lan a dress.*

   (*Lit.*: Mrs. Ba buy for Miss Lan one pre-determiner dress.)

d. Mrs. Ba wrote *Miss Lan three letters.*

   (*Lit.*: Mrs. Ba write for Miss Lan three pre-determiner letter.)

Examples 73c and 73d show that prepositional phrases often keep the preposition in both the shifted and non-shifted complement positions. However, after verbids like *cho* 'give', *biểu* 'give as a gift', and *tặng* 'give as a gift', complement units regularly occur in the shifted C̃ position without a preposition. After such verbids, in fact- and especially after the verbid *cho* 'give' — a shifted complement with no preposition is more common than a non-shifted complement preceded by a preposition. For example:

                V   C̃   O

U: (74) a. Bà Ba   cho *Lan*   một cái ví.

       b. Ông Ba   tặng *cô Lan* một bó hoa hồng.

       c. Anh Hai biểu *ông Ba* một giỏ cam.

Trans.: (74) a. Mrs. Ba gave *Lan* a bag.

             (*Lit.*: Mrs. Ba give Lan one pre-determiner bag.)

       b. Mr. Ba gave *Miss Lan* a bunch of roses.

             (*Lit.*: Mr. Ba give as a gift Miss Lan one bunch flower rose.)

       c. Hai gave *Mr. Ba* a basket of oranges.

             (*Lit.*: Older brother Hai give as a gift Mr. Ba one basket orange.)

When there are two prepositional phrases in the complement position, either or both may shift to the shifted C̃ position. When both shift, they occur in the normal order. For example:

            S   V   C̃   O   C

U: (75) a. Ba cầm   cái lược *lên gác cho mợ*.

       b. Ba cầm *lên gác cho mợ* cái lược.

       c. Ba cầm *lên gác*   cái lược   *cho mợ*.

       d. Ba cầm   *cho mợ* cái lược *lên gác*.

Trans.: (75) a. Ba took the comb *upstairs to his mother*.

             (*Lit.*: Ba take pre-determiner comb up stairs for mother.)

       b. *Ba took *upstairs to his mother* the comb.

             (*Lit.*: Ba take up stairs for mother pre-determiner comb.)

       c. *Ba took *upstairs* the comb *to his mother*.

             (*Lit.*: Ba take up stairs pre-determiner comb for mother.)

       d. *Ba took *to his mother* the comb *upstairs*.

             (*Lit.*: Ba take for mother pre-determiner comb up stairs.)

Possessives with *của* 'belonging to' may also shift from the C to the shifted C̃ position. For example:

            S   V   C̃   O   C

U: (76) a. Ông Ba mượn   ba quyển sách *của tôi*.

       b. Ông Ba mượn *của tôi* ba quyển sách.

Trans.: (76) a. Mr. Ba borrowed three books *from me*.

             (*Lit.*: Mr. Ba borrow three book book belonging to I.)

       b. Mr. Ba borrowed *from me* three books.

             (*Lit.*: Mr. Ba borrow belonging to I three book book.)

Ambiguity may result when the possessive occurs in the non-shifted C position since the possessive may then be taken to be part of the object unit. In sentence 76a above, for example, *ba quyển sách của tôi* may be a noun cluster in the object position instead of the separate units occurring in two different positions. The noun cluster could then be analyzed as follows:

K: |⟨ba quyển sách của tôi⟩|
            → *   ←   ←—
            nu n   n

R: ⟨của tôi ⟩
                                 r   pN

Trans.:   my three books
            (*Lit.*: three book book belonging to I.)

But in sentences in which *của tôi* can be shifted to the shifted C̃ position, it is not part of the noun cluster in the object position.

   Ambiguity may also occur when a prepositional phrase in the non-shifted C position may be taken to be a part of the preceding object, as in the following example:

U: (77) a. Cô Lan nhìn thấy *ba cái áo ở trong tủ.*

Trans.: (77) a. Miss Lan saw (*the*) *three dresses in the closet.*
            (*Lit.*: Miss Lan see three pre-determiner dress in closet.)

The prepositional phrase *ở trong tủ* 'in the closet' may be analyzed as functioning either as part of the object noun cluster *ba cái áo ở trong tủ* 'three dresses in the closet,' or as a complement unit in the non-shifted C position. This ambiguity can be removed if the prepositional phrase *ở trong tủ* can be shifted to the shifted C̃ position. The sentence will then become:

U: (77) b. Cô Lan nhìn thấy *ở trong tủ ba cái áo.*

Trans.: (77) b. Miss Lan saw *in the closet three dresses.*
            (*Lit.*: Miss Lan see in closet three pre-determiner dress.)

A prepositional phrase in the shifted C̃ position places certain requirements on the unit in the object position. An object unit, for example, may consist of a single noun when the prepositional phrase is in the non-shifted C position. But when the prepositional phrase shifts to the shifted C̃ position, the noun cluster in the object position must be a normal noun cluster — that is, it must include one or more preceding and/or following adjectivals modifying the nucleus noun. For example:

```
                    S  V        O           C
U: (78) a.  Ba viết       thơ         cho bạn.
        b.  Ba viết cho bạn cái thơ.
        c.  Ba dắt        trâu        ra đồng.
        d.  Ba dắt ra đồng mấy con trâu.
```

Trans.: (78) a. Ba wrote *letters to friends.*
            (*Lit.*: Ba write letter to friend.)

b. Ba wrote *friends the letters*.
   (*Lit.*: Ba write to friend pre-determiner letter.)
c. Ba led *the buffaloes to the field*.
   (*Lit.*: Ba lead buffalo out to field.)
d. *Ba led *to the field several buffaloes*.
   (*Lit.*: Ba lead out to field several pre-determiner buffalo.)

Modifiers and modifier clusters may also shift from the C to the shifted C̃ position. For example:

	S	V	C̃	O	C
U: (79) a.	Chúng tôi	sơn		cái xe đạp	*trắng*.
b.	Chúng tôi	sơn	*trắng*	cái xe đạp.	
c.	Ông Ba	ăn		ba cái kẹo	*thật nhanh*.
d.	Ông Ba	ăn	*thật nhanh*	ba cái kẹo.	

Trans.: (79) a. We painted the bicycle *white*.
   (*Lit.*: We paint pre-determiner bicycle white.)
b. *We painted *white* the bicycle.
   (*Lit.*: We paint white pre-determiner bicycle.)
c. Mr. Ba ate three pieces of candy *very fast*.
   (*Lit.*: Mr. Ba eat three pre-determiner candy real fast.)
d. *Mr. Ba ate *very fast* three pieces of candy.
   (*Lit.*: Mr. Ba eat real fast three pre-determiner candy.)

5.5.1. *Similarities and differences between complements in English and Vietnamese*

As was stated in section 2.16.4., seven kinds of constructions may occur in the complement sector in English. These are noun clusters, adjectives or adjective clusters, complement adverbs, phrases or pro-phrases, complement clauses, complement verbids, and complement predicatids. English also has a shifted complement position, which is the position for prepositional phrases that have lost their introducers and have become clusters — the so-called 'indirect objects'. When the object in a sentence is a pro-nominal, however, a complement phrase is usually not shifted to the shifted complement position, either with or without its preposition.[17]

The complement position in Vietnamese is a position for noun clusters, modifiers or modifier clusters, verbids, predicatids, clausids, prepositional phrases or pro-phrases, and question words. Vietnamese also has a shifted complement position, which is the position for modifiers or modifier clusters, for prepositional phrases, and — after verbids like *cho*, *biểu*, and *tặng* — for nouns and noun clusters derived from phrases that have lost their prepositions.

In both languages, the complement position follows the object position, and the shifted complement position precedes the object position.

[17] Robert L. Allen, *A Modern Grammar of Written English* (New York, The Macmillan Company, in press), p. 559.

As was pointed out in section 4.4.6., modifiers and modifier clusters in Vietnamese may occur in any of several different positions: within noun clusters, in certain adverbial positions (i.e., in the M_2 and D sectors), and in the complement position. In English adjectives and adjective clusters normally occur within noun clusters or in the complement position, while adverbs and adverb clusters occur in the complement position or in adverbial positions. Vietnamese modifiers thus seem to perform functions similar to those performed by both adjectives and adverbs in English.

The shifted complement positions in both languages are alike in that both precede the object position. But while most prepositional phrases that shift from the complement position to the shifted complement position in English lose their prepositions (as so-called 'indirect objects'), the same thing happens to only a very limited number of prepositional phrases in Vietnamese. Most prepositional phrases in Vietnamese retain their prepositions when shifting to the shifted complement position.

In English, a prepositional phrase does not normally shift to the shifted complement position when the unit in the object position is a pronominal. As was stated in section 4.3.3., pro-nominals in English replace constructions which refer to things and animals as well as to persons; the 'personal pronouns' in Vietnamese are used only as substitutes for constructions which refer to human beings. Therefore, secondary substitutes in Vietnamese — that is, substitutes which are parts of the constructions or units they represent — are used more often than 'personal pronouns'. When these substitutes occur in the object position, a prepositional phrase may shift from the C to the shifted $\tilde{C}$ position. For example:

	S	V	$\tilde{C}$	O	C
U: (80) a.	Tôi	mua		*cái đồng hồ đó cho bà Hai.*	
b.	Tôi	mua		*cái đó*	*cho bà Hai.*
c.	Tôi	mua	*cho bà Hai*	*cái đó.*	

Trans.: (80) a. I bought *that watch for Mrs. Hai.*
  (*Lit.*: I buy pre-determiner watch that for Mrs. Hai.)
  b. I bought *it for Mrs. Hai.*
  (*Lit.*: I buy pre-determiner that for Mrs. Hai.)
  c. *I bought *Mrs. Hai it.*
  (*Lit.*: I buy for Mrs. Hai pre-determiner that.)

A prepositional phrase, however, does not shift to the shifted complement position if the unit in the object position is a single noun. It can shift only when the object is a noun cluster.

Moreover, modifiers and modifier clusters regularly occur in the shifted complement position in Vietnamese, while adjectives and adjective clusters in English do not.

5.6. THE B AND SHIFTED $\tilde{B}$ SECTORS

The B and shifted $\tilde{B}$ sectors are positions for particles. Like the particles in English, Vietnamese particles are similar in form to prepositions but differ from prepositions in that they do not have objects. The following is a list of some of the Vietnamese particles:

Dưới	under	*Trên*	over
Lên	up	*Vaò*	in
Ra	out	*Về*	toward
		Xuồng	down

In the first sentence below, *lên* 'up' is a preposition, while in the second sentence *lên* is a particle:

U: (81) a. Cầm cái lược *lên gác.*
   b. Cầm cái lược *lên.*

Trans.: (81) a. Take the comb *upstairs.*
   (*Lit.*: Take pre-determiner comb up stairs.)
   b. Take the comb *up.*
   (*Lit.*: Take pre-determiner comb up.)

The first *lên* is a preposition since it has an object (*gác* 'stairs'). The second *lên* cannot be considered to be the introducer of an elliptical prepositional phrase since no object can be supplied from the immediate linguistic context. The second *lên*, therefore, must be a particle.

As in English, the B sector in a Vietnamese sentence follows the object sector. The shifted B̃ sector, however, does not follow the shifted complement sector in Vietnamese but precedes it. For example:

```
              V      B̃        O          B
U: (82) a. Cầm       cái lược  xuồng.
        b. Cầm xuồng  cái lược.
              V      O         B          C
        c. Cầm cái lược         xuồng nhà cho Mợ.
        d. Cầm cái lược xuồng               cho Mợ.
              V      B̃        C̃                      O
        e. Cầm       xuồng nhà cho Mợ    cái lược.
        f. Cầm xuồng          cho Mợ    cái lược.
```

Trans.: (82) a. Take the comb *down.*
   (*Lit.*: Take pre-determiner comb down.)
   b. Take *down* the comb.
   (*Lit.*: Take down pre-determiner comb.)
   c. Take the comb *downstairs to Mother.*
   (*Lit.*: Take pre-determiner comb down house to Mother.)
   d. Take the comb *down to Mother.*
   (*Lit.*: Take pre-determiner comb down to Mother.)
   e. *Take *downstairs to Mother* the comb.
   (*Lit.*: Take down house to Mother pre-determiner comb.)

f. *Take *down to Mother* the comb.

(*Lit.*: Take down to Mother pre-determiner comb.)

	V	B̃	Č	O	C
U: (82) g.	Cầm	*xuồng nhà*		cái lược	*cho Mợ*.
h.	Cầm *xuồng*			cái lược	*cho Mợ*.

Trans.: (82) g. *Take *downstairs* the comb *to Mother*.

(*Lit.*: Take down house pre-determiner comb to Mother.)

h. Take *down* the comb *to Mother*.

(*Lit.*: Take down pre-determiner comb to Mother.)

When the object of a preposition is not expressed, the preposition automatically becomes a particle. As can be seen from sentences 82d and 82f, particles often precede prepositional phrases and seem to be closely related to the phrases — that is, the particle and the phrase seem to function as a unit. However, the particle cannot be said to be part of the following phrase since, when both a particle and a phrase co-occur, either the particle or the phrase may be left out of the sentence. For example:

	V	O	B	C
U: (83) a.	Cầm	cái lược	*xuồng*	*cho Mợ*.
b.	Cầm	cái lược	*xuồng*.	
c.	Cầm	cái lược		*cho Mợ*.

Trans.: (83) a. Take the comb *down to Mother*.

(*Lit.*: Take pre-determiner comb down for Mother.)

b. Take the comb *down*.

(*Lit.*: Take pre-determiner comb down.)

c. Take the comb *to Mother*.

(*Lit.*: Take pre-determiner comb for Mother.)

Since in such sentences the verbid requires, in addition to the object, either a particle or a prepositional phrase (but not necessarily both), it seems preferable to consider both the particle and the prepositional phrase as forming part of the predicatid nucleus rather than to consider the prepositional phrase as belonging to the D sector.

Most of the particles may shift from the B to the shifted B̃ position, but in certain contexts a particle may occur only in the B sector. For example:

		B	
U: (84) a.	Mở	cửa	*ra*.
But not:	*Mở *ra*	cửa.	
b.	Khép	cửa	*vào*.
But not:	*Khép *vào*	cửa.	

Trans.: (84) a. Open the door.

(*Lit.*: Open door out.)

b. Close the door.

(*Lit.*: Close door in.)

In these examples, the particles may be considered to form the second part of the verbids that precede them. These verbids with their particles are similar to the verb-plus-particle combinations in English which are sometimes called 'two-word verbs'. (See section 5.2.).

There are three special lexemes, *được*, *ngay*, and *luôn*, which may either precede an object and/or complement, or follow an object and/or complement. The meanings of *được* and *luôn* change according to their position relative to the object or complement. Preceding an object and/or complement, *luôn* means 'straight (away), immediately', and *được* means 'capable of, able to'. But following the object and/or complement, *luôn* means 'often', and *được*, 'possible'. *Ngay*, however, has the same meaning — 'immediately' — regardless of whether it precedes or follows the object and/or complement.

The following examples show different uses of *luôn* and *ngay*:

$$\tilde{B} \qquad O \qquad \qquad B$$

U: (85) a. Tôi viết *luôn* thơ về nhà.
        b. Tôi viết   thơ về nhà *luôn*.

$$\tilde{B} \qquad C \qquad \qquad B$$

        c. Tôi vào *ngay* trong vườn.
        d. Tôi vào   trong vườn *ngay*.

Trans.: (85) a. I wrote a letter home *immediately*.
            (*Lit.*: I write at once letter toward house.)
        b. I *often* wrote letters home.
            (*Lit.*: I write letter toward house often.)
        c. I went *immediately* into the garden.
            (*Lit.*: I enter at once into garden.)
        d. I went into the garden *immediately*.
            (*Lit.*: I enter into garden at once.)

When *ngay*, *luôn*, and *được* precede the object and/or complement, they may be considered to be particles in the shifted B position, or else single words functioning in the shifted complement position since they are not, strictly speaking, words that can be used with objects as prepositions and should therefore, perhaps, not be called particles. When one of these words follows the object or complement, it may be considered to be a unit in the complement position, or else a unit in the D position since it can then be dropped from its sentence without affecting the grammaticality of the sentence.

5.6.1. *Similarities and differences between the uses of the B Sector in English and Vietnamese*

The B and shifted $\tilde{B}$ positions in an English sentence are positions for particles (see section 2.3.3.). It is usually possible to shift a particle from the B position following the object position to the shifted $\tilde{B}$ position preceding the object position when the latter is filled by a nominal, but not when it is filled by a pro-nominal.[18]

The B and shifted $\tilde{B}$ positions in a Vietnamese sentence are also positions for particles. In Vietnamese, as in English, the B position follows the object position. But unlike the shifted $\tilde{B}$ position in English, the shifted $\tilde{B}$ position in Vietnamese precedes the shifted complement position instead of following it. Except for certain special particles which occur either in the B position or in the shifted $\tilde{B}$ position (but not in both), particles can usually be shifted from the B position to the shifted $\tilde{B}$ position in Vietnamese.

[18]   Robert L. Allen, *A Modern Grammar of Written English* (New York, The Macmillan Company, in press), p. 546.

6

A GRAMMAR OF PRESENT-DAY WRITTEN VIETNAMESE: THE Q AND 'EM.' SECTORS, AND MINOR SENTENCES

The preceding chapters have dealt with the sectors found in Vietnamese sentences on the trunk level, the predicatid level, and the predicatid nucleus level, and also with most of the sectors on the sentence level. There are two more sectors on the sentence level which have not been analyzed as yet: the Q sector and the 'Em.' sector. These are potential positions which are not filled in ordinary, non-emphatic statements but which can be filled in questions or in emphatic sentences.

6.1. THE Q SECTOR

The Q or Question sector is the position for question words other than those that occur in the sectors described previously. The latter have already been discussed in the appropriate places, together with the sectors in which they occur. The following question words, however, occur in a special sector of their own, the Q sector:

à	nhé
chăng	nhỉ
chứ	ư
hả (hở, hử)	có phải không (phải không)
không[1]	nghe không

6.1.1. The question word 'chăng'

Chăng is a question word that is used to express doubt as to whether something has already occurred or not. It follows either an affirmative or negative statement. For example:

$$\text{Q}$$

Qn: (1) a. Ông Ba ốm *chăng*?
       b. Ông Ba không biết tiếng Anh *chăng*?

---

[1] Besides its use as a question word in the Q position, *không* is also used as a negator in the 'Neg.' position (see section 5.3.2.), and as a negator before the question word *ai* 'who' or before an honorific noun in the subject position (see section 4.5.5.).

Trans.: (1) a. *Could it* (*really*) *be that* Mr. Ba was sick?
            (*Lit.*: Mr. Ba sick question word?)
        b. *Could it* (*really*) *be that* Mr. Ba didn't know English?
            (*Lit.*: Mr. Ba no know sound England question word?)

6.1.2. *The question word 'không'*

Không occurs in the Q position at the end of an affirmative statement to change it into a yes-no question. Generally, in a yes-no question with *không*, the emphatic lexeme *có* also occurs, in the 'Neg.' position. But as was stated in Section 5.5. (b), the emphatic lexeme *có* may also occur before a modifier or modifier cluster in the complement position, to show that the emphasis in the question is on the unit or units following *có*. For example:

	Neg.		C	Q
Qn: (2) a. Ông Ba	*có*	nói tiếng Anh		*không?*
b. Ông Ba	*có*	ngủ	ngon	*không?*
c. Ông Ba		ngủ	*có* ngon	*không?*

Trans.: (2) a. *Does* Mr. Ba speak English?
            (*Lit.*: Mr. Ba emphatic lexeme speak sound England question word?)
        b. *Did* Mr. Ba sleep well?
            (*Lit.*: Mr. Ba emphatic lexeme sleep well (delicious) question word?)
        c. *Did* Mr. Ba have *a* (*really*) *good sleep*?
            (*Lit.*: Mr. Ba sleep emphatic lexeme well (delicious) question word?)

When the equative verbid *là* occurs in the verbal position in a yes-no question with *không*, *có phải* occurs in the 'Neg.' position instead of *có*.[2] For example:

	Neg.	V	Q
Qn: (3) a. Ông Ba	*có phải là*	người Mỹ	*không?*
b. Cô Lan	*có phải là*	con bà Hai	*không?*

Trans.: (3) a. *Is* Mr. Ba an American?
            (*Lit.*: Mr. Ba emphatic lexeme is person America question word?)
        b. *Is* Miss Lan Mrs. Hai's daughter?
            (*Lit.*: Miss Lan emphatic lexeme is child Mrs. Hai question word?)

The lexeme *có phải* may also be used in a yes-no question containing a verbid other than the equative verbid *là*. In such a case, the lexeme *có phải* does not occur in the 'Neg.' position but shifts to the 'Em.' position (i.e., the position for emphatic units). The emphasis in the question is then not on the unit following the 'Neg.' sector, but on the whole question. For example:

[2]   Although *có* is not a negator, it is here analyzed as occurring in the 'Neg.' position instead of in a separate 'Em.' (emphatic position) for the following reason: *có* is replaced by *có phải* before the verbid *là* just as the negator *không* is replaced by *không phải* before *là*; both *có phải* and *không phải*, therefore, seem to occupy the same position.

```
            Em.                                    Q
Qn: (4) a.  Có phải hôm qua ông Ba nói tiếng Tàu không?
        b.  Có phải bà Ba mua ba con gà        không?
```

Trans.: (4) a. *Was it true that* Mr. Ba spoke Chinese yesterday?
(*Lit.*: Emphatic lexeme day past Mr. Ba speak sound China question word?)
        b. *Was it true that* Mrs. Ba bought three chickens?
(*Lit.*: Emphatic lexeme Mrs. Ba buy three pre-determiner chicken question word?)

As has been stated, *không* regularly occurs in the Q position and signals a yes-no question. It may do so even in questions containing other question words in the F, E, S, O, or C sectors, but not in questions formed with question words in the I or D sectors. The addition of the question word *không* to a sentence containing another question word changes that question word into a indefinite determiner, an indefinite numeral, or an indefinite pronoun. When *không* is added to a question having another question word in the F or S sector, the emphatic lexeme *có* shifts to the 'Em.' position. The following are examples of yes-no questions with question words in the F, E, S, O, and C sectors:

(1) *With question words in the F position*:

```
            Em.  F                              Q
Qn: (5) a.       Bao giờ  ông Ba về Việt Nam?
        b.  Có  bao giờ   ông Ba về Việt Nam  không?
        c.       Hôm nào ông Ba đi?
        d.  Có  hôm nào ông Ba đi              không?
```

Trans.: (5) a. *When* will Mr. Ba go back to Vietnam?
(*Lit.*: When Mr. Ba return Vietnam?)
        b. *Will* Mr. Ba *ever* go back to Vietnam?
(*Lit.*: Emphatic lexeme ever Mr. Ba return Vietnam question word?)
        c. (*On*) *what* day will Mr. Ba go away?
(*Lit.*: Day which Mr. Ba go?)
        d. *Will* Mr. Ba *ever* go away?
(*Lit.*: Emphatic lexeme day any Mr. Ba go question word?)

(2) *With question words in the E position*:

```
            Neg.                 E        Q
Qn: (6) a. Ông Ba      về Việt Nam bao giờ?
        b. Ông Ba có    về Việt Nam bao giờ  không?
        c. Ông Ba      mua cam      ở đâu?
        d. Ông Ba có    mua cam      ở đâu     không?
```

Trans.: (6) a. *When* did Mr. Ba go back to Vietnam?
         (*Lit.*: Mr. Ba return Vietnam when?)
      b. *Did* Mr. Ba *ever* go back to Vietnam?
         (*Lit.*: Mr. Ba emphatic lexeme return Vietnam ever question word?)
      c. *Where* did Mr. Ba buy oranges?
         (*Lit.*: Mr. Ba buy orange where?)
      d. *Did* Mr. Ba buy oranges *anywhere*?
         (*Lit.*: Mr. Ba emphatic lexeme buy orange anywhere question word?)

(3) *With question words in the S position*:

        Em. S   Q

Qn: (7) a.   Con *gì* đang ăn cỏ?
      b. *Có* con *gì* đang ăn cỏ *không*?
      c.   *Ai*   có xe hơi?
      d. *Có* ai   có xe hơi *không*?

Trans.: (7) a. *What* animal was eating grass?
         (*Lit.*: Animate pre-determiner what in the process of eat grass?)
      b. *Was* there *any* animal eating grass?
         (*Lit.*: Animate pre-determiner any in the process of eat grass question
         word?)
      c. *Who* has a car?
         (*Lit.*: Who have car?)
      d. *Is* there *anyone* (who) has a car?
         (*Lit.*: Emphatic lexeme anyone have car question word?)

(4) *With question words in the O position*:

              Neg.   O Q

Qn: (8) a. Ông Ba   gặp người *nào*?
      b. Ông Ba *có*   gặp người *nào không*?
      c. Ông Ba   học   *gì*?
      d. Ông Ba *có*   học   *gì*   *không*?

Trans.: (8) a. *Whom* did Mr. Ba meet?
         (*Lit.*: Mr. Ba meet person which?)
      b. *Did* Mr. Ba meet *anyone*?
         (*Lit.*: Mr. Ba emphatic lexeme meet person any question word?)
      c. *What* did Mr. Ba study?
         (*Lit.*: Mr. Ba study what?)
      d. Did Mr. Ba study *anything*?
         (*Lit.*: Mr. Ba emphatic lexeme study any question word?)

(5) *With question words in the C position*:

              Neg.   C Q

Qn: (9) a. Ông Ba   đi   *đâu*?

    b. Ông Ba *có*   đi   *đâu không*?
    c. Ông Ba   đi với người *nào*?
    d. Ông Ba *có*   đi với người *nào không*?

Trans.: (9) a. *Where* did Mr. Ba go?
              (*Lit.*: Mr. Ba go where?)
           b. *Did* Mr. Ba go *anywhere*?
              (*Lit.*: Mr. Ba emphatic lexeme go anywhere question word?)
           c. *Whom* did Mr. Ba go with?
              (*Lit.*: Mr. Ba go with person which?)
           d. *Did* Mr. Ba go with *anyone*?
              (*Lit.*: Mr. Ba emphatic lexeme go with person whichever question
              word?)

The examples given above show that the 'yes-or-no' meaning signaled by the presence
of the question word *không* in the Q position seems to override any other kind of
questioning that may be signaled by some other question word occurring in the
F, E, S, O, or C sector. In other words, *không* is a stronger question word than any
other question word that might occur in one of the sectors mentioned above.

6.1.3. *The question word 'à'*

As was stated in the last section, the question word *không* forms yes-no questions
from affirmative statements. To form yes-no questions from negative statements,
Vietnamese speakers use the question word *à*. In addition to being a question word,
à expresses the notion of surprise. For example:

                    Neg.   Q
  Qn: (10) a. Ông Ba *không*   ăn cam   *à*?
           b. Ông Ba *chưa*   về Việt Nam   *à*?
           c. Cô Lan *không phải* là con bà Hai *à*?

Trans.: (10) a. *Didn't* Mr. Ba eat oranges?
               (*Lit.*: Mr. Ba no eat orange question word?)
            b. *Hasn't* Mr. Ba gone back to Vietnam?
               (*Lit.*: Mr. Ba not yet return Vietnam question word?)
            c. *Isn't* Miss Lan Mrs. Hai's daughter?
               (*Lit.*: Miss Lan no is child Mrs. Hai question word?)

6.1.4. *The question words 'chứ', 'nhé', 'nhỉ', 'ư', and 'hả' ('hở', 'hử')*

These question words, when added to statements, change them into questions that
expect confirmation or agreement. For example:

                              Q
  Qn: (11) a. Ông Ba không đi câu cá *hả*?

            b. Cô Lan đẹp   *nhỉ?*

Trans.: (11) a. Mr. Ba didn't go fishing, *did he?*

             (*Lit.*: Mr. Ba no go fish (verbid) fish (noun) question word?)

            b. Miss Lan is beautiful, *isn't she?*

             (*Lit.*: Miss Lan beautiful question word?)

The question word *nhé* is used only when the speaker is addressing the person who is the referent of the subject in the question. For example:

$$Q$$

Qn: (11) c. Ông Ba ăn cam *nhé?*

Trans.: (11) c. *Will* you have an orange, *Mr. Ba?*

             (*Lit.*: Mr. Ba eat orange question word?)

The question words *nhỉ* and *hả* (and the two variants of *hả*, *hở* and *hử*) are regularly added to yes-no questions which have *không* in the Q position, or *chưa* in the D position, or some other question word in the F, E, S, I, O, or C sector. *Nhỉ* and *hả* strengthen the notion of questioning. For example:

                         Q_1 Q_2

Qn: (12) a. Ông Ba có biết tiếng Anh *không nhỉ?*

                      D   Q

            b. Ông Ba về Việt Nam *chưa nhỉ?*

                                Q

            c. *Bao giờ* ông Ba về Việt Nam *hả?*

                           E Q

            d. Ông Ba về Việt Nam hôm *nào nhỉ?*

Trans.: (12) a. *Did* Mr. Ba know English?

             (*Lit.*: Mr. Ba emphatic lexeme know sound England question word question word?)

            b. *Has* Mr. Ba gone back to Vietnam *yet?*

             (*Lit.*: Mr. Ba return Vietnam yet question word?)

            c. *When will* Mr. Ba go back to Vietnam?

             (*Lit.*: When Mr. Ba return Vietnam question word?)

            d. *(On) what* day did Mr. Ba go back to Vietnam?

             (*Lit.*: Mr. Ba return Vietnam day which question word?)

              S   Q

Qn: (12) e. Con *gì* đang ăn cỏ *nhỉ?*

              I   Q

            f. *Sao* ông Ba đi Dalat *hả?*

                    O   Q

            g. Ông Ba gặp *ai*   *hả?*

                         C Q

            h. Ông Ba nói chuyện với *ai nhỉ?*

Trans.: (12) e. *What* animal was eating grass?
    (*Lit*.: Animate pre-determiner what in the process of eat grass question
     word?)
    f. *Why did* Mr. Ba go to Dalat?
     (*Lit*.: Why Mr. Ba go Dalat question word?)
    g. *Whom did* Mr. Ba meet?
     (*Lit*.: Mr. Ba meet who question word?)
    h. *Whom did* Mr. Ba talk to?
     (*Lit*.: Mr. Ba talk with who question word?)

Even negative questions which have become statements as a result of the addition of emphatic lexemes in the D position (as described in sections 5.4. (e) and 5.5. (h)) become questions again with the addition of the question word *à*, *há*, or *nhỉ* in the Q position. For example:

       Neg.   D Q
Qn: (13) a. Ông Ba *không gập ai?*
U: b. Ông Ba *không gập ai cả.*
Qn: c. Ông Ba *không gập ai cả à?*
   d. Ông Ba *không làm gì hết nhỉ?*
   e. Ông Ba *không đi đâu cả hả?*

Trans.: (13) a. *Whom* didn't Mr. Ba meet?
     (*Lit*.: Mr. Ba no meet who?)
    b. Mr. Ba did *not* meet *anyone at all*.
     (*Lit*.: Mr. Ba no meet anyone at all.)
    c. *Didn't* Mr. Ba meet *anyone at all*?
     (*Lit*.: Mr. Ba no meet anyone at all question word?)
    d. *Didn't* Mr. Ba do *anything at all*?
     (*Lit*.: Mr. Ba no do whatever at all question word?)
    e. *Didn't* Mr. Ba go *anywhere at all*?
     (*Lit*.: Mr. Ba no go anywhere at all question word?)

6.1.5. *Tag Questions*

In Vietnamese, tag questions are formed by the addition of the following lexemes to statements:

  có phải không (*or* phải không)
  nghe không

Nghe không is usually used as a tag question following an order, command, or recommendation, while *phải không* and *có phải không* are used as tag questions that ask for confirmation or agreement. For example:

Q

Qn: (14) a. Ông Ba là người Việt Nam, *phải không?*

b. Ông Ba về Việt Nam rồi,   *phải không?*

c. Hoa hồng không đắt lắm,   *có phải không?*

d. Con phải ở nhà,   *nghe không?*

Trans.: (14) a. Mr. Ba is Vietnamese, *isn't he?*

(*Lit.*: Mr. Ba is person Vietnam, tag question word?)

b. Mr. Ba has gone back to Vietnam, *hasn't he?*

(*Lit.*: Mr. Ba return Vietnam already, tag question word?)

c. Roses are not very expensive, *are they?*

(*Lit.*: Flower rose no expensive very, tag question word?)

d. You must stay home, *do you hear?*

(*Lit.*: Child must stay house, tag question word?)

6.1.6. *The Interrogative Coordinator 'Hay'*

The coordinator *hay* (or *hay là*) 'or' functions as a question word when it occurs in the subject, complement or object sector. But when *hay* (or *hay là*) occurs in some other sector, such as, for example, the F or E sector, the sentence in which it occurs will be taken to be either a statement or a question depending on the intonation (in speech) or on the final punctuation (in writing). That is, if a period appears at the end of such a sentence, it will be taken to be a statement, but if it ends in a question mark, it will be taken as a question. For example:

C   C

Qn: (15) a. Bài này *dễ* HAY *khó?* Or: Bài này *dễ* HAY LÀ *khó?*

V O + V O

b. Ông Ba ăn cam HAY ăn táo?

S

c. *Cô Ba* HAY LÀ *cô Mai* sắp đi Pháp?

E

d. Ông Ba sẽ về Việt Nam *ngày mai* HAY LÀ *ngày kia?*

or:

St: Ông Ba sẽ về Việt Nam *ngày mai* HAY LÀ *ngày kia.*

Trans.: (15) a. Is this lesson *easy* OR *difficult?*

(*Lit.*: Lesson this easy or difficult?)

b. Does Mr. Ba *eat oranges* OR *apples?*

(*Lit.*: Mr. Ba eat orange or eat apple?)

c. Is *Miss Ba* OR *Miss Mai* going to France?

(*Lit.*: Miss Ba or Miss Mai immediate later time-relationship particle go France?)

 d. Will Mr. Ba go back to Vietnam *tomorrow* OR *the day after tomorrow*?
  (*Lit.*: Mr. Ba later time-relationship particle return Vietnam day
  tomorrow or day other?)

or:

  Mr. Ba will go back to Vietnam *tomorrow* OR *the day after tomorrow*.
  (*Lit.*: Mr. Ba later time-relationship particle return Vietnam day
  tomorrow or day other.)

To change questions with *hay* or *hay là* into statements, the coordinator *hay* or *hay là* is replaced by the coordinator *hoặc* or *hoặc là* 'or, either', which is repeated before each alternative item. For example:

U: (15) e. Bài này HOẶC LÀ *dễ* HOẶC LÀ *khó*.
  f. Ông Ba HOẶC LÀ *ăn cam* HOẶC LÀ *ăn táo*.

or:

  Ông Ba ăn HOẶC LÀ *cam* HOẶC LÀ *táo*.
  g. HOẶC LÀ *cô Ba* HOẶC LÀ *cô Mai* sắp đi Pháp.

Trans.: (15) e. This lesson is EITHER *easy* OR *difficult*.
  (*Lit.*: Lesson this either easy or difficult.)
  f. Mr. Ba EITHER *ate an orange* OR (*ate*) *an apple*.
  (*Lit.*: Mr. Ba either eat orange or eat apple.)

or:

  Mr. Ba ate EITHER *an orange* OR *an apple*.
  (*Lit.*: Mr. Ba eat either orange or apple.)
  g. EITHER *Miss Ba* OR *Miss Mai* is going to France.
  (*Lit.*: Either Miss Ba or Miss Mai immediate later time-relationship
  particle go France.)

6.1.7. *Similarities and differences between the use of question words in English and Vietnamese*

Yes-no questions in English are most commonly signaled by the occurrence of X words in the shifted $\tilde{X}$ position (see section 2.9. above). The order X-word — subject is referred to as 'inverted order' since in a statement the X word generally follows the subject.[3] Tag questions in English are formed by statements to which have been added appropriate tag-question forms in the Z position.[4] Yes-no questions in Vietnamese, on the other hand, are signaled by the occurrence of the question word *không* in the Q position. In English, shifted X words occur in both affirmative and negative yes-no questions. In Vietnamese, however, the question word *không* occurs only in affirmative yes-no questions. A different question word — the question word *à* — is used in negative yes-no questions.

[3] Robert L. Allen, *A Modern Grammar of Written English* (New York, The Macmillan Company, in press), pp. 325, 330.
[4] *Ibid.*, pp. 325, 329.

Vietnamese also has other question words which are used in the Q position to change statements into questions, and, in certain cases, also to strengthen the notion of questioning. These question words are somewhat similar to tag questions in English, which are formed by adding the appropriate 'tags' to the ends of statements. Vietnamese has, in addition, two special lexemes — (có) *phải không* and *nghe không* — which are added at the ends of statements to form tag questions. But unlike English 'tags', these lexemes keep the same form regardless of the sentences to which they are added. Besides the question words in the Q position, Vietnamese also has other question words, which — unlike the question words in English — do not introduce the questions in which they appear but instead occur in different sectors, namely, in those sectors in which the units answering the questions would occur.

6.2. THE 'EM.' SECTOR

The 'Em.' (or 'emphatic') sector is the position for elements which are shifted from other sectors for the purpose of giving them an emphasis or 'focus' that they would not have if they remained in their normal positions. (In speech, stress also helps to express emphasis.) The 'Em.' sector occurs at the beginning of a sentence; a unit from any one of the following sectors may shift to the 'Em.' sector: the subject, the verbal, the object, the complement, and the negator sectors.

When a unit from the subject position shifts to the 'Em.' position, it is replaced (in the subject position) by a primary or secondary substitute. If the shifted item is itself a substitute, the same substitute is repeated in the empty subject position. The shifted subject is usually but not always followed by the lexeme *thì* or *là* in the I position. For example:

```
              Em.        I   S
U: (16) a. Tôi        thì tôi    chỉ muốn về Việt Nam.
        b. Ông Ba        ông ấy hay đi Dalat lắm.
        c. Con bò ấy    nó     ăn ít cỏ lắm.
```

Trans.: (16) a. *I* only wanted to return to Vietnam.
        (*Lit.*: I then I only want return Vietnam.)
    b. *Mr. Ba* went to Dalat very often.
        (*Lit.*: Mr. Ba Mr. that often go Dalat very.)
    c. *That cow* did not eat much grass.
        (*Lit.*: Animate pre-determiner cow that it eat few grass very.)

Verbids in the verbal position may also shift to the 'Em.' position. The shifted verbid is usually followed by the lexeme *thì* in the I position; the shifted verbid is repeated in the verbal position. For example:

```
              Em. I        V
U: (17) a. Ăn  thì ông Ba ăn  khỏe lắm.
```

   b. *Nói thì* bà Ba *nói* rất nhiều.

Trans.: (17) a. Mr. Ba *has* an enormous appetite.
    (*Lit.*: Eat then Mr. Ba eat healthy very.)
   b. Mrs. Ba *talks* a lot.
    (*Lit.*: Speak then Mrs. Ba speak very much.)

Units in the object position may also shift to the 'Em.' position. There are two types of shifted objects: those that do not force other changes in the sentence, and those that do.

 Objects of the first type remain exactly the same in form when they are shifted to the 'Em.' position. For example:

     Em.   O
 U: (18) a.   Tôi đọc *quyển truyện đó* rồi.
   b. *Quyển truyện đó* tôi đọc   rồi.
     Em. I   O
   c.   Tôi chưa xem *phim này*.
   d. *Phim này thì* tôi chưa xem.

Trans.: (18) a. I have already read *that novel*.
    (*Lit.*: I read book story that already.)
   b. I have already read *that novel*.
    (*Lit.*: Book story that I read already.)
   c. I have not seen *this film*.
    (*Lit.*: I not yet read film this.)
   d. I have not seen *this film*.
    (*Lit.*: Film this then I not yet read.)

Objects of the other type cause certain changes in the sentence in which they occur when they are shifted to the 'Em.' position. There are, for example, objects which contain indefinite numerals expressing the notion of totality. If such an object shifts to the 'Em.' position unchanged, the M_2 lexeme *đều* 'all' must be added to the sentence. Again, when the object position is filled by a question word used as an indefinite determiner (see section 5.4. (e)), either the M_1 lexeme *cũng* 'also' or a negator must be added to the sentence if the object is shifted to the 'Em.' position. (If the sentence is in the negative, the lexeme *cũng* must be added in addition to the negator.) For example:

(a) With an unchanged object:

           O
 U: (19) a.   Ông Ba biết *tất cả mọi thứ*.
    Em. M_2
   b. *Tất cả mọi thứ thì* ông Ba *đều* biết.

		Em.	M₁ Neg.	O	D
c.		Ông Ba	*chẳng* biết *điều gì cả.*		
d.	*Điều gì ông Ba*		*cũng chẳng* biết.		

Trans.: (19) a. Mr. Ba knew *everything.*
    (*Lit.*: Mr. Ba know all thing.)
  b. Mr. Ba knew *everything.*
    (*Lit.*: All all thing then Mr. Ba all know.)
  c. Mr. Ba did *not* know *anything at all.*
    (*Lit.*: Mr. Ba no know reason (thing) whatever at all.)
  d. Mr. Ba did *not* know *anything at all.*
    (*Lit.*: Reason (thing) whatever Mr. Ba also no know.)

(b) With a changed object:

		Em.	M₁ Neg.	O
U: (20) a.		Ông Ba	biết *tất cả mọi điều.*	
b.	*Điều gì ông Ba cũng*		biết.	
or:	c. *Điều gì ông Ba*		*chẳng* biết.	

Trans.: (20) a. Mr. Ba knew *everything.*
    (*Lit.*: Mr. Ba know all all reason (thing).)
  b. Mr. Ba knew *everything.*
    (*Lit.*: Reason (thing) whatever Mr. Ba also know.)
  c. Mr. Ba knew *everything.*
    (*Lit.*: Reason (thing) whatever Mr. Ba no know.)

It should be noted that in all the examples with a shifted object in the 'Em.' position, the object position remains empty.

Both the subject and the object may shift to the 'Em.' position. The subject position may then be left empty or else be filled by a substitute; the object position always remains empty. In the 'Em.' position, the subject unit precedes the object unit. For example:

		Em.	S	M₁	O
U: (21) a.		Ông Ba		biết *tất cả mọi điều.*	
b.	*Ông Ba điều gì ông ấy*		*cũng* biết.	
c.	*Ông Ba điều gì*		*cũng* biết.	

Trans.: (21) a. Mr. Ba knew *everything.*
    (*Lit.*: Mr. Ba know all all reason (thing).)
  b. Mr. Ba knew *everything.*
    (*Lit.*: Mr. Ba reason (thing) whatever Mr. that also know.)
  c. Mr. Ba knew *everything.*
    (*Lit.*: Mr. Ba reason (thing) whatever also know.)

Both the verbid and the object may shift to the 'Em.' position. But if the verbal unit consists of an auxiliary and a verbid, the auxiliary will remain in the verbal position.

The verbid and the object occur in their normal order — that is, with the former preceding the latter — in the 'Em.' position. For example:

	Em.	I	V	O
U: (22) a.		Ông Ba không	*dám làm việc ấy*	đâu.
b.	*Làm việc ấy thì*	ông Ba không	*dám*	đâu.
c.	*Làm việc ấy thì*	ông Ba không	*dám làm*	đâu.

Trans.: (22) a. Mr. Ba does not *dare to do that work* at all.

(*Lit.*: Mr. Ba no dare do work that at all.)

b. Mr. Ba does not *dare to do that work* at all.

(*Lit.*: Do work that then Mr. Ba no dare at all.)

c. Mr. Ba does not *dare to do that work* at all.

(*Lit.*: Do work that then Mr. Ba no dare do at all.)

Units in the complement position may also shift to the 'Em.' position. Such shifted complements are always repeated in the complement position. The lexeme *thì* is usually added immediately following the shifted complement in the 'Em.' position. For example:

U: (23) a.		Bà Ba *đẹp* lắm.
b.	*Đẹp thì*	bà Ba *đẹp* lắm.
c.		Ai cũng muốn *ăn.*
d.	*Ăn thì*	ai cũng muốn *ăn.*

Trans.: (23) a. Mrs. Ba is very *beautiful.*

(*Lit.*: Mrs. Ba beautiful very.)

b. Mrs. Ba is very *beautiful.*

(*Lit.*: Beautiful then Mrs. Ba beautiful very.)

c. Everybody wants *to eat.*

(*Lit.*: Everybody also want eat.)

d. Everybody wants *to eat.*

(*Lit.*: Eat then everybody also want eat.)

As was stated in section 6.1.2., the lexemes *có* and *có phải* may shift from the 'Neg.' sector to the 'Em.' sector in yes-no questions with *không*. When *có phải* is used in such questions with a verbid other than the equative verbid *là*, it always occurs in the 'Em.' position. For example:

	Em.	S	Neg.	V	Q
Qn: (24) a.		Con gì	*có*	ăn cỏ	*không?*
b.	*Có*	con gì		ăn cỏ	*không?*
c.		Ông Ba	*có phải là*	người Mỹ	*không?*
d.	*Có phải*	ông Ba		*là* người Mỹ	*không?*
e.		Bà Ba	*có*	mua ba con gà	*không?*
f.	*Có phải*	bà Ba		mua ba con gà	*không?*

Trans.: (24) a. Did that animal *eat grass*?

          (*Lit.*: Animate pre-determiner whatever emphatic lexeme eat grass question word?)

      b. *Was there any animal* eating grass?

          (*Lit.*: Emphatic lexeme animate pre-determiner whatever eat grass question word?)

      c. Is Mr. Ba *an American*?

          (*Lit.*: Mr. Ba emphatic lexeme is person America question word?)

      d. Is *Mr. Ba* an American?

          (*Lit.*: Emphatic lexeme Mr. Ba is person America question word?)

      e. Did Mrs. Ba *buy three chickens*?

          (*Lit.*: Mrs. Ba emphatic lexeme buy three animate pre-determiner chicken question word?)

      f. Did *Mrs. Ba* buy three chickens?

          (*Lit.*: Emphatic lexeme Mrs. Ba buy three animate pre-determiner chicken question word?)

6.2.1. *Similarities and differences between the expression of emphasis in English and Vietnamese*

In spoken English, emphasis is most commonly expressed by means of stress (which is often suggested in writing by underlining or italics). The entire predication expressed by the predicate of a sentence can be made emphatic — or can be emphatically denied — by stressing the X word. (In the absence of any other X word, either *do*, *does*, or *did* is supplied to carry this emphatic stress.)

Stress is also used in spoken Vietnamese to emphasize one or another unit in a sentence. But where an English speaker emphasizes (or emphatically denies) the predication expressed by the predicate of a sentence by stressing the X word, a Vietnamese speaker expresses such emphasis by inserting (and stressing) the emphatic lexeme *có*. This lexeme normally occurs in the 'Neg.' position, although it may occur in the C position before a modifier or a modifier cluster in yes-no questions. (See section 5.3.2.).

Unlike English in which units remain in their normal positions even when they receive emphatic stress, Vietnamese has a separate position, the 'Em.' sector, to which almost any unit that a speaker wishes to emphasize can be shifted. (Items occurring in the 'Em.' position regularly receive emphatic stress.)

All the sectors that occur in a Vietnamese sentence have now been described and contrasted with the equivalent sectors in English sentences. (It should be remembered that sectors are merely POTENTIAL positions for different kinds of units. Almost any sector may remain vacant in a given sentence.) There remain two sectors in English that have no equivalents in Vietnamese. These are the two PP sectors, which are the positions for postponed subjects and postponed objects. (See section 2.16.7.). Subjects and objects in Vietnamese can be shifted only to the 'Em.' position (for emphasis), not to any other position, although C and B units may be shifted to the shifted Č and shifted B̃ positions. (See sections 4.5.7., and 5.4.1., and 6.2.).

6.3. MINOR SENTENCES

The discussion so far has dealt only with major sentences. Minor sentences occur more in spoken and informal Vietnamese than in formal written Vietnamese. Some of the most common types of minor sentences are described below.

Commands and requests make up the group of minor sentences most frequently used in spoken Vietnamese. (See sections 5.2. and 5.3.3.). Such sentences occur both with and without subjects. When they have subjects, they usually contain also one of the negators *đừng* and *chớ*, or the modal auxiliary *hãy*. For example:

> (25) a. Hãy đợi một chút nữa.
>   b. Mở cửa ra.
>   c. Xin Trời phù hộ chúng ta.
>   d. Chớ đi nhanh quá.
>   S
>   e. *Con* đừng thức khuya quá.
>   f. *Con* hãy đợi một chút nữa.

Trans.: (25) a. Let's wait for a little while longer.
             (*Lit.*: Let's wait one little more.)
         b. Open the door.
             (*Lit.*: Open door out.)
         c. May God protect us.
             (*Lit.*: Beg God protect us.)
         d. Don't go too fast.
             (*Lit.*: No go fast very.)
         e. Don't *you* stay up too late.
             (*Lit.*: *Child* no stay up late very.)
         f. *You* should wait a little while longer.
             (*Lit.*: *Child* let's wait one little more.)

'Half-questions' — that is, questions containing no subjects and possibly also no verbids — may also be classified as minor sentences. For example:

	O D		V Q
(26) a.	Cơm chưa?	c.	Ăn không?
	V C Z		C
b.	Đi đâu đấy?	d.	Đẹp thế nào?

Trans.: (26) a. Eaten yet?

            (*Lit*.: Eat question word?)

        b. Where (are you) going?

            (*Lit*.: Go where final particle?)

        c. Want to eat?

            (*Lit*.: Eat question word?)

        d. How beautiful (is that lady)?

            (*Lit*.: Beautiful how?)

Such half-questions consist of units occurring in various sectors of the predicatid. They may be changed into major sentences by the addition of subjects (or by the addition of subjects and verbids). For example:

                             S   V Q

(1)   Minor sentence: Ăn không?

        Major sentence: Anh ăn không?

                             S   C

(2)   Minor sentence: Đẹp thế nào?

        Major sentence: Cô ấy đẹp thế nào?

                         S   V O   D

(3)   Minor sentence: Cơm chưa?

        Major sentence: Anh ăn cơm chưa?

Trans.: (1)   Want to eat?

               (*Lit*.: Eat question word?)

               Do you want to eat?

               (*Lit*.: Older brother eat question word?)

      (2)   How beautiful (is that lady)?

               (*Lit*.: Beautiful how?)

               How beautiful is that lady?

               (*Lit*.: Miss that beautiful how?)

      (3)   Eaten yet?

               (*Lit*.: Rice question word?)

               Have you eaten yet?

               (*Lit*.: Older brother eat rice question word?)

Besides the half-questions described above, there are also half-questions consisting only of question words (or question word units) occurring in the subject, object, or complement position followed by Z lexemes. For example:

            S/O/C Z

      (27) a. *Ai*   đấy?

          b. Con *gì* thế?

Trans.: (27) a. *Who* is it?

            (*Lit*.: Who final particle?)

        b. *What* (kind of) animal is it?

           (*Lit.*: Animate pre-determiner what final particle?)

Questions 27a and 27b may be changed into major sentences by the addition of subjects and verbids. For example:

                            S/O/C Z

(1)   Minor sentence: *Ai*   đẩy?

                           S TR V   Z

        Major sentences: *Ai* đang cười *đẩy?*

                           S   V   O Z

                           Anh gập *ai đẩy?*

                           S   V C Z

                         Người kia là *ai đẩy?*

                             S/O/C Z

(2)   Minor sentence: *Con gì* thế?

                           S   TR V O Z

        Major sentences: *Con gì* đang ăn cỏ *thế?*

                           S   V   O   Z

                         Anh mua *con gì thế?*

                         S V C   Z

                         Vện là *con gì thế?*

Trans.: (1)   *Who* is it?

               (*Lit.*: Who final particle?)

               Who was laughing?

               (*Lit.*: Who in the process of laugh final particle?)

               Whom did you meet?

               (*Lit.*: Older brother meet who final particle?)

               Who was that person?

               (*Lit.*: Person there is who final particle?)

    (2)   *What* (kind of) animal is it?

               (*Lit.*: Animate pre-determiner what final particle?)

               What animal was eating grass?

               (*Lit.*: Animate pre-determiner what in the process process of eat grass final particle?)

               What (kind of) animal did you buy?

               (*Lit.*: Older brother buy animate pre-determiner final particle?)

               What (kind of) animal is Vện?

               (*Lit.*: Ven is animate pre-determiner what final particle?)

There is one question formula which cannot be changed into a major sentence and which is used both in formal written Vietnamese and in spoken informal Vietnamese to ask for the time. This formula consists of the noun cluster *mấy giờ* 'what time' followed by the lexeme *rồi* 'already'. The answer to such a question commonly consists of a numeral indicating the time asked, followed by *rồi*. For example:

Question: *Mấy giờ rồi?*
Answer: *Ba giờ   rồi.*

Trans.:   *What time is it?*
(*Lit.*: What hour already?)
It is already three o'clock.
(*Lit.*: Three hour already.)

One may also ask for the time by means of the question in 28a, below, but such a question is rarely used in Vietnamese unless one wants to compare the time of one's own watch with that of someone else's:

                        S   V O
U: (28) a. Question: Đồng hồ anh chỉ *mấy giờ?*
       b. Answer: Đồng hồ tôi chỉ *ba giờ.*

Trans.: (28) a. *What time* does your watch indicate?
                (*Lit.*: Watch older brother indicate what hour?)
             b. My watch indicates *three o'clock.*
                (*Lit.*: Watch I indicate three hour.)

One other type of minor sentence that should be mentioned is the two-part sentence each part of which is introduced by the lexeme *càng* followed by a modifier or by a clausid. This type of minor sentence is similar to the two-part sentences in English introduced by *the ... the ...*, as in *The more, the merrier*. For example:

(29) a. *Càng* đông *càng* vui.
     b. *Càng* nhiều *càng* tốt.
     c. *Càng* đọc thơ tôi *càng* nhớ nhà.

Trans.: (29) a. The more, the merrier.
                (*Lit.*: The more crowded the more gay.)
             b. The more, the better.
                (*Lit.*: The more plenty the more good.)
             c. The more letters I read, the more homesick I feel.
                (*Lit.*: The more read letter I the more miss home.)

7

CONCLUSION

7.1. RECAPITULATION

The description of Vietnamese presented in the preceding chapters shows that there are both similarities and differences between English and Vietnamese on every level of analysis.

In both languages, the positions in which functional units occur relative to each other prove to be the most important grammatical signals.

Most of the important sectors occurring on the four top levels in a sentence — that is to say, the S, V, O, B, C, F, and E sectors — exist in both languages, and the order of occurrence of these sectors is approximately the same in both English and Vietnamese.

According to Allen, English sentences can be classified into various 'patterns' on the basis of the kinds of units that may occur in the sectors in the predicate-nucleus that is, in the sectors $V + \tilde{C} + \tilde{B} + O + B + C$.[1] Taking into consideration the fact that any one or more of these sectors may be vacant in a given sentence, Allen is able to list fourteen sentence patterns for English.[2] He also states that a larger number of 'patterns' could be identified if one were to carry the classification further on the basis of the kinds of units that may fill the object and complement sectors appearing in some of the basic patterns.[3] Following Allen's method of classification, the present writer has found eleven 'basic' sentence patterns for Vietnamese:

(1) V

(2) C

(3) V + O

(4) V + B

(5) V + C

(6) V + $\tilde{C}$ + O

(7) V + $\tilde{B}$ + O

(8) V + $\tilde{B}$ + $\tilde{C}$ + O

(9) V + O + B

(10) V + O + C

(11) V + O + B + C

[1] Robert L. Allen, *A Modern Grammar of Written English* (New York, The Macmillan Company, in press), pp. 611-612.

[2] *Ibid.*, p. 612.

[3] *Ibid.*

Of these eleven patterns, ten are similar to ten of the patterns that Allen has identified as English patterns. Pattern 8, however, does not occur in English (although English does have the pattern $V + \tilde{C} + \tilde{B} + O$).

But aside from these similarities, there exist sectors in English that do not have any equivalent in Vietnamese, and also sectors in Vietnamese that do not have any equivalent in English. Moreover, even in the case of sectors that occur in both English and Vietnamese, not all the units or constructions that fill such sectors are the same in both languages.

On the clause level, included clausids and non-included clausids occur in both English and Vietnamese. The order of units within such clausids is the same for each language as the order found in its sentences. Since time-orientation is important in English, one must distinguish in that language between constructions that show time-orientation (such as clauses and predicates) and those that do not (such as clausids and predicatids). Every major sentence in English must include at least one clause since every major sentence must be oriented with relation to time. In Vietnamese, however, time-orientation is never expressed by a verb form. Thus Vietnamese has only clausids and predicatids. Clausids function in the S, O, C, F, and E sectors — and as adjectivals within noun clusters — in Vietnamese, as do clauses in English, although clausids in English function only in the S, O, F, and E sectors.

A phrase in both English and Vietnamese consists of an introducer or preposition followed by an object. This object may consist of either a noun cluster, a verbid, or a predicatid (or even, in English, of a clause or a clausid). In both languages, a phrase may occur in the F, E, C, and D sectors (in the S sector also in English), and may function as an adjectival within a noun cluster. The chief differences between English and Vietnamese on this level are to be found in the kinds of units that make up the object of a preposition, and in the order of occurrence of such units.

A noun cluster in both English and Vietnamese consists of a noun functioning as a nucleus preceded and/or followed by modifiers. Similarly, a verb or verbid cluster consists of a verb or verbid functioning as a nucleus preceded by auxiliaries; an adverb cluster consists of an adverb functioning as a nucleus preceded by a modi-modifier; and an adjective cluster in English — and a modifier cluster in Vietnamese — consists of an adjective or modifier functioning as a nucleus preceded and/or followed by modi-modifiers. However, the kinds of modifiers that occur within clusters — and the order in which they occur — are not the same in English and Vietnamese.

Both English and Vietnamese have listable and non-listable lexemes. The class to which a lexeme belongs is identified by the position(s) in which the lexeme occurs in higher-level constructions or units — that is, its function and word class are determined by its occurrence before or after other kinds of words or units on a higher level. Both English and Vietnamese use other grammatical devices in addition to position to show certain grammatical relationships. Vietnamese makes much use of listable lexemes, especially of those called 'particles' in this study; English makes use of listable lexemes, too, but it also makes use of inflections, which Vietnamese lacks.

While English verbs inflect for time, Vietnamese verbids do not. While different kinds of time are expressed in English by different forms of the verbs and by auxiliaries as well as by time expressions, they are expressed in Vietnamese by time-relationship particles, by time-expressions, and by the context.

While number is expressed by inflections in English, it is expressed by plural particles in Vietnamese. Furthermore, its expression is obligatory in English, but optional in Vietnamese. The necessity for agreement between a subject and its verb or between a pronoun and its antecedent causes difficulties for many students learning English, but Vietnamese has no such problem since all Vietnamese words are invariable.

Nouns in English are commonly classified as count nouns, mass nouns, or proper nouns. To this classification Vietnamese adds that of animate nouns versus inanimate nouns. As a result, the use of determiners in Vietnamese differs from the use of determiners in English. Again, in Vietnamese the relative age, sex, and social status of speaker and listener plays an important part in the selection of nouns of address, whereas English speakers largely ignore such distinctions.

While adjectives in English regularly occur only within noun clusters or in the C position, modifiers in Vietnamese, besides occurring within noun clusters and in the C position, also fill the M_2 or middle adverb position.

In both English and Vietnamese, a higher-level unit such as a clause or clausid, predicate or predicatid, or phrase, may function as part of a unit on the same level or on a lower level, and a lower-level unit may function as part of a unit on a higher level.

7.2. SUGGESTIONS FOR FURTHER STUDIES

This study has been an exploratory attempt at classifying the units which occur on different syntactical levels in Vietnamese, at stating the order in which they normally occur, and at contrasting the arrangements and functions of such units with the arrangements and functions of corresponding units in English. The study has been limited to the analysis of grammatical units from the sentence level down to the word level. No attempt has been made to analyze units on levels higher than the sentence level (such, for example, as the paragraph), nor has any attempt been made to analyze units on levels lower than the word level. Intonation has also been ignored in this study.

7.3. SUGGESTIONS FOR TEACHING AND FOR THE PREPARATION OF MATERIALS

As was stated above, there are many differences between English and Vietnamese, as well as many similarities. It is the hypothesis of many linguists and teachers that these differences inevitably interfere with the attempts of Vietnamese students to learn English. A corollary to this hypothesis is that in order to learn English effectively, students need not only well-trained teachers but especially materials that have been based on an accurate, systematic contrastive analysis of the two languages.

This study has been attempted to present just such an analysis. It is hoped that, from the results of this study, a teacher may be able to predict those areas or details of English structure which will cause the most difficulty for Vietnamese students. By noting the degree of difference between an English pattern and the corresponding Vietnamese pattern, a teacher may be able to organize his materials so as to start with the least troublesome patterns and from there to move gradually to the more troublesome ones. Structural patterns that are similar in both languages should probably be introduced at an earlier stage since they will be easy to learn and will require little re-learning. Those patterns that are dissimilar should be introduced at a later stage since they will be more difficult to learn. The range of differences must be considered not only on one level, but on different levels, from the sentence level down to the word level.

The chief emphasis in this study has been on the positions in which functional units occur on the different grammatical levels of English and Vietnamese. But other grammatical devices such as the use of listable lexemes and of inflections have also been taken into consideration. Considerable attention has also been devoted to the similarities and differences between statement patterns and question patterns in English and Vietnamese.

It is hoped that the description of Vietnamese presented in this study — and the comparison of the structure of Vietnamese sentences with that of English sentences — will be helpful not only to English teachers in Vietnam in their preparation of teaching materials and in their classroom teaching, but also to advanced Vietnamese students who are studying English, and even, perhaps to non-speakers of Vietnamese who are trying to learn Vietnamese.

BIBLIOGRAPHY

1. BOOKS AND ARTICLES ON LANGUAGE AND LINGUISTICS

1.1. *Books*

Allen, Harold B. (ed.), *Readings in Applied English Linguistics* (New York, Appleton-Century-Crofts, 1958).

Bally, Charles, *Linguistique générale et linguistique française*, 2nd ed., revised (Berne, A. Francke, 1944).

Black, Max, *Language and Philosophy: Studies in Method* (Ithaca, N.Y., Cornell University Press, 1940).

Bloch, Bernard, and Trager, George L., *Outline of Linguistic Analysis* (Baltimore, Md., Linguistic Society of America, 1942).

Bloomfield, Leonard, *Language* (New York, Henry Holt and Company, 1933).

Boas, Franz, *Race, Language, and Culture* (New York, The Macmillan Company, 1940).

Carroll, John B., *The Study of Language: A Survey of Linguistics and Related Disciplines in America* (Cambridge, Mass., Harvard University Press, 1955).

Chomsky, Noam, *Syntactic Structures* ('s-Gravenhage, Mouton and Company, 1957).

de Saussure, Ferdinand, *Cours de linguistique générale*, edited posthumously by Charles Bally and Albert Séchehaye with the collaboration of Albert Riedlinger, 4th edition (Paris, Payot, 1949).

Elson, Benjamin, and Pickett, Velma B., *Beginning Morphology-Syntax* (Santa Ana, Calif., Summer Institute of Linguistics, 1960).

——, *An Introduction to Morphology and Syntax* (Santa Ana, Calif., Summer Institute of Linguistics, 1964).

Gleason, H. A., Jr., *An Introduction to Descriptive Linguistics* (New York, Henry Holt and Company, 1955).

——, *An Introduction to Descriptive Linguistics*, revised edition (New York, Holt, Rinehart and Winston, 1961).

Graff, Willem L., *Language and Languages: An Introduction to Linguistics* (New York, D. Appleton and Company, 1932).

Gray, Louis H., *Foundations of Language* (New York, The Macmillan Company, 1939).

Greenberg, Joseph H., *Essays in Linguistics* (Chicago, The University of Chicago Press, 1957).

Hall, Edward T., *The Silent Language* (Garden City, N.Y., Doubleday and Company, Inc., 1959).

Hall, Robert A., Jr., *Leave Your Language Alone!* (Ithaca, N.Y., Linguistica, 1950).

——, *Linguistics and Your Language*, 2nd revised edition of *Leave Your Language Alone!* (Garden City, N.Y., Doubleday and Company, 1960).

Harris, Zellig S., *Methods in Structural Linguistics* (Chicago, The University of Chicago Press, 1951).

——, *Structural Linguistics*, formerly *Methods in Structural Linguistics* (Chicago, University of Chicago Press, 1960).

Hill, Archibald A., *Introduction to Linguistic Structures* (New York, Harcourt, Brace and Company, 1958).

Hockett, Charles F., *A Course in Modern Linguistics* (New York, The Macmillan Company, 1958).

Jakobson, Roman, *Shifters, Verbal Categories, and the Russian Verb*. (Cambridge, Mass., Department of Slavic Languages and Literature, Harvard University, 1957).

Jespersen, Otto, *The Philosophy of Grammar* (London, George Allen and Unwin, 1924).

——, *The System of Grammar* (London, George Allen and Unwin, 1933).

——, *Analytic Syntax* (Copenhagen, Levin and Munksgaard, Ejnar Munksgaard, 1937).

——, *Language, Its Nature, Development and Origin* (London, George Allen and Unwin, 1952).

Joos, Martin (ed.), *Readings in Linguistics: The Development of Descriptive Linguistics in America Since 1925* (Washington, D.C., American Council of Learned Societies, 1957).

Meillet, [A]ntoine, *Linguistique historique et linguistique générale*, 2 vols. (Paris, La Société de Linguistique de Paris, 1921, 1936).

Nida, Eugene A., *Linguistic Interludes* (Glendale, Calif., Summer Institute of Linguistics, 1947).

——, *An Outline of Descriptive Syntax* (Glendale, Calif., Summer Institute of Linguistics, 1951). (Mimeographed.)

Pickett, Velma, *An Introduction to the Study of Grammatical Structure* (Glendale, Calif., Summer Institute of Linguistics, 1956).

Pike, Kenneth L., *Language in Relation to a Unified Theory of the Structure of Human Behavior*, preliminary edition, 3 vols. (Glendale, Calif., Summer Institute of Linguistics, 1954, 1955, 1960).

Sapir, Edward, *Language: An Introduction to the Study of Speech* (New York, Harcourt, Brace and Company, 1921). (Reprinted as a Harvest Book, 1949).

Sturtevant, Edgar H., *An Introduction to Linguistic Science* (New Haven, Yale University Press, 1949).

Trager, George L., *The Field of Linguistics* (Studies in Linguistics, Occasional Papers, No. 1, 1949).

Weinreich, Uriel, *Languages in Contact: Findings and Problems* (New York, Linguistic Circle of New York, 1953).

Whorf, Benjamin Lee, *Collected Papers on Metalinguistics* (Washington, D.C., Foreign Service Institute, Department of State, 1952).

——, *Language, Thought, and Reality: Selected Writings of Benjamin Lee Whorf*, edited and with an introduction by John B. Carroll, foreword by Stuart Chase (Cambridge and New York, The Technology Press of Massachusetts Institute of Technology and John Wiley and Sons, 1956).

1.2. *Articles*

Bazell, C. E., "On Form and Function", *Journal of English and Germanic Philology*, XXXVII (1938), 329-331.

——, "On the Problem of the Morpheme", *Archivum Linguisticum*, I (1949), 1-15.

Bloch, Bernard, "Contrast", *Language*, XXIX (1953), 59-62.

——, "Linguistic Structure and Linguistic Analysis", *Monograph Series on Languages and Linguistics*, No. 4, pp. 40-44. (Washington, D.C., Georgetown University Press, 1953).

Bloomfield, Leonard, "Language or Ideas?", *Language*, XII (1936), 89-95.

——, "A Set of Postulates for the Science of Language", *Language*, II (1926), 153-164.

Boas, Franz, "Language", in *General Anthropology*, edited by Franz Boas (Boston, D. C. Heath and Company, 1938).

Bolinger, Dwight L., "On Defining the Morpheme", *Word*, IV (1948), 18-23.

Cassirer, Ernst A., "Structuralism in Modern Linguistics", *Word*, I (1945), 99-120.

Chatman, Seymour, "Immediate Constituents and Expansion Analysis", *Word*, XI (1955), 377-385.

Collinson, W. E., "Some Recent Trends in Linguistic Theory with Special Reference to Syntactics", *Lingua*, I (1948), 306-332.

Dykstra, Gerald, "Perspective on the Teacher's Use of Contrast", *Language Learning*, VI (1956), 1-6.

Fowler, Murray. Review of Zellig Harris, *Methods in Structural Linguistics*, in *Language*, XXVIII (1952), 504-509.

Francis, W. Nelson, "An Interim Syntax for the Classroom", *Monograph Series on Languages and Linguistics*, No. 9, pp. 39-47 (Washington, D.C., Georgetown University Press, 1957).

Fries, Charles C., "Implications of Modern Linguistic Science", *College English*, VIII (1947), 314-320.

——, "Meaning and Linguistic Analysis", *Language*, XXX (1954), 57-68.

——, "Linguistic Science and the Teaching of English", in *Perspectives on English*, edited by Robert C. Pooley, pp. 135-155 (New York, Appleton-Century-Crofts, 1960).

——, "Advances in Linguistics", *College English*, XXIII (1961), 30-37.

Halliday, M. A. K., "Some Aspects of Systematic Description and Comparison in Grammatical Analysis", in *Studies in Linguistic Analysis*, Special Volume of the Philological Society, pp. 54-67. (Oxford, Basil Blackwell, 1957).

Harris, Zellig, "Morpheme Alternants in Linguistic Analysis", *Language*, XVIII (1942), 169-180.

——, "Discontinuous Morphemes", *Language*, XXI (1945), 121-127.

——, "From Morpheme to Utterance", *Language*, XXII (1946), 161-183.

——, "Distributional Structure", *Word*, X (1954), 146-162.

——, "From Phoneme to Morpheme", *Language*, XXI (1955), 190-222.

Hatcher, Anna Granville, "Syntax and the Sentence", *Word*, XII (1956), 234-250.

Hill, Leslie A., "Form-Classes and Sub-Classes", *Language Learning*, VIII (1958), 5-13.

Hjelmslev, Louis, "Structural Analysis of Language", *Studia Linguistica*, I (1947), 69-78.

——, "La stratification du language", *Word*, X (1954), 163-188.

Hockett, Charles F., "Problems of Morphemic Analysis", *Language*, XXIII (1947), 321-343.

——, "Two Models of Grammatical Description", *Word*, X (1954), 210-234.

——, "Linguistic Elements and Their Relations", *Language*, XXXVII (1961), 29-53.

Jespersen, Otto, "The System of Grammar", in his *Linguistica: Selected Papers in English, French, and German*, pp. 304-345 (Copenhagen, Levin and Munksgaard, 1933).

Joos, Martin, "Description of Language Design", *Journal of the Acoustical Society of America*, XXII (1950), 701-708.

Lehmann, W. P., "Linguistics and the Study of Language", *Texas Quarterly*, II (1959), 23-36.

Lloyd, Donald J., "The Uses of Structure and the Structure of Usage", *The English Record*, VI (1955), 41-46.

Longacre, Robert E., "String Constituent Analysis", *Language*, XXXVI (1960), 63-88.

Lotz, John, "On Language and Culture", *International Journal of American Linguistics*, XXI (1955), 187-189.

Martinet, André, "Elements of a Functional Syntax", *Word*, XVI (1960), 1-10.

Mathesius, Vilem, "On Some Problems of the Systematic Analysis of Grammar", *Travaux du Cercle Linguistique de Prague*, No. 6 (1936), 95-107.

Nida, Eugene A., "The Analysis of Grammatical Constituents", *Language*, XXIV (1948), 168-177.

Pike, Kenneth L., "Taxemes and Immediate Constituents", *Language*, XIX (1943), 65-82.

——, "Grammemic Theory", *General Linguistics*, II (1957), 35-41.

——, "Grammemic Theory in Reference to Restricted Problems of Morpheme Classes", *International Journal of American Linguistics*, XXIII (1957), 119-128.

——, "On Tagmemes, Née Gramemes", *International Journal of American Linguistics*, XXIV (1958), 273-292.

Voegelin, C. F., "Linguistics Without Meaning and Culture Without Words", *Word*, V (1949), 36-42.

Wells, Rulon S., "Immediate Constituents", *Language*, XXIII (1946), 81-117.

——, "Meaning and Use", *Word*, X (1954), 235-250.

Ullmann, S., "Word-Form and Word-Meaning", *Archivum Linguisticum*, I (1949), 126-139.

2. BOOKS, OTHER STUDIES, AND ARTICLES ON ENGLISH

2.1. *Books*

Allen, Robert L., *The Verb System of Present-Day American English* (The Hague, Mouton and Company, 1966).

——, *A Modern Grammar of Written English* (New York, The Macmillan Company, in press).

Baugh, Albert C., *A History of the English Language*, 2nd edition (New York, Appleton-Century-Crofts, 1957).

Bryant, Margaret, *A Functional English Grammar* (Boston, D. C. Heath and Company, 1945).

Brown, Dona Worrall, Brown, Wallace C., and Bailey, Dudley, *Form in Modern English* (New York, Oxford University Press, 1958).

Christophersen, Paul, *The Articles: A Study of Their Theory and Use in English* (Copenhagen, Ejnar Munksgaard, 1939).

Curme, George O., *Syntax*, Vol. III of *A Grammar of the English Language* (Boston, D. C. Heath and Company, 1931).

——, *Parts of Speech and Accidence*, Vol. II of *A Grammar of the English Language* by Hans Kurath (Vol. I) and George O. Curme (Vols. II and III), (Boston, D. C. Heath and Company, 1935).

Francis, W. Nelson, *The Structure of American English* (New York, The Ronald Press Company, 1958).

Fries, Charles C., *American English Grammar: The Grammatical Structure of Present-Day American English with Especial Reference to Social Differences or Class Dialects* (New York, D. Appleton-Century-Crofts, Inc., 1940).

——, *The Structure of English: An Introduction to the Construction of English Sentences* (New York, Harcourt, Brace and Company, 1952).

Grattan, J. H. G., and Gurrey, P., *Our Living Language* (London, Thomas Nelson and Sons, 1925).

Hill, Archibald A., *Introduction to Linguistic Structures: From Sound to Sentence in English* (New York, Harcourt, Brace and Company, 1958).

Hook, J. N., and Mathews, E. G., *Modern American Grammar and Usage* (New York, The Ronald Press Company, 1956).

Jespersen, Otto, *Essentials of English Grammar* (New York, Henry Holt and Company, 1933).

——, *A Modern English Grammar on Historical Principles*, 7 vols. (Copenhagen, Ejnar Munksgaard, 1909-1949).

——, *Growth and Structure of the English Language*, 9th edition, Anchor Book (Garden City, N.Y., Doubleday and Company, 1955).

Kennedy, Arthur G., *Current English: A Study of Present-Day Usages and Tendencies, Including Pronunciation, Spelling, Grammatical Practice, Word-Coining, and the Shifting of Meanings* (Boston, Ginn and Company, 1935).

Kittredge, George Lyman, and Farley, Frank Edgar, *An Advanced English Grammar with Exercises* (Boston, Ginn and Company, 1913).

Krapp, George P., *Modern English: Its Growth and Present Use* (New York, Charles Scribner's Sons, 1909).

Kruisinga, E., *A Handbook of Present-day English*, 5th edition, 4 vols. (Groningen, P. Noordhoff, 1931-1932).

Lloyd, Donald J., and Warfel, Harry R., *American English in Its Cultural Setting* (New York, Alfred A. Knopf, 1956).

Long, Ralph B., *The Sentence and Its Parts: A Grammar of Contemporary English* (Chicago, The University of Chicago Press, 1961).

Marckwardt, Albert H., *Introduction to the English Language* (Toronto and New York, Oxford University Press, 1942).

——, *American English* (New York, Oxford University Press, 1958).

Nida, Eugene A., *A Synopsis of English Syntax* (Norman, Oklahoma, Summer Institute of Linguistics, 1960).

Onions, C. T., *An Advanced English Syntax* (New York, The Macmillan Company, 1911).

Palmer, Harold E., *A Grammar of Spoken English on a Strictly Phonetic Basis*, 2nd edition, revised by Harold E. Palmer and F. C. Blandford. (Cambridge, England, W. Heffer and Sons, 1939). (1st edition: 1924).

Poutsma, H., *A Grammar of Late Modern English for the Use of Continental, Especially Dutch, Students*, 5 vols. (Groningen, P. Noordhoff, 1904-1916).

Roberts, Paul, *Understanding Grammar* (New York, Harper and Brothers, 1954).

——, *Patterns of English* (New York, Harcourt, Brace and Company, 1956).

——, *Understanding English* (New York, Harper and Brothers, 1958).

——, *English Sentences* (New York, Harcourt, Brace and World, 1962).

——, *English Syntax*, alternate edition (New York, Harcourt, Brace and World, Inc., 1964).

Robertson, Stuart, *The Development of Modern English*, 2nd edition, revised by Frederic G. Cassidy (Englewood Cliffs, N.J., Prentice-Hall, inc., 1954).

Sledd, James, *A Short Introduction to English Grammar* (Chicago, Scott, Foresman and Company, 1959).

Sørensen, Holger Steen, *Word-Classes in Modern English* (Copenhagen, G. E. C. Gad, 1958).

Sweet, Henry, *A New English Grammar, Logical and Historical*, 2 vols. (Oxford, The Clarendon Press, 1892, 1898).

Trager, George L., and Smith, Henry Lee, Jr., *An Outline of English Structure* (= *Studies in Linguistics, Occasional Papers*, 3), (Norman, Oklahoma, Battenburg Press, 1951).

Whitehall, Harold, *Structural Essentials of English* (New York, Harcourt, Brace and Company, 1956).

Zandwoort, R. W., *A Handbook of English Grammar*, unilingual edition, third impression with minor corrections (London, Longmans, Green and Company, 1960).

2.2. *Other Studies and Articles*

Allen, Robert L., "The Classification of English Substitute Words", *General Linguistics*, V (1961), 7-20.

——, *Lecture Notes on Sector Analysis* (Course No. TL 4102), (New York, N.Y., Teachers College, Columbia University, Spring Session, 1965).

Barritt, Carlyle Westbrook, "The Order Classes of Modifiers in English" (Unpublished doctoral dissertation, The University of Virginia, Charlottesville, 1952).

Cartledge, H. A., "The Articles in English", *English Language Teaching*, XIV (1960), 107-117.

Chatman, Seymour, Review of Paul Roberts, *Patterns of English*, in *Language Learning*, VII (1956-1957), 143-154.

Crymes, Ruth, "Some Systems of Substitution Correlations in Modern American English" (Unpublished doctoral dissertation, Teachers College, Columbia University, New York, N.Y., 1965).

El-Araby, Salah Abdel Megid, "A Taxonomy of Adverbial Units in Contemporary American English with Special Emphasis on Their Order in Post-Verbal Positions" (Unpublished doctoral dissertation, Teachers College, Columbia University, New York, N.Y., 1963).

Greene, Olive, "The Problem of the Article in the Teaching and Learning of English as a Foreign Language" (Unpublished Master's thesis, The Kennedy School of Missions of the Hartford Seminary Foundation, Hartford, Connecticut, 1957).

Hatcher, Anna Granville, "An Introduction to the Analysis of English Noun Compounds", *Word*, XVI (1960), 356-373.

Hungerford, Harlan M., "The Verb-Head Construction and Its Modificational Patterns in Present-Day English with Special Reference to the Marked Infinitive and Single Word Verbs" (Unpublished doctoral dissertation, University of Michigan, Ann Arbor, Michigan, 1949).

Lees, R. B., "A Multiple Ambiguous Adjectival Construction in English", *Language*, XXXVI (1960), 207-221.

Long, Ralph B., "The Clause Patterns of Contemporary English", *American Speech*, XXXII (1957), 12-30.

McIntosh, Lois, "A Description and Comparison of Question Signals in Spoken English, Mandarin Chinese, French, and German for Teachers of English as a Second Language" (Unpublished doctoral dissertation, The University of Michigan, Ann Arbor, Michigan, 1953).

Sørensen, Holger Steen, "The Function of the Definite Article in Modern English", *English Studies*, XL (1959), 401-420.

Traver, Alice Aileen, "The Modificational Patterns of the Substantive Head Construction in Present-Day American English" (Unpublished doctoral dissertation, University of Michigan, Ann Arbor, Michigan, 1944).

Whitehall, Harold, "The English Language", in *Webster's New World Dictionary of the American Language*, College edition (Cleveland, The World Publishing Company, 1956 [and 1953, 1954, 1955]), pp. xv-xxxiv.

3. BOOKS AND ARTICLES ON VIETNAMESE

Bulteau, R., *Cours d'annamite (Langue vietnamienne)*, 4th printing (Paris, Editions Larose, 1953).

Cadière, L., *Syntaxe de la langue vietnamienne* (Paris, Publications de l'École Française d'Extrême-Orient, 1958).

Chính, Trương Văn, and Lê, Nguyễn Hiên, *Khảo Luận về Ngữ Pháp Việt Nam* (Huê, Đại Học Huê, 1963).

Đặc, Phạm Tất, *Phân Tích Tự Loại & Phân Tích Mệnh Đê*, 4th printing (Saigon, Nhà Xuất Bản ABC, 1950).

Day, Arthur Colin, *Final Consonants in Northern Vietnamese* (= *Transactions of the Historical Research Institute*, No. 3), (Saigon, The Historical Research Institute, 1962).

Emeneau, M. B., *Studies in Vietnamese (Annamese) Grammar* (= *University of California Publications in Linguistics*, Vol. 8), (Berkeley and Los Angeles, University of California Press, 1951).

——, "Homonyms and Puns in Annamese", *Language*, XXIII (1947), 239-244.

Gage, William W., and Jackson, Merrill H., *Verb Constructions in Vietnamese* (*Southeast Asia Program, Data Paper*: Number 9), mimeographed (Ithaca, N.Y., Department of Far Eastern Studies, Cornell University, July, 1953).

Hòa, Nguyễn Đình, *Speak Vietnamese* (Saigon, Publications of the School of Languages, 1957).

——, "Classifiers in Vietnamese", *Word*, XIII (1957), 321-343.

——, *Vietnamese Phrase Book* (Saigon, Vietnamese-American Association, 1959).

——, *The Vietnamese Language* (= *Vietnamese Cultural Series*, No. 2), (Saigon, Department of National Education, 1961).

Hợi, Đào Thị, "Representation of Time and Time Relationship in English and in Vietnamese" (Unpublished doctoral project report, Teachers College, Columbia University, New York, N.Y., 1965).

Honey, Patrick J., "Word Classes in Vietnamese", *Bulletin of the School of Oriental and African Studies*, XVIII (1956), 534-544.

Jones, Robert B., Jr., and Thông, Huỳnh Sanh, *Introduction to Spoken Vietnamese*, revised edition (Washington, D.C., American Council of Learned Societies, 1960).

Kim, Trần Trọng, Kỷ, Bùi, and Khiêm, Phạm Duy, *Việt Nam Văn Phạm*, 8th printing (Saigon, Tân Việt, n.d.).

——, Kỷ, Bùi, and Oánh, Nguyễn Quang, *Tiểu-Học Việt-Nam Văn-Phạm*, 3rd printing (Saigon, Tân Việt, n.d.).

Lê, Nguyễn Hiên, *Để Hiểu Văn-Phạm* (Saigon, P. Văn Tươi, 1952).

Lý, Lê Văn, *Le parler vietnamien (Sa structure phonologique et morphologique fonctionnelle)* (Saigon, Bộ Quốc-Gia Giáo-Dục, Viện Khảo-Cổ, 1960).

Miller, John D., "Word Tone Recognition in Vietnamese Whispered Speech", *Word*, XVII (1961), 11-15.

Thanh, Nguyễn Trúc, *Văn Phạm Mới* (Saigon, Liên-Hiệp, 1956).

Thomas, David D., "On Defining the 'Word' in Vietnamese", *Văn Hóa Nguyệt San*, 70 (1962), 519-523.

Thompson, Laurence C., "Saigon Phonemics", *Language*, XXXV (1959), 454-476.

——, "A Grammar of Spoken South Vietnamese" (Unpublished doctoral dissertation, Yale University, New Haven, Connecticut, 1954).

Tịnh, Bùi Đức, *Những Nhận Xét về Văn-Phạm Việt Nam* (Saigon, Đại Chúng, 1949).

——, *Văn Phạm Việt Nam* (Saigon, P. Văn Tươi, 1952).

——, *Văn Phạm Việt Nam cho các Lớp Trung-Học* (Saigon, Vĩnh Bảo, 1956).

Trụ, Nguyễn Ngọc, *Chánh Tả Việt Ngữ* (Saigon, Nhà Xuất Bản Nam Việt, 1951).

Tụy, Nguyễn Bạt, *Ngôn Ngữ Việt Nam* (Saigon, Ngôn Ngữ, 1958).

4. BOOKS ON THE TEACHING OF ENGLISH AS A FOREIGN LANGUAGE

Abercrombie, David, *Problems and Principles* (London, Longmans, Green, Ltd., 1956).

Allen, Virginia F. (ed.), *On Teaching English to Speakers of Other Languages* (Champaign, Illinois, National Council of Teachers of English, 1965).

Billows, F. L., *The Techniques of Language Teaching* (London, Longmans, 1961).

Bloomfield, Leonard, *Outline Guide for the Practical Study of Foreign Languages* (Baltimore, Linguistic Society of America, 1942).

Brooks, Nelson, *Language and Language Learning* (New York, Harcourt, Brace and Company, 1960).

Cochran, Anne, *Modern Methods of Teaching English as a Foreign Language* (Washington, Educational Services, 1954).

French, F. G., *The Teaching of English Abroad*, in 3 Parts (London, Oxford University Press, 1948-1950).

Fries, Charles C., *Teaching and Learning English as a Foreign Language* (Ann Arbor, University of Michigan Press, 1947).

Gatenby, Edward V., *English as a Foreign Language: Advice to Non-English Teachers* (London, Longmans, Green, Ltd., 1944).

Gauntlett, J. O., *Teaching English as a Foreign Language* (London, Macmillan and Company, Ltd., 1957).

Gurrey, P., *Teaching English as a Foreign Language* (London, Longmans, Green, Ltd., 1955).

Huebener, Theodore, *How to Teach Foreign Language Effectively* (New York, New York University Press, 1959).

Jespersen, Otto, *How to Teach a Foreign Language* (London, Allen and Unwin, 1904).

Lado, Robert, *Annotated Bibliography for Teachers of English as a Foreign Language* (Washington, United States Department of Education, 1955).

——, *Linguistics Across Cultures: Applied Linguistics for Language Teachers* (Ann Arbor, Michigan, University of Michigan Press, 1957).

Leavitt, Leslie W., *The Teaching of English to Foreign Students* (London, Longmans, Green, Ltd., 1941).

Morris, Isaac, *The Art of Teaching English as a Living Language* (London, Macmillan and Company, 1954).

Palmer, Harold E., *The Scientific Study and Teaching of Languages* (Yonkers-on-Hudson, N.Y., World Book Company, 1926).

——, *The Oral Method of Teaching Languages* (Yonkers-on-Hudson, N.Y., World Book Company, 1926).

——, *Classroom Procedures and Devices in Connection with English Teaching* (Tokyo, Institute of Research in English, 1930).

Stack, Edward M., *The Language Laboratory and Modern Language Teaching* (New York, Oxford University Press, 1960).

Stevick, Earl W., *Helping People Learn English* (Nashville, Tenn., Abingdon Press, 1957).

The Board of Education of the City of New York, *Teaching English as a New Language to Adults*, Fundamental Adult Education Series. Curriculum Bulletin, 1963-1964 Series, No. 5 (New York, The Board of Education of the City of New York, 1964).

5. TEXTBOOKS FOR TEACHING ENGLISH AS A FOREIGN LANGUAGE

Allen, Virginia F., and Allen, Robert L., *Review Exercises* (New York, Thomas Y. Crowell Co., 1961).

Allen, W. Stannard, *Living English Structure: Practice Book for Foreign Students and Key* (London, Longmans, Green and Company, 1955).

——, *Living English Structure for Schools* (London, Longmans, Green and Company, Ltd., 1958).

American Council of Learned Societies, *Structural Notes and Corpus: A Basis for the Preparation of Materials to Teach English as a Foreign Language* (Washington, D.C., American Council of Learned Societies, 1952).

Campbell, Russell N., *English for Vietnamese Speakers*, Vol. I., experimental edition, Southeast Asian Regional English Project (Ann Arbor, Michigan, University of Michigan, 1960).

Crowell, Thomas Lee, Jr., *Notes on English for Advanced Foreign Students*, 3rd edition (New York, Saxon Press, 1960).

Dixon, Robert J., *Complete Course in English*, 2 vols. (New York, Latin American Institute Press, 1953).

English Language Institute Staff, *English Sentence Patterns — understanding and producing English grammatical structures — An Oral Approach*, revised edition, 3rd printing (Ann Arbor, The University of Michigan Press, 1959).

Fries, Charles C., *Teaching and Learning English as a Foreign Language* (= *Publications of the English Language Institute* No. 1), (Ann Arbor, University of Michigan Press, 1945).

——, *An Intensive Course in English for Latin-American Students*, 6 vols. (Ann Arbor, English Language Institute, University of Michigan, 1953).

——, Kitchin, Aileen Traver, and French, Virginia, *A Syllabus for English Through Practice*, 2 vols. (New York, Teachers College, Columbia University, 1947). (Mimeographed.)

——, and the Research Staff of the English Language Institute. *Cumulative Pattern Practices*, Lessons I-XX from *An Intensive Course in English* (Ann Arbor, English Language Institute, University of Michigan, 1954).

——, and Fries, Agnes C., *Foundations for English Teaching*, published for the English Language Exploratory Committee (Tokyo, Kenkyusha, 1961).

Hayden, Rebecca E., Pilgrim, Dorothy, and Haggard, Aurora Q., *Mastering American English: A Handbook-Workbook of Essentials* (Englewood Cliffs, N.J., Prentice-Hall, 1956).

Hornby, A. S., *A Guide to Patterns and Usage in English* (London, Oxford University Press, 1954).

——, *The Teaching of Structural Words and Sentence Patterns*, 3 vols. (London, Oxford University Press, 1959-1962).

King, Harold V., *The Verb Forms of English: Lessons and Oral Drills* (London, Longmans, Green and Company, 1957).

Millington-Ward, John, also Ward, John Millington, *The Use of Tenses in English: A New Approach for Intermediate Students* (London, Longmans, Green and Company, 1954).

Mitchell, Elizabeth Gillilan, *Beginning American English* (Englewood Cliffs, N.J., Prentice-Hall, 1957).

National Council of Teachers of English, *English for Today: Teacher's Text*, 3 vols. (New York, McGraw-Hill Book Company, 1962-1964).

Ogden, C. K., *The System of Basic English* (New York, Harcourt, Brace and Company, 1934).

——, *Basic English: A General Introduction with Rules and Grammar*, 9th edition (London, Kegan Paul, Trench, Trubner and Company, 1944).

Praninskas, Jean, *Rapid Review of English for Foreign Students* (Champaign, Ill., Stipes Publishing Company, 1957). (Mimeographed.)

——, *Rapid Review of English Grammar: for Students of English as a Second Language* (Englewood Cliffs, N.J., Prentice-Hall, Inc., 1961).

Prator, Clifford H., *Manual of American English Pronunciation*, revised edition (New York, Holt, Rinehart and Winston, 1960).

Walpole, Hugh R., *Foundations of English for Foreign Students* (Chicago, University of Chicago Press, 1946).

Wright, Audrey L., *Practice Your English* (New York, American Book Company, 1952).

——, and McGillivray, James H. *Let's Learn English*, Part I (New York, American Book Company, 1955).

6. OTHER MATERIALS CONSULTED

Alston, William P., *Philosophy of Language* (Englewood Cliffs, N.J., Prentice-Hall, Inc., 1964).

Ayer, Alfred Jules, *Language, Truth and Logic* (New York, Dover Publications, Inc., 1952).

Hayakawa, S. I., *Language in Thought and Action* (New York, Harcourt, Brace and Company, Inc., 1949).

Hjelmslev, Louis, *La catégorie des cas: étude de grammaire générale*, Aarskrift for Aarhns Universitet, *Acta Jutlandica*, Vol. VII, No. 1 (1935); Vol. IX, No. 2 (1937).

Huyên, Nguyễn Văn, *Chants alternés des garçons et des filles en Annam* (Paris, Librairie Orientaliste, Paul Guethner, 1933).

Ives, Sumner, *A New Handbook for Writers* (New York, Alfred H. Knopf, 1960).

Landes, A., *Contes et légendes annamites* (Saigon, Imprimerie Coloniale, 1886).

Langer, Suzanne, *Philosophy in a New Key: A Study in the Symbolism of Reason, Rite, and Art*, Mentor Books (New York, The New American Library of World Literature, 1942).

——, *Feeling and Form: A Theory of Art Developed from Philosophy in a New Key* (New York, Charles Scribner's Sons, 1953).

Lewis, M. M., *Language and Society: The Linguistic Revolution and Social Change* (New York, Social Science Publishers, 1948).

Morris, Charles, *Signs, Language, and Behavior* (New York, George Braziller, 1955).

Reichenbach, Hans, *Elements of Symbolic Logic* (New York, The Macmillan Company, 1947).

Shoemaker, Francis, and Forsdale, Louis (eds.), *Communication in General Education: College Composition and Communication* (Dubuque, Iowa, William C. Brown Company, 1960).

Sturt, Mary, *The Psychology of Time* (London, Kegan Paul, Trench, Trubner and Company, 1925).